T0340930

Growing and Managing Foreign Purchasing

The Global Warrior Series

Growing and Managing Foreign Purchasing

Thomas A. Cook

CRC Press
Taylor & Francis Group
Boca Raton   London   New York

CRC Press is an imprint of the
Taylor & Francis Group, an **informa** business

CRC Press
Taylor & Francis Group
6000 Broken Sound Parkway NW, Suite 300
Boca Raton, FL 33487-2742

© 2017 by Taylor & Francis Group, LLC
CRC Press is an imprint of Taylor & Francis Group, an Informa business

No claim to original U.S. Government works

Printed on acid-free paper
Version Date: 20160314

International Standard Book Number-13: 978-1-4822-2625-6 (Hardback)

Library of Congress Cataloging-in-Publication Data

Names: Cook, Thomas A., 1953- author.
Title: Growing and managing foreign purchasing / Thomas A. Cook.
Description: Boca Raton, FL : CRC Press, 2016. | Includes bibliographical references and index.
Identifiers: LCCN 2016004969 | ISBN 9781482226256 (hardcover : alk. paper)
Subjects: LCSH: Purchasing. | Imports--Management. | Exports--Management. | Business logistics--Management.
Classification: LCC HF5437 .C658 2016 | DDC 658.7/2--dc23
LC record available at http://lccn.loc.gov/2016004969

Visit the Taylor & Francis Web site at
http://www.taylorandfrancis.com

and the CRC Press Web site at
http://www.crcpress.com

Printed and bound in the United States of America by Publishers Graphics, LLC on sustainably sourced paper.

Dedicated to Kelly Raia, a loyal, responsible, consummate professional, and a beautiful person. I am very grateful for her skill sets, capabilities, and attitude which are all a great support!

Contents

Foreword

I have read all of Tom's books and articles and have been at a number of his seminars and presentations. His knowledge of world trade is impressive, but even more discerning is his ability to articulate the complicated nature of international business and put it into words and meaning that is very comprehensible.

This book, focusing on international procurement and global logistics, could not come at a more important time in the history of international trade and transportation, which has been and is more recently an ever-growing need and discipline for all companies worldwide.

Global supply chain has become an increasing area of growth in all sizes of companies, and there is a need to control cost, risk, and business development. Tom addresses these topics very comprehensively within the chapters of this very important publication.

Business executives are increasingly developing purchasing targets in overseas markets, particularly in Asia. This increased activity in buying finished goods, raw materials, and components in foreign locations poses numerous challenges in logistics, trade compliance, distribution, and profitable sales. Tom covers all these subjects in depth, in an easy-to-comprehend order that I believe every one who imports and exports should be reading and implementing in their business operations.

This book will be kept on my desk along with a number of extra copies for handing out to clients, staff, and business colleagues, as a *must-read* for the supply chain, logistics, and trade professional who wants to have a first-class global procurement, sourcing and logistics program that becomes *best in class*.

Spencer Ross
Chairman, National Institute of World Trade/New York

Preface

Corporations, multinationals, and businesses of all sizes feel the pressure of world competition and the need to reduce costs and produce products less expensively. A key to success and survival is managing these issues and successfully operating an inbound global supply chain.

Almost every American and foreign national company is beginning to source goods, parts, and traditional American-made products from other countries or is even further expanding its overseas manufacturing and purchasing program.

The driving force in this quest is cheaper unit costing.

Along with cheaper pricing come inherited risks. The author, whose supply chain and logistics experience now spans four decades, identifies these risks and provides hands-on solutions to transfer, eradicate, or mitigate them.

It is a must-read for corporate purchasing, sourcing, trade compliance, legal, customer service, supply chain, logistics, risk management, and import/export executives.

It becomes a *blueprint* for creating the necessary SOPs for managing the risks of inbound supply chains.

There are numerous benefits to sourcing products overseas. There are also alternatives to keep the manufacturing or assembly of finished products here. Irrespective, the consequences of sourcing foreign finished products or components for assembly present some dilemmas for supply chain operators.

Those companies that manage the skill sets of operating global supply chains by proactively managing the risks are much more likely to produce better profits and sustainable growth objectives.

With an increasing volume of goods being purchased in Asia, this book also reviews the necessary disciplines that are necessary to successfully source, purchase, and ship from Asia, particularly China, to North America.

Near-sourcing is also becoming a direction for many companies with the leveraging of free trade agreements, which is covered in many of the chapters.

This book provides the necessary *information flow and tools* to successfully manage inbound global supply chains and obtain a competitive advantage in world trade.

Thomas A. Cook

Acknowledgments

Kelly Raia has been very helpful in providing valuable content and editing.

Material support has come from the US government and various online resources.

Many organizations, such as but not limited to the American Management Association, *The Journal of Commerce* (JOC), and *American Shipper*, have been helpful in developing the relevant topics, material, and structure to this book.

Many government agencies, professionals, and periodicals have given me invaluable information flow that has become part of this important project.

To all, you are most appreciated, and thank you.

1

Purchasing, Sourcing, and Vendor Management 101

1.1 INTRODUCTION

This chapter outlines in an overview format all the considerations to manage purchasing and sourcing in operating in a global supply chain. It states the case for the balance of this book and creates the foundation for all the granular issues that one would deal with in leveraging the purchasing and sourcing responsibilities.

1.2 THE CASE FOR MANAGING, PURCHASING, AND SOURCING

As we enter the second decade of the new millennium, companies wishing to grow and prosper in a very competitive economy recognize the importance of impacting the costs and risks in their global supply chains.

Strategically, this concept is easy to grasp, but tactically, it means investing in developing their prowess in three key areas: (1) purchasing, (2) sourcing, and (3) vendor/supplier management.

These three areas are very different from one another yet intensely connected.

As companies first enter into purchasing management as a serious vertical within their company, typically, sourcing and vendor management are part of that person(s) responsibilities.

As the company grows, these disciplines become separated and are handled as their own facility or fiefdom within the company.

Purchasing can be defined as the acquisition of goods or services on behalf of a company for the maintenance and operation of their supply chains without any interference to operational success.

Sourcing is the discipline that is associated with finding vendors and suppliers to fulfill the companies' procurement needs.

Vendor management is the structure that is determined on handling the vendors and suppliers once their relationships move from opportunity to a closed deal.

The *connection* between all these concerns is very evident, but so are the differences. In larger companies, it is recognized that these three disciplines can require very different skill sets in managing them successfully.

For example, purchasing management requires strong negotiation and management skill sets, so do vendor/supplier relations. But in sourcing, this may not be quite as important.

In sourcing, resource development, travel, outreach, exploring prowess, and persistence may be the more important skill sets to have.

In smaller companies, purchasing or procurement may encompass all three areas, and therefore, the purchasing team will be required to master all the three components of purchasing, sourcing, and vendor management.

The typical order in the overall procurement process is as follows:

1. We find alternative sources.
2. We create requests for proposal (RfPs) and/or bidding structures.
3. We choose the suppliers.
4. We create statements of work (SOWs).
5. We finalize contracts.
6. We create vendor/supplier management programs.

These areas will be reviewed in greater detail as this chapter moves forward.

1.3 THE CRITICAL RESPONSIBILITIES OF PURCHASING, SOURCING, AND VENDOR MANAGEMENT

1.3.1 Purchasing

The key responsibility in purchasing is to manage the process of creating an uninterrupted flow of goods and services into a company so that it can deliver its products and services for growth and profit.

The secondary responsibilities include the following:

- Creating greater value in vendor relationships
- Lowering costs and risks in vendor relationships
- Allowing for sustainability in vendor relationships
- Building partnerships and long-term relationships

The purchasing manager must keep a number of balls up in the air to maintain open and performing global supply chains.

1.3.2 Global Sourcing

The sourcing manager typically has two specific overriding responsibilities:

1. Transactionally assisting internally on finding suppliers for particular needs. This is typically done with short notice.
2. Perform via enterprise proactive business process in developing various vendor/supplier options anticipating future needs and internal demands.

At the end of the day, a successful sourcing manager always does the following:

- Searches out vendor/supplier options
- Reaches out internally so that future needs can be determined
- Explores the marketplace and turns stones over to be able to respond to internal demands

- Creates futuristic options in alternative suppliers and vendors who can reduce purchasing costs and risks
- Finds suppliers and vendors who can offer creative options in sourcing that might provide competitive advantages

Keep in mind that sourcing globally creates potentially huge advantages, particularly in cost. But it also creates a huge risk.

Management of that risk is a very critical component of overseas sourcing and is outlined in great detail in every chapter of this book.

1.3.3 Vendor Management

Once the supplier is picked and a contract is placed, we have to manage the relationship.

Our primary goal in vendor management is to assure that all the deliverables are met and the pricing is honored.

The secondary goals are as follows:

- A robust relationship ensues.
- Sustainability is obtained.
- Quarterly business reviews (QBRs) and accountability systems in place to assure ongoing performance.
- Renewal of relationships and developing long-term partnerships.
- All regulatory and administrative responsibilities are maintained.
- Risks and costs are continually minimized.
- Innovation and contemporary deliverables are brought into the relationship.

1.4 SKILL SETS NECESSARY FOR SUCCESSFUL PURCHASING, SOURCING, AND VENDOR MANAGEMENT

The necessary skill sets of purchasing, sourcing, and vendor managers are as follows:

- Project management
- Negotiation prowess
- Mastering communications: oral and written presentations
- Basic legal understanding: for Statement of Works (SOWs) and contracts
- Time management
- Strengths, weaknesses, opportunities, and threats analysis and specific, measurable, achievable, realistic and time-scaled objectives
- Organization
- Problem resolution
- Risk management
- Basic technology
- Your companies' product and service offerings and basic understanding at a detailed level of comprehension
- Inventory, demand planning, and supply chain management basics
- Sales and marketing

1.5 KEY CONSIDERATIONS FOR WORLD-CLASS PURCHASING, SOURCING, AND VENDOR MANAGEMENT

There are 10 considerations for operating a first-class/world-class/Sarbanes–Oxley procurement business model:

1. Develop significant leadership and management skill sets.
2. Always bring metrics into the decision-making process (when feasible).
3. Seek vendors and suppliers who offer a similar cultural and mantra operating profile.
4. Manage RfPs based on value add and service over cost.

5. Cost should be competitive, not necessarily the least expensive or cheapest.
6. Be transparent in your approach to managing vendor relationships.
7. Change can be very costly. Seek vendors and suppliers who offer long-term sustainability.
8. Sourcing needs to be accomplished consistently and aggressively and being very *proactive.*
9. Learn the difference between value and price in your business model and practice it responsibly.
10. Master negotiation skills and the psychology of how people make decisions.

1.6 BEST PRACTICES IN RfP MANAGEMENT

RfPs are a vastly accepted practice in choosing vendors and suppliers, and the author affirms that they are a *best practice* to follow in managing procurement decisions.

Keep in mind that RfPs are a tool, not necessarily an *end-all*, in the decision-making process for choosing suppliers and vendors.

Outlined in the following list is an 18-step process that we have developed to help companies manage the RfP process consistently with the most favorable outcomes.

The following 18 steps focus on making sure that you obtain your needs, high levels of value add, and eventually the pricing that you require:

1. *Determine goals of RfP*
2. *Determine RfP needs and requirements*
3. *Identify stakeholders*
4. *Obtain senior management support*
5. *Internal reach*
6. *Create RfP committee*
7. *Create RfP strategy*: identify deliverables and create scorecard
8. *Create RfP action plan*: goals, actions, and timeline
9. *Identify initial list of RfP participants*
10. *Initial contact to RfP*
11. *Create RfP outline that is given to initial list of RfP participants*
12. *Scrutinize responses*: reduce list to a manageable amount
13. *On-site meetings with RfP finalists*
14. *Bring price into the equation*
15. *Final selection process (revisits)*
16. *Implementation and transition strategy development*
17. *Act on RfP*
18. *Follow up, tweaking, revisions, and QBR*

1.7 CONTRACTS AND SOWs

SOWs typically precede contracts. They can be utilized as an entry point to an agreement with a basic outline of expectations and deliverables between both parties: (a) you, the principal, and (b) the supplier and/or vendor.

This becomes the prelude to the contract that will provide a greater structure of the agreement at a more detailed, granular level.

Keep in mind that SOWs, simply stated, are a *promises-met, promises-delivered document*.

The following outline provides a set of instructions to consider in creating SOWs.

[Insert company logo]

Statement of Work

Date	[insert date]
Client	[insert client's name]
Job Name	[insert project name]
Requested by	[insert your client sponsor's name]
From	[insert your name]

Summary

(Provides the "why"—include an introduction, the marketing or business objectives of the project, and a very brief overview of the scope [only a sentence or two].)

Project Scope

This SOW covers the following activities and deliverables.

(Include a detailed description of the scope. Include as many assumptions to clearly define what is, and what is not, included. Also, include a detailed list of deliverables, including a description of each deliverable.)

Schedule

(Include the schedule. Minimally, it needs to include the client and the client partner touch points. It should include the task name and the end date. This can either be inserted as a table, or as a screen print of the Microsoft Project Plan.)

Task	Finish Date

Pricing

All the costs listed below are based on the scope and assumptions that are included in this SOW.

Item		Price	Cost Structure
Agency fees:		$99,999	Fixed-fee basis
Out-of-pocket fees:		$99,999	Time and materials basis
	[Include breakdown of expenses]	$99,999	
	[Include breakdown of expenses]	$99,999	
TOTAL		$99,999	

(Include the payment terms.)

The following is the payment schedule.

Invoice Date	Invoice Amount

Key Assumptions

This agreement is based on the following assumptions.
(List all the key assumptions that are not mentioned in this document.)

Acceptance

The client named below verifies that the terms of this statement of work are acceptable. The parties hereto are each acting with proper authority by their respective companies.

[Client name]	[Agency information]
Company name	Company name
Full name	Full name
Title	Title
Signature	Signature
Date	Date

1.8 SOW GUIDELINES

The SOW is a critical document outlining the basic understanding and agreements of both parties, and mirroring that basic fact is what it should do.

Writing an SOW is one of the most important things that an agency does. Frequently, it is the first deliverable that a client sees. It is crucial that your SOW is telling the client a story. It starts with the "why" and then moves to the "how" and "what," followed by the "when" and "how much."

Everything should be cohesive with a flow so that it is easy to follow. Do not treat the SOW as a *form* that you simply fill in the blanks. This article explains what is contained with an SOW and provides an SOW template that you can download and use.

Contrary to what many people believe, the SOW is not a sales tool. It should only be given to clients after you have their agreement as to the scope, schedule, key assumptions, and price. Many people believe that the SOW is where you first present this information. *Wrong.* The SOW is a legal contract that is used to document the agreement only after the business terms have been agreed upon.

This preliminary agreement can be verbal. This means that if there are price issues (and there always are), have those negotiations before the SOW is presented. Yes, you could ignore this advice and use the SOW to negotiate the contract, but doing so will always take more time.

As input to the SOW, it is important to have the following:

- A timeline developed either in Microsoft Project®, Excel®, or a similar program that can be utilized for project management or related topics
- Client verbal agreement as to the scope, schedule, key assumptions, and price

All SOWs contain the following sections:

- Objectives
- Scope
- Schedule
- Price
- Key assumptions
- Acceptance

STATEMENT OF WORK

- Task 1: Assist in the development of information-preserving transformation rules for merging heterogeneous schemas.
- Task 2: Assist in the development of security/privacy policy model.
  Review and comment on standby request for information's (SRI's) work on trusted query mediation.
- Task 3: Assist in obtaining sample healthcare databases or schemas as testbeds.
  Participate in the development of the demo system.
  Assist in testing and evaluating the demo system.

Each section is explained in detail.

1.8.1 Objectives

Defines the "why." This section states the marketing or business objectives of the project and a high-level overview of the solution. This ensures that we have clarity as to why we are performing this work and begins to weave the story.

1.8.2 Scope Including Inline Assumptions and Deliverables

Defines the "how" and "what" of the story. This section defines the work that is being done and the process for how it will be performed. This is your task list, and it should be written in process form so that it flows as follows:

- Kick off the project
- Develop creative brief and present it to client for review and approval
- Develop up to three creative concepts

Assumptions are the most important part of any SOW, and any assumptions that you made when scoping and estimating the project should be included here. The assumptions should be included in line with the tasks. It is also important to state exactly what deliverables are being produced, including the details that accurately describe each deliverable, such as the description and size (either expressed as an approximate number of pages or number of designs, and should be expressed using the term *up to* so that if you produce less, you are still fulfilling the contract).

Many people include tasks within the list of deliverables. This is incorrect. Deliverables are just that; they are items that you hand off to the client for their review and approval. For example, the *creative brief* is a deliverable; however, *presenting the creative brief* is not a deliverable because it is a task. One litmus test to verify if something is a deliverable or not is, "Can it be emailed?" Also, never make status reports deliverables as you do not want to be in a position where you are asking the client to review and approve every single status report. (I'm not saying that status reports are not important because they are crucial. They are just not a deliverable.)

Do not give the client options or alternatives in the scope. All of the decisions should have been made by now. The SOW should be written as a definitive statement.

1.8.3 Schedule

Defines the "when." This section provides a detailed schedule. Minimally, it should include all of the client's and their partner's touch points. The format is less important as you can either develop this as a table in Microsoft Word®, or you can copy and paste images directly from Microsoft Project into the SOW document. The data should include the task and the end date. The task start dates are optional.

1.8.4 Price

Defines the "how much" of the story. This section needs to include the price, including both the time of staff and outside expenses. It should also discuss the pricing assumptions such as if this is fixed fee or time and materials, how outside expenses are handled, payment terms including a payment schedule, and if payments are based on a milestone/deliverable or a schedule. (If you are an agency, you generally want date based; if you are a client, you want milestone/deliverable based.)

1.8.5 Key Assumptions

Assumptions that are not related to the scope are included here. Any scope-related assumptions should have already been included in Section 1.8.2. Do not repeat assumptions as this will lead to errors. Instead, use this section to document any general assumptions that are not stated elsewhere.

Also, if you do not have a master services agreement (MSA) or professional services agreement (PSA) executed with the client, you can use this space to document the key MSA/PSA terms.

1.8.6 Acceptance

This section contains the client signature and the signature from the agency's key executives overseeing the project. You should not start the project without having the client signature. Doing so is asking for trouble. So if you have any exceptions, you want to be sure that the agency management team agrees to doing so, since they are accepting a significant risk by starting without having a signature. Also, when you are audited, the auditors will look to ensure that all signatures are obtained (including the internal agency signatures).

1.8.7 Other Important Considerations

The SOW should not reference any external documents as its basis. All materials should be built into the SOW. For example, do not refer or link out to a separate schedule; instead, put the schedule directly into the SOW. The reason is that since this is a legal contract, it makes it much more difficult to refer to outside documents.

Make sure that the SOW is proofread carefully from different perspectives. First, it should tell a story. Second, make sure that the solution is actually solving the client's problem. Third, be sure that you are not overcommitting the agency. Make sure that you can deliver on the price. Finally, make sure that all the "T"s are crossed and the "I"s are dotted.

2

Developing Foreign Sourcing

2.1 INTRODUCTION

This chapter sets the stage for the comprehensive and critical material that is covered in the balance of this book. It explains in an overview format just why companies look to sourcing overseas, how they will interface with foreign companies, and what options exist in finding and managing these vendor relationships. There is also an intensive guide to finding and qualifying overseas partners.

2.2 OVERVIEW

In the current global marketplace, all companies need to strive to gain competitive advantage. A revolution took place in the late 1990s and continues into the second decade of the new millennium so that the logistics options in corporate supply chains could easily make or break a company's manufacturing and supply chain model.

This book examines the layers of issues that corporate executives need to consider in the decision-making process to source overseas and, if they do, how to make sure that they do it by reducing risk, thereby mitigating exposures and maximizing the opportunities for favorable outcomes and more competitive landed costs.

There has been a trend in US manufacturing for over five decades to find less expensive sources of the products and services that are consumed by American and global demands. This trend has seen exponential growth in the past decade as the global markets continue to expand, and corporate executives are competitively forced to reduce costs and supply products at lower prices. This is almost comparable to a never-ending economic spiral—where it will end and the consequences, nobody knows.

One can argue from varied perspectives on what is driving this trend, but it is clear that retailers and consumers are finding greater market share, growth, and new business development as the primary beneficiaries of cheaper wholesale product costs.

Many US-based manufacturers have met this need for lower costs by moving to foreign countries where there is less regulation that interferes with the manufacturing process; cheaper labor; and overall lower basic plant, personnel, and operation costs.

As this trend has matured and grown, two basic methods of foreign manufacturing have developed—(1) sourcing and (2) outsourcing. We need to study this to make the best choices for our global supply chains.

2.3 SOURCING VERSUS OUTSOURCING

The main ingredient for companies looking to source in foreign markets is the unit cost of products being produced overseas at a substantially lower price. The two phenomena that occur in that search for lower price are sourcing and outsourcing. The similarities and differences between sourcing and outsourcing need to be studied before companies make the decision to move their production or manufacturing operations offshore:

- *Sourcing* is transferring the site of your manufacturing to a foreign location but maintaining some or all of the control over ownership of the manufacturing process.
- *Outsourcing* is transferring the site of your manufacturing to a foreign location and transferring most or all of the control of the manufacturing process to a foreign entity.

In sourcing, US companies have certain protections that are built in to control proprietary rights. In outsourcing, the controls are fewer or non-existent. In practice, the ability to *contract out* foreign exposure, particularly in proprietary rights issues, is very dismal.

Most companies will control the proprietary rights issues, such as patents, trademarks, formulizations, product specifications, and so on, by maintaining ownership of the manufacturing and distribution process rather than providing this to a third-party manufacturer and attempting to have attorneys contract out the exposures. If sourcing is a necessary evil, then ownership of manufacturing is a much more secure method than transferring it to a third party and having it outsourced. What happens if the relationship deteriorates, or if a major economic downfall occurs in that country, or a political event strains or breaks ties with the United States? Will the US companies be able to retain their proprietary rights?

Based on global precedence, when social or political events occurred in countries such as Peru, Iran, Russia, and Nigeria, foreign companies whose interests were not protected experienced major losses.

With the potential reopening of Cuba in 2015–2016, the events back in the early 1960s will have a current impact on how the relationship develops in the new millennium, with political discourse dominating the business development plans.

2.3.1 Criteria in the Decision to Source or Outsource

Some of the criteria to consider in deciding whether to source or outsource are the following:

- *The legal climate of the foreign location.* Does the legal system of the foreign company provide protections for proprietary rights, penalties for violators, and recourses for abusers?
- *Overall access to the specific manufacturing process, technology, or patent, and so on.* In other words, can the product be easily duplicated?
- *Control over ingredients, raw materials, formularizations, and so on so that they cannot be altered or found alternatively, and control over options to another source.* An example would be that a main ingredient of the manufacturing process has only one source and the company controls that source, compared to a main ingredient that could be easily sourced in five other countries.

- *Dependence of the foreign-based facility on the US company's capability, knowledge, and wherewithal to produce the product.*
- *The economic and political stability of that country and the relationship that it enjoys with the United States.*
- *Over the long term, the degree that the foreign government will invest in the various infrastructures that will allow maintaining an effective presence in that country, such as transportation (roads, airports, and seaports), communication and advanced technology capabilities, and worker skill set enhancements.*
- *Standard of living and accommodation that is available if business requires locating Americans or other Westerners in the foreign market.*

It is important for a company to develop a checklist of these basic criteria and then add the company's specific needs. The checklist allows viewing of all of the issues to make the best decision on sourcing or outsourcing.

2.3.2 Other Factors Affecting the Decision to Source or Outsource

Some of the other factors that affect the decision to source or outsource are as follows:

- *Sourcing is generally more expensive than outsourcing.* It may require construction, plant relocation, asset transfers, and personnel relocation.
- *Outsourcing generally provides a quick resolution and faster turnaround in the short term.* It is important to find a suitable outsourcing partner. Minimal time to set up and begin manufacturing right away is a potential option.
- *Outsourcing is easier to do away with or modify in the short term.* If the performance is not acceptable and change cannot be implemented, then a new partner should be sought.
- *Some outsourcing options provide benefits.* For example, the outsource partner may have processes and capabilities that add value to the company; it may have personnel with the skill sets that are required, and it may have potentially fewer regulatory concerns, making it easier for the company to do business.

- *The long-term prospects of duty, tax, and special treaty considerations between the United States and the country that the company is considering sourcing from and other competitive areas of the world.*

Making the decision to source or outsource will have a major impact on a company's decision to manufacture and purchase overseas. Sufficient time must be allotted to properly collect and analyze data on all the aspects that are related to the move. The decision-making process should include factors that affect both short- and long-term financial consequences.

It is imperative that the decision-making process consider carefully relevant information on special treaty programs such as the North American Free Trade Agreement, the Central American Free Trade Agreement, the Israeli Free Trade Agreement, and so on, which have far-reaching effects on where and how companies will source.

International business done successfully means paying attention to detail. Nowhere is paying attention to detail of greater importance to a company considering sourcing or outsourcing than the decision-making process in global sourcing options because decisions in this area will determine both short- and long-term competitiveness.

2.4 GLOBAL PURCHASING MANAGEMENT 101

The purchasing manager position of the new millennium requires a far different type of person from the previous years. The skill sets required must be much broader in scope and much more detailed in execution.

In most corporations that decide to source from foreign markets, the decision-making process is typically within the scope of the purchasing manager. If this is not the case, he or she will generally have a significant influence on the options that are considered and the final business model.

In purchasing management, the goal is generally to find the best source at the best price. But, in the current global market, the purchasing manager may need to speak foreign languages; learn about the customs, traditions, and etiquette of foreign countries; work 80 hours per week; travel to multiple countries over several days; know how ocean carriers work; be an expert on US customs law; understand international contract law; memorize International Commercial Terms (INCOTerms); be knowledgeable about geography; be able to provide information on packing, marking, and labeling requirements in over 30 countries; master foreign exchange information; and try to maintain sanity when many of those things change every day.

Throughout the 1990s, management expounded on the *value-added* concept and the *best-spend* policies, which were ingrained into corporate purchasing credos. This has continued into the second decade of the new millennium.

Purchasing domestically is arduous, but purchasing internationally is dramatically more complicated, with serious consequences for bad decisions.

2.4.1 Skill Sets for Purchasing Managers

Purchasing managers engaged in global sourcing must have the following skill sets:

- Negotiation skills in numerous cultures
- Basic, and in some cases, more expanded, knowledge of foreign cultural issues
- An understanding of how to access information on legal, political, economic, and social factors in various countries
- Ability to develop partnerships with consultants, attorneys, bankers, and accountants with contacts and expertise in foreign markets
- Knowledge of US and foreign customs regulations, duty, tax, and value-added tax implications
- Ability to select the best partners in freight forwarding, carriers, customhouse brokers, and other related transportation providers
- An understanding of all the issues affecting global supply chains, such as freight and carrier options, weather patterns, longshoreman actions, and warehouse options
- Skill in contract management and risk mitigation and ability to work with specialized legal counsel on related matters
- Possibly speaking a foreign language or acquiring rudimentary foreign language skills, such as how to say hello, thank you, please, my name is…, and so on
- Ability to adapt to travel to a foreign country, if required, including skills in cell phone, computer, and Internet use

The successful purchasing managers of 2016 and beyond will need diverse skills. They will surround themselves with those with qualified expertise and who take the time to know all of the basics and the areas in which enhanced knowledge must be gained.

Some companies are elevating the position of purchasing manager to the highest levels of the corporate ladder. As global sourcing becomes even more critical, this position will continue to gain prominence in the corporate structure.

2.5 WHY DEVELOP SOURCING OPTIONS IN FOREIGN MARKETS?

Many steps make up the global sourcing process. The following list provides an overview of why companies source in foreign markets:

- *Unit cost*. Products can be made cheaper—period.
- *In some cases, products can be made cheaper and "quicker."*
- *Regulatory controls can be significantly less cumbersome or even nonexistent.*
- *Moving plants to foreign locations spreads the risk.* Diversification is a long-time risk mitigation factor. For example, consider an oil production company with plants in New Orleans, Louisiana, and Naples, Florida. The hurricanes of 2005 could have stopped production. If the company also had a production facility in Europe that could pick up the load during reconstruction and revamping, the company could mitigate the risk of the hurricanes and perhaps prevent serious losses.
- *Labor issues may be diminished.* In some countries, the labor laws are much less restrictive. Issues such as employee benefits, workers' compensation, life and health requirements, working hours,

child labor laws, safety- and Occupational Safety and Health Administration–related controls, and other government agency matters all add costs to production in the United States or other Western locations and, in some places, may be far less restrictive or not even exist.

- *Research and development matters are less restrictive and cumbersome.* In the United States, in some industries such as the food, pharmaceutical, and chemical industries, lead times, documentary controls, and trial sample laws prove costly and complicated. In other countries, these controls greatly favor the manufacturer or the producer.
- *Local politics may have considerable influence.* In some countries, politics is more controlled and favors industrialists, big businesses, and new business developments. The politics of certain countries might favor expansion and foreign engagement, making it easier for a US or Western company to do business.
- *Local tax laws sometimes favor foreign investment, making it financially attractive to develop manufacturing in that country.*

Along with all of these reasons why a company should consider foreign sourcing, the following concerns should be examined as well in the foreign sourcing decision:

- Do not compromise short-term gains or solutions for long-term ill effects.
- Verify information using multiple sources. Exercise due diligence.
- Engage experts.
- Investigate political and economic uncertainties that may prove impossible to manage successfully. Legal, currency, and governmental restrictions may be barriers.
- Investigate the availability of qualified labor.
- Determine whether weather considerations, power resources, and transportation and communication infrastructures will meet the company needs.

The company examining foreign sourcing should create a checklist of all the issues that the company may face in a particular market. Having qualified expertise or access to expertise is a critical element to assessing the risks correctly.

2.5.1 Locating Manufacturing Sources

There are numerous methods of finding manufacturing options in foreign markets. Some of them are as follows:

- *Hire employees who have specific contacts and prior experience in foreign sourcing in the products and manufacturing that you require.*
- *Engage consultants who can provide the specific expertise that you need.*
- *Find specialty sourcing agents who represent foreign manufacturers.* These are typically foreign nationals of that country living in the United States and having the connections to locate manufacturing partners. They often work on a commission basis or are paid by the manufacturer.
- *Contact US consulates in foreign countries who can provide introductions and basic local manufacturing contacts.* This option is viable only on a very limited basis.
- *Contact the Department of Commerce (DoC) (http://www.doc.gov).* They provide expertise through the Foreign Commercial Service and their outreach programs. The DoC actively pursues connections for US companies that are interested in foreign sourcing or outsourcing. The Foreign Commercial Service has numerous personnel and resources that are planted in overseas gateways to provide assistance to US corporations in developing foreign sourcing or markets.

   This local connection and database of companies seeking business ventures with the United States can be an invaluable resource in finding foreign manufacturers. The DoC has other internal entities, outlined within the chapters of this book and the Appendix, such as the International Trade Administration, which runs overseas fairs, exhibitions, and trade missions to put US companies in contact with potential foreign partners.

- *Trade shows in particular industries also provide a concentration of people and companies that are looking to provide access to their markets, plants, and manufacturing sites.* These shows often have foreign manufacturers' and buyers' pavilions where contact and introductions can be facilitated.

- *Placing advertisements in local papers, trade journals, and industry publications can produce contacts.*
- *Internet search engines can supply information on available options, although contact would still have to be made independently.*

Foreign business dealings will likely entail travel to the countries with which the company is involved. This is discussed in the following section.

2.5.2 Developing Relationships with Foreign Partners

I cannot emphasize enough the importance of building solid relationships with foreign partners. The term *partner* describes the mature business relationship. In most foreign cultures, the business world operates on a much more personal basis than it does in the United States. In my lectures and supply chain classes, I often say, "In the United States, we tend to buy from Coca-Cola because of their reputation. Overseas, they tend to buy from Bob from Coca-Cola because of their relationship."

Contracts and legal resolve are the way that business is done in American culture. In most foreign markets, excluding some western European countries, the contract is only a starting point of the relationship. It can be altered and modified as circumstances change.

Functionally, this means that it is nearly impossible to hold a company in China to the exact points of a contract, but there is an opportunity to develop a good working relationship that will make the arrangement more successful.

In other words, spend more money on *breaking bread* than on attorneys.

I am not downplaying the importance of sound, qualified legal advice in international business; I am rather emphasizing that in international business, contracts have little functional value over the monies and time that are invested in developing the relationship. In this process, it is important to do the following:

- Learn the specific cultural and business guidelines of the countries that are involved.
- Learn basic language skill sets—hello, goodbye, please, thank you, my name is, where, how, and so on.

- Identify the local differences within the country, particularly if the company has multiple sites. In China, for example, there are major cultural differences among Hong Kong, Beijing, and Shanghai provinces. In Italy, there are major cultural differences between northern Italy, for example, Milan, and the southern part of the country, for example, Rome. In Brazil, the culture of the people of São Paulo is very different from that of the people in Rio de Janeiro.
- Budget correctly for time, commitment, travel, and entertainment in foreign countries.

These costs could be considerable. Chapter 4 addresses the overall cost considerations in deciding to source internationally, which can be a factor against overseas sourcing. Companies frequently do not factor these costs into their overall bottom-line landed costs and thus are unable to truly determine the most cost-effective manufacturing option.

Developing a quality working relationship with a foreign partner will go a long way in mitigating problems and allow a long-term partnership to flourish, which will always make for the most cost-effective manufacturing option.

2.6 JOINT VENTURE, OWN, OR CONTRACT OUT?

The decision to enter a joint venture, own, or contract out is one of the most complex issues that a corporation will face in developing a global supply chain. Company executives often struggle with these issues, and the answers are more often the result of opportunity rather than strategy. However, a company must have a strategy when entering into foreign manufacturing.

Assuming that a company has already identified foreign manufacturing as an option, the executives must choose among joint venture, ownership, or a third-party relationship.

In some countries, for example, Peru, Saudi Arabia, and Libya, foreign ownership would not be an option. In other countries, such as Russia, China, and Vietnam, ownership would be very difficult to achieve. In South Korea, South Africa, and Israel, for example, ownership is allowed but is typically not prudent because of complicated politics, currency factors, and labor stability.

From a control standpoint, then, ownership would typically be the best option, but the following factors must be considered:

- Local and regional politics
- Local and regional economics
- Current and historic relationships with the United States and other supply chain countries
- Energy, communication, and transportation infrastructure
- Government posture on related issues, such as environment, regulatory controls, partnership mentality, and ease of doing business
- Legal complexities and proprietary rights matters

Ownership will typically provide the most control and influence in managing the business. However, is it feasible? What are the costs to make it a longer-term consideration?

In the short term and for companies considering their first venture into the foreign market, the best option is typically third-party or contract manufacturing, in which a third party handles the work in the foreign country. In this situation, the company provides the manufacturing specifications, requirements, and parameters for the product, and the foreign site handles the manufacturing process. The US-based company might share the technology, wherewithal, and capability or perhaps loan, lease, sell, or give the equipment that is required to the manufacturer.

The major risk or exposure in this option involves proprietary rights, trademarks, and patent issues because the company may potentially lose control over these matters. Good legal advice and contracts will help mitigate these issues but will not eliminate them.

Chapter 4 discusses deemed export regulations in detail. In brief, these are the US government regulations regarding the transfer of capability, technology, and wherewithal to foreign nationals for utilization outside of the United States. Restrictions are in place regarding how US companies and their executives can transfer any of these benefits to overseas facilities or foreign nationals. In addition, there are serious penalties and consequences for noncompliance and breaking of deemed export regulations.

A middle-ground option is to enter into a joint venture. This can be done in a number of ways, in tandem with friendly competitors or directly with the foreign manufacturers. A joint venture can involve a wide range of relationships or be specific to a product, trade lane distribution supply chain, and so on. It provides a compromise and balance between owner-ship and a relationship with a third party.

From an initial cash outlay/capital expenditure basis, ownership bears the largest fixed expense, followed by joint venture, and then a third-party relationship, which clearly is the least costly.

For a company considering its initial entry into overseas production, I suggest considering a third party or outsourcing first. This option pro-vides the following:

- The least amount of fiscal investment in the beginning.
- Initial reduction of a certain amount of risk.
- Ease of ending the relationship if it fails.
- Ability to limit information flow to such a time that the company is comfortable with the partnership.
- Affords an adjustment period before the company must seriously commit.
- Joint ventures are a less expensive option than ownership because the costs and commitment can be shared. However, joint ventures will typically require heavy initial legal costs in structuring and making the operation functional. Thus, it might be best for a company to first engage in a third-party relationship or contract out and then later consider a joint venture, leading into ownership. These steps provide the least exposure and initial cost until the company has sufficient experience to make a larger, riskier commitment.

3

Global Sourcing Model

3.1 INTRODUCTION

This chapter begins the process of dissecting the risks of global sourcing, framing the issues, and providing the necessary benchmarking ideas for evaluating the importance of global sourcing to an organization's supply chain. Case studies are reviewed to examine the various aspects of global sourcing to be considered in an organization's decision-making processes.

3.2 IDENTIFYING THE RISKS OF GLOBAL SOURCING

The main reason that most companies source overseas is to maintain or gain competitive product pricing. We know that this is true just by looking at how much of what we buy every day at Sears, Wal-Mart, and Target originates in China, Pakistan, or Mexico. And, from the specific companies, we worship their products: Apple, Samsung, Motorola, and Crocs, to name a few.

Our trade deficit (the difference between what we import versus what we export) grows every day. American companies have found a virtually limitless supply of inexpensive labor, less government interference, and low-cost manufacturing outside the United States.

But, our exports continue to grow, neutralizing the impact of our import mentality and practice, which is a good occurrence for all of North America.

But, with these benefits come risks. Those companies that actively analyze these exposures, mitigate the risks, and proactively engage them will be in a far better position to maintain competitive supply chains and profitable bottom lines. Each supply chain will have both risks that are common to all other companies that source globally and some that are unique to their supply chain.

In the area of commonality, supply chain executives must recognize that the extent of the influence of risks could vary dramatically in their supply chains from those of other companies. In other words, risks that are common to all companies could affect one company more than another.

For example, consider two companies that source in China. One has a single factory in Shanghai; the other's factory is in Beijing. The one that is in Shanghai has only a short inland move from factory to port. The company that has the plant in Beijing has an inland move of over 1000 miles. The risk facing the second company in Beijing is much greater than the risk to the company in Shanghai because the Beijing company will have more exposures from weather, communications, road conditions, the availability of haulage and drivers, and the state of the overall transportation infrastructure.

China faces unique problems regarding inland transit. The roads are not yet developed to American or European standards. As manufacturing has expanded, the transportation infrastructure has not been able to keep up on certain trade lanes. There is a capacity problem of vehicles and qualified drivers. These issues are being addressed, but they do have an impact on the supply chain performance of companies that source from various points in China.

The conclusion to this example is that the supply chain executive should analyze this potential problem, understand what effects it might have on the inbound supply chain, and determine the proactive steps to mitigate the problem.

Sections 3.2.1 through 3.2.13 describe the risks and exposures that a company faces in globalization.

3.2.1 Competition for Resources

The entire world is looking for less expensive manufacturing. This places a greater demand on resources in China, Pakistan, India, Vietnam, Sri Lanka, Malaysia, and other countries, often pitting, for example, a German company against an American company for access to resources and local manufacturing partners.

3.2.2 Lack of Expertise

Many US companies enter globalization and foreign sourcing without the necessary skills to develop a successful inbound supply chain. The learning curve can prove to be both costly and ineffective.

3.2.3 *Force Majeure*

The effects of *acts of God*, such as weather conditions, climate, environmental conditions, and the potential effects of physical geography, could present significant risks overseas that do not affect business in the United States or do so to a much lesser extent. Tsunamis, earthquakes, rainy seasons, monsoons, flooding, droughts, and typhoons all have potentially disastrous effects in other parts of the world.

3.2.4 Local and Regional Politics

Events in the Middle East, North African countries, and Venezuela, for example, give evidence to the way that local politics can affect how companies manage commercial relationships with these countries.

Few US companies are prepared to manufacture in Lebanon, Sudan, or Peru because of political conditions that potentially work against a favorable trade environment. There are probably more than 50 countries around the world, at any given time, in which the political environment is not conducive to partnering with local business.

3.2.5 Currency Issues

Money has to be moved between the United States and a company's foreign manufacturing partners. Stability of currency provides *ease* of trade.

Instability makes it more complex, which introduces risk. If the money changing hands amounts to tens of millions of dollars, a 5% deviation could affect the profitability of the supply chain or the specific transactions that are involved. A 4% deviation could prove disastrous.

Larger companies have specific personnel in their financial departments who watch and manage information on currency valuations. A smaller company that may not have specific personnel still must set up systems, internally or outsourced, that protect and hedge against currency fluctuations. The opposite of risk is also present when discussing currency issues.

Many times, companies can put themselves in an advantageous position by managing currency to their favor.

3.2.6 Local and Regional Economics

Local and regional economics can be a major risk factor because developing countries, where manufacturing is less expensive, may also experience a volatile economic potential. In 1999, over one weekend, almost every Asian economy and currency declined sharply.

A number of banking and economic events took place, causing the crash of many Asian economies. In 2016, although most countries have regained their economic well-being, many still have not fully recovered. Many American companies were financially hurt by the occurrence.

Many US companies are reluctant to invest in offshore manufacturing in Latin America and Africa because of the instability of regional and local economies. Large companies engage specific personnel to watch local economies. Although the risks are just as great for medium and smaller companies, they must find support channels through consultants or accounting and financial firms that can provide third-party support in this risk area.

3.2.7 Relationships between the United States and Other Countries

The relationship that the United States has with the country that a company chooses to source from is a critical factor in the decision-making process. That relationship will affect the partners, the subsidiaries, the parents, and the operating units that the company has located in other countries. For example, consider the North American subsidiary of a German company that wants to source product from a country with which the United States has unfavorable political and economic ties, such as Iran, North Korea, or Libya. Although the German parent can do business there, the American subsidiary will have difficulty in doing so.

This will create a complex problem of points of origin, ultimate consignees, *de minimis* rules, deemed exports, US principal parties of interest (PPIs), and technology transfers, all relating to US import and export regulations. If these are not managed correctly, the consequences could prove to be disastrous, in the form of fines, penalties, and loss of supply chain privileges.

The consequences of the September 11, 2001 terrorist attacks have made this whole subject area a major concern for firms that are active in global trade, even as we approach some 15 years later.

3.2.8 Language and Culture

Language and cultural issues are manageable but must be recognized as concerns that must be dealt with. Good international business management requires that respect be shown to the people, culture, and language of the countries in which a company operates.

This means taking the time to learn basic information about the culture and possibly learning some basic language skills, such as how to say hello, goodbye, thank you, my name is, and so on.

The ability to successfully interact on a personal level with foreign nationals and local personnel will go a long way in developing a good working relationship, which maximizes the opportunity for developing a successful supply chain.

3.2.9 Energy, Communication, and Transportation Infrastructure

Not all countries, particularly those offering low-cost manufacturing, have good internal systems for providing consistent and state-of-the-art energy, communication, and domestic transportation infrastructure options.

China is an example of this; development is occurring so quickly that it has been difficult for the country to keep pace with providing quality support infrastructure capabilities.

A company may find a very capable factory to manufacture a product, but if consistent communication is not possible, electricity frequently fails, or there is limited availability of transport, it will all be for naught. In addition, a company must evaluate the commitment of the local government and its ability to develop sufficient capital requirements to support long-term infrastructure needs.

3.2.10 Government Posture

It is critical that a company evaluate the local government's posture on all matters that are related to foreign investment and, in particular, foreign investment by American companies. Most countries welcome US investment and will provide incentives for foreign firms to partner with local manufacturers and invest in business development. These incentives can include tax breaks, personnel deployment and training, research and development monies, and capital investment. Determining that a government is either investment friendly or understands partnering is an important criterion in due diligence regarding the decision to engage in foreign sourcing.

3.2.11 Legal and Proprietary Rights

How does a company protect proprietary rights, patents, trademarks, formulizations, trade secrets, and so on? To each company, the answers to these questions can pose very little exposure or very significant exposure. These factors must be reviewed and examined in great detail. A quality, experienced law firm specializing in international business can be invaluable in the endeavor.

This book continually makes the point that companies need to invest more heavily in developing relationships with foreign business partners and less in attorneys.

However, due diligence requires allocating time and resources to working through the complexities of the legal issues of offshore manufacturing plants.

Understanding a foreign country's legal system, contract law, patent law, personnel issues, and so on is key to developing a successful overseas supplier relationship.

The more complex a company's product is and the more committed the company is to the partnership, such as in ownership or a joint venture option, the more critical it is that the company make sure that all legal issues are handled carefully and correctly. For example, if a company was making tennis balls from a technology that is available from numerous sources with little complexity to their supply chain, their legal concerns might exist but be minimal. However, for a company building electronic surveillance systems that are protected under US patent laws, with proprietary specifications, the legal concerns are more complicated, and penalties more severe, and thus legal issues must be handled with a much higher level of due diligence.

In some countries, such as Canada, Great Britain, and the Netherlands, there is an excellent opportunity to protect proprietary rights on a scale that is similar to that of the United States. But in Pakistan, India, or China, this not only is more difficult but also may be impossible.

For a company with high-end, high-value products with proprietary technical profiles, the choice of foreign sourcing can be very much influenced by the country's approach to legal protection of foreign commercial proprietary rights.

Many companies have general counsels who focus on domestic business matters and find external expertise in law firms that have a global reach and practice.

3.2.12 US Customs

When a company sources from an overseas market, it then has the responsibility to manage the inbound clearance process, which engages an interface with US Customs and Border Protection (CBP). Those who have experience in dealing with the CBP know that it is best described as frustrating, arduous, difficult, and very demanding. Frequent importers have dedicated personnel to manage the CBP interface.

Issues related to the importing of goods include the following:

- Choice of suppliers
- Currency convertibility
- Documentation
- Recordkeeping
- Choice of customhouse brokers
- Valuation
- Food and Drug Administration compliance
- Classification
- Customs–Trade Partnership Against Terrorism
- Points of origin and substantial transformation

These are but a few of the due diligence and reasonable care standards with which an importer must comply. If a company has a complex product that requires interface with other government agencies, for example, chemicals, food products, weapons, pharmaceuticals, or medical supplies, the clearance process is very demanding and quite detailed.

3.2.13 The Physical Risks of Transporting Goods from Overseas to the United States

No matter how technology manages a global trade that is electronically driven, there is still a physical movement of goods from overseas to the US point of destination. This movement can be from over 10,000 miles, through several time zones, under the influence of variable climatic conditions, and subject to severe physical abuse from the environment and the handling that takes place through the transportation infrastructure.

A company cannot ship goods from China into the United States in the same manner that it would ship them from Columbus, Ohio, to Knoxville, Tennessee. *The level of packing, stowage, material handling, routing, and marking and labeling and the choice of carriers must be enhanced to a much greater extent for the product to consistently survive the international inbound journey.*

Damaged cargo vessel and freight containers

3.3 PUTTING THE RISKS INTO PERSPECTIVE

Where opportunity exists, there will also be risk. If a company mitigates the risks, it can increase the opportunity for successful supply chains. Risks have to be taken in context—they exist, and most cannot be controlled but only influenced. A company must be able to assess risks and how they will affect the global supply chain. To a certain extent, most of this analysis is subjective. However, science can be applied.

3.3.1 Cook's Law of Global Risk

Cook's law of global risk provides a mathematical formula for evaluating risk in the supply chain. A quantitative analysis profile can be developed for global risk to assist in determining the significance of certain exposures and how a particular supply chain compares to others.

First, secure a risk matrix. Using a scale of 1 to 5, with 1 being the least and 5 being the most, outline the risks and apply the formula. The key in this *Cook's matrix* is the use of *salience*, which allows a weight that is given to the degree of concern, unique to that supply chain. For example, suppose that a company has put its foreign manufacturing risks into five areas of concern—(1) location, (2) availability of qualified local talent, (3) currency risk, (4) proprietary rights issues, and (5) final classification of the product by the CBP.

Areas of Concern	Importance	Salience	Total
Location of plant	3	1	3
Availability of qualified local talent	5	4	20
Currency risk	2	3	6
Proprietary rights issues	2	2	4
Final classification of the product by US CBP	3	5	15
Total			48

The total risk factor is 48. Compared to other models in which 31.25 is a normal risk assessment total for placing a plant overseas, in this case, the risk would be considered somewhat high. If the total changed to 58 or higher, that would raise serious concern.

Determining what would be normal is subjective. This model uses a scale of 1 to 5 and has five categories; an average gives 31.5 (2.5, 3, 2.5, 3, 5).

If the company moves forward with outsourcing, the matrix also allows a prioritization of risk mitigation. In this example, the areas of availability of qualified local talent and the final classification by CBP appear to be more serious concerns.

This would then be clearly identified to the import supply chain executives and purchasing, risk management, and logistics personnel, allowing them to develop a strategy to mitigate or minimize the risk to the company. In any event, at least the corporation would understand where its greatest risk potentials were. Where they could not proactively mitigate, they could develop contingency plans for the future.

This matrix allows for the creation of as many line items as desired. The scale can go from 1 to 3, 1 to 5, 1 to 10, or to any amount, as long as it is consistently applied. The *importance* is defined as the importance of the risk in general to all similar supply chains. Salience is defined as how this risk is received in a company's specific situation and supply chain. The total gives a combined and weighted amount to the line item category.

The math to find the normal reference point involves determining an average depending on the 1 to 5 grading multiplied by each other in importance and salience, multiplied by the total number of line category items. The example used a 1 to 5 scale, with five line category items. The 1 to 5 or 50% is 2.5. Thus, 2.5 times two categories times five line items is 31.25, for the normal reference point. If a scale of 1 to 10 is used with 20 line items, the norm would be 5, 3, 5, 3, 20 or 500.

A company can adjust the normal reference point as a guide to be more liberal or conservative on its risk management profile or how the company chooses to view risk and engage it. The matrix is to be used only as a guide to help assess the degree of risks that a company is incurring in its supply chain. It is not meant to determine an overall risk profile. It is one of the many tools to use in risk assessment.

3.3.2 Case Studies

3.3.2.1 *Where Foreign Sourcing Makes Sense*

Allen Manufacturing has a low-end product being manufactured in several plants in the Midwest. The product is simple, with very little advanced technology and no components, being made of one-piece plastic extrusion.

One of its plants has been running for 65 years with *band-aids* that are used over the past 20 years to keep the plant running effectively. The work force is mature, at the top of the pay scale. Although the employees are unionized, there have been no serious union problems in over 10 years. The unit wholesale cost of the product is $10.00.

The manufacturing process has a nonusable by-product that is classified as a biohazard. The removal and disposal of this by-product are costly, becoming the second highest cost of the manufacturing process. The Environmental Protection Agency (EPA), which governs these regulations, along with various state and local authorities has made it increasingly more difficult to manufacture this product because the disposal costs and processes involved are increasing in both the direct cost and the indirect cost of administering the EPA paperwork.

Allen Manufacturing has been contacted by a company in India that advises that it can produce the product at 20% of Allen's costs.

Moving this type of manufacturing overseas is a perfect example of one that would fit any business model, compelling one to develop overseas sources. The following circumstances are involved:

- Aging plant
- Aging work force
- Low-end, nontechnical product
- Few proprietary issues
- An increasing cost and concern with the EPA regulations

This set of circumstances suggests great benefit in looking overseas for manufacturing. Any business model would support the steps that are necessary to build a plant overseas, outsource, or engage in a joint venture.

3.3.2.2 Where Foreign Sourcing Makes Little Sense

Watson, Inc.'s plants are located in New York, Illinois, and California. Watson produces a piece of high-tech diagnostics equipment. Wholesale cost is over $10,000 per unit.

It is protected under US patents, and the company holds exclusive technical expertise in the assembly process. The unit is composed of over 40 pieces, of which 10 are manufactured by Watson, and the balance comes from various third-party suppliers.

Watson is thus approximately 25% pure manufacturing and 75% assembly.

Watson's plant is 30 years old but was upgraded and modernized 7 years ago.

The work force is nonunion and mostly made up of younger, college-educated or technically trained workers.

Watson has been approached by a Taiwanese company that advises that it has the capability to manufacture the product at 50% of Watson's costs.

This scenario does not favor offshore production. The following circumstances are involved:

- Young plant.
- Young work force, college educated and technically trained.
- High-end product with high-dollar value.
- Proprietary issues with the product.
- The product has a complex assembly process, and more components are purchased from third parties than produced by Watson.

One of the problems with US-based manufacturing is the age of plants. In this case, that is not an issue. Watson has access to a highly qualified, youthful work force. The value of the product is high. Patent issues are involved, and Watson holds proprietary rights to a highly technical assembly process.

In this case, the gain from offshore production may be very minimal compared to what could potentially be lost. When the additional expenses of importing, taxes, duties, insurance, transportation, logistics, customs clearance, and so on are considered, that might bring the savings down to only 20%. When the indirect costs of travel, communications, and legal expense are added to subcontracting overseas, that 20% savings is reduced even further. With the potential loss of proprietary rights, the minimal savings may not prove enough to contract and manufacture offshore.

Watson might want to consider placing some of the component manufacturing offshore, but retaining control of the assembly process, in which the proprietary rights issue is of more serious concern. This would provide the benefit of lower costs in components but does not involve sharing processes and technical information.

In Section 3.5, we will discuss the use of foreign trade zones, which could provide a more lucrative and viable option in this scenario. However, this scenario does not favor offshore manufacturing. Where the benefit is marginal and there is risk to lose an advantage or competitive edge, the better decision is to remain in the United States.

3.4 OPTIONS TO GLOBAL SOURCING

Since the 1960s, US manufacturers have sought low-cost foreign options for their manufacturing locations. But, at no point since then has this overseas initiative been so largely a part of the American business model as in the new millennium. It almost seems that companies are outsourcing supply chain functions initiated by Purchasing Management. The rush has grown so large and dominant that sometimes overseas placement is being done even when there is little or no benefit, almost as if it was done because that is what companies are supposed to do rather than as a result of a decision that is made strategically, with the benefits and consequences clear.

The US competition is in China, so US companies must be there too. Senior management knows that production costs will be reduced by outsourcing to India. Cheaper production costs mean less expensive landed costs in the United States. Attorneys will write contracts that protect all of the company's interests. Although in some cases all of this may be true, in many instances, it is not. Each company and each supply chain have its own manufacturing and related issues. It is critical that when deciding to produce offshore, *all* factors are considered.

Many US companies have brought manufacturing back to the United States after determining that foreign manufacturing was not as expected. Many companies have extreme difficulties in successfully managing foreign manufacturing. When companies examine the indirect costs of managing the problems, frustrations, and complexities, the move overseas may not have been worthwhile.

Numerous companies have provided technical expertise or other proprietary rights capabilities, only to later regret having entered into those agreements. Some have discovered the hard way how local courts deal with foreign contracts and experienced the lack of enforceability in the local market.

So, what options to foreign manufacturing exist?

- Find ways to make manufacturing competitive in the United States.
- Negotiate with employees and unions who want to protect jobs.
- Invest in plants and machinery in the United States.
- Work with government incentives, tax relief, and other benefit programs to keep manufacturing in the United States.
- Find government programs that favor production and assembly in the United States, such as foreign trade zones.
- Build *out-of-the-box* business models that favor US manufacturing, such as assembly operations using foreign-made components.

There are many ways to make manufacturing work in the United States. Companies are perhaps too quick to look for overseas manufacturing options, when more lucrative choices and business models may exist in the United States.

3.5 FOREIGN TRADE ZONES

Most governments have some sort of foreign trade zones or free trade zones that allow certain economic, duty, and tax relief to companies that participate in these programs.

These trade programs are designed to keep a certain amount of manufacturing, assembly work, warehousing, and so on in the local economies. Although the details of these programs vary from one country to another, they are based on the same concept.

Companies are allowed to import spare parts, raw materials, components, assemblies, and so on tax and duty free, with ease of clearance, into a designated foreign trade zone, where a final product is manufactured. Once the product enters the local economy for sale or use, the tax or duty is levied, but it applies only to the cost of the components and materials, not the final price of the completed product.

The following are a few of the major advantages that US companies find when managing some or all of their supply chain in foreign trade zones:

- Taxes and duties are deferred to a later point in time.
- Tax and duty amounts overall are much less compared to those for importing fully completed goods.
- Control is exercised in an environment under company and US control and influence.
- Stability is maintained for infrastructure concerns—energy, transportation, and communications.
- Clearances are accomplished much easier.
- The final product inventory is close to point of end use.
- The regulatory environment is known and consistent.
- The legal system is able to settle commercial disputes fairly.
- The work force is stable.
- Logistics and landed costs are potentially lower.

A financial business model works as follows. Consider a company that manufactures steam turbines in China. Bringing in completed units and spare parts has an associated cost of approximately 7% in duties and taxes. The company imports $100 million worth of completed equipment and spare parts over the course of a year.

On top of the logistics inbound costs, the company pays approximately $7 million a year in duties and taxes. They have ongoing problems with the supplier on completed product delivery times, some quality control problems, and the occasional loss and damage of completed products. In addition, the completed turbines are large and not easy to handle, and because of their size, there are additional carrier surcharges because of the size of the finished product. In this model, 60% of the purchase cost is components and raw materials, and the balance is labor, quality control, and export handling.

When this company figures its landed costs, it adds up the following.

If the company elected to operate in an approved foreign trade zone, it would be eligible for financial benefits and numerous other advantages. First, it would still import from China but not the completed turbines. Rather, it would import all of the raw materials and components. Obviously, US-supplied raw materials and components would be reviewed, as well, to see if any efficiencies or advantages could be gained. It would then assemble the finished product in this foreign trade zone, located at its US plant site.

This would reduce inbound freight costs because the spare parts, raw materials, and components carry no freight-related surcharges, and less weight is being shipped.

Using American labor to assemble the product will raise labor costs but will allow the deferral of duties and taxes until the completed goods are ready for sale in the foreign trade zone. Problems are seriously reduced in quality control, timely manufacturing, and loss and damage.

The new financial model looks like this.

The model is overly simplistic but does fairly represent the potential direct savings over building completed goods on foreign shores versus in the United States.

For example, consider the foreign car manufacturers who build the cars and trucks to sell in the United States—in domiciled foreign trade zones. In almost every industry—from heavy manufacturing to high-tech electronics to the chemical, food, and pharmaceutical industries—companies are taking advantage of the multitude of benefits of using foreign trade zones in their global supply chains. This does add financial benefit to the bottom line, which one could estimate, because some costs will decrease, such as travel, communications, internal follow-ups, and so on.

Some companies, in their evaluation matrix, assign values to the following:

- Stability of the work force
- Better and more dependable transportation infrastructure
- Consistent energy sources
- Access to better technology and government resources

A company must evaluate the specific details of its supply chain to accomplish a true *apples-to-apples* comparison to create a checklist that outlines the issues in its inbound supply chains.

Ex-works plant	$100,000,000.00
Inland freight	$1,500,000.00
Free on board (FoB) cost Shanghai	$101,500,000.00
Ocean freight	$2,500,000.00
Oversize surcharges	$350,000.00
Clearance charges	$50,000.00
Duties and taxes	$7,105,000.00
On forwarding	$250,000.00
Total landed cost	**$110,755,000.00**

Global Sourcing Model	
Ex-works plant	
Components only	$60,000,000.00
Inland freight	$1,000,000.00
FoB cost Shanghai	$61,000,000.00
Ocean freight	$2,000,000.00
Oversize surcharges	$10,000.00
Clearance charges	$50,000.00
Duties and taxes	$4,270,000.00
On forwarding	$150,000.00
Total landed cost to foreign trade zone	$67,480,000.00
US labor plus additional costs	$41,000,000.00*
Total landed costs through foreign trade zone	$108,480,000.00
Savings	**$2,275,000.00**

*US labor costs are approximately $1 million higher than in China.

4

Landed Costs

4.1 INTRODUCTION

Landed cost (LC) becomes the key factor in making sure that foreign sourcing provides a competitive advantage. It is the total aggregate of all the costs to develop and bring a product to utilization or revenue. Understanding how LC works is a key ingredient to ensure that offshore production is viable and to ensure competitive inbound supply chains.

4.2 DEVELOPING LC MODELS

A company must develop LC models to clearly and more accurately understand the cost to manufacture and import goods into the United States. Too often, purchasing executives make decisions based on ex-works purchase price, which is normally much less in overseas markets compared to US-produced goods, but fail to include many incremental costs that could override the benefit of overseas manufacturing.

When companies both here and abroad purchase merchandise and services, a common goal is to ensure competitive pricing. More often than not, an evaluation is not done to make an informed decision on whether or not competitive pricing has been achieved. The primary reason for this shortfall in the decision-making process is failure to factor in the total costs in the import and export supply chain. Very clear, identifiable costs and varied and numerous hidden costs make up the total accumulated costs that are relative to determining what it actually costs to import or export competitively. It is imperative for companies to perform a complete evaluation to make sure that it is exercising good judgment in purchasing options, as well as to fairly compare vendor and supplier choices and all of the other variables in the global supply chain.

All companies look for a less expensive purchase. But, the purchase price is only one component of the cost to import and export products and services. Depending on the products, weights, densities, dimensions, freight, duties and taxes, and other supply chain variables, the purchase price could be incremental to the total LC.

To obtain the best supply chain option, companies and global supply chain executives must build a matrix that does the following:

- Identifies the supply chain options
- Outlines all the variables in the options that can influence LCs
- Indicates how the supply chain can affect pricing
- Organizes all of the variable cost factors into a detailed structure

The sample matrix costing outlines are as follows.

4.2.1 Import LC Matrix

Likelihood / Consequence	Level	**Rare** The event may occur in exceptional circumstances / Less than once a year	**Unlikely** The event could occur at some time / At least once a year	**Moderate** The event will probably occur at some time / At least once in 6 months	**Likely** The event will occur in most circumstances / At least once per month	**Certain** The event is expected to occur in all circumstances / At least once per week
		1	2	3	4	5
Negligible No injuries. Low financial loss.	0	0	0	0	0	0
Minor First-aid treatment. Moderate loss.	1	1	2	3	4	5
Serious Medical treatment required. High financial loss. Moderate environment implications. Moderate loss of reputation. Moderate business interruption.	2	2	4	6	8	10
Major Excessive, multiple long-term injuries. Major financial loss. High environmental implications. Major loss of reputation. Major business interruption.	3	3	6	9	12	15
Fatality Single death.	4	4	8	12	16	20
Multiple Multiple deaths and serious long-term injuries.	5	5	10	15	20	25

Legend

Risk rating	Risk priority	Description
0	N	No risk: The costs to treat the risk are disproportionately high compared to the negligible consequences.
1–3	L	Low risk: May require consideration in any future changes to the work area or processes, or can be fixed immediately.
4–6	M	Moderate: May require corrective action through planning and budgeting process.
8–12	H	High: Requires immediate corrective action.
15–25	E	Extreme: Requires immediate prohibition of the work, process and immediate corrective action.

- Purchase price
- Method and cost for payment
- Currency exchange costs
- Foreign vendor packing charges
- Foreign inland transportation charges
- Foreign loading charges
- Foreign inspection fees
- Foreign port charges for Customs and Border Protection (CBP) examination and no-load containers
- International transportation charges (air, ocean, and ground transportation)
- *Ad valorem* duties and taxes based on import value, specific duties and taxes based on import quantity, and compound duties based on both value and quantity
- Merchandise processing fees based on 0.125% of import value
- Harbor maintenance fee for ocean shipments based on 0.3464% of import value
- Antidumping fees based on CBP investigation into fair market price value methods, countervailing duty fees based on CBP investigation into foreign bounty grants, and subsidies that are paid to foreign vendors that may affect the price paid or payable
- Security manifest fees
- Fuel surcharge fees
- Handling and freight transfer fees
- Storage fees that are incurred on freight that are not picked up from the pier in three days from date of availability
- International freight
- US inland transportation fees
- US warehousing, deconsolidation, storage, distribution, and break-bulk fees

- Messenger fees
- US CBP examination fees
- Other government agency examination fees (Agriculture, Fish and Wildlife Service, Environmental Protection Agency)

4.2.2 Export LC Matrix

- Export packing
- Warehouse in/out fee
- Fumigation
- Foreign inland freight
- Automated Export System filing fee
- Foreign loading
- Foreign documentation fees (legalization, consularization), inspection fee
- Insurance
- Bank fees (letter of credit fees, confirmation fees, messenger fees)
- Ocean freight fees: currency adjustment factor, bunker fee, wharfage container fees (exceeding free time for loading)
- Fuel fees
- Security fees
- Automated manifest system fee
- Delivery charges (including accessorial charges: inside delivery, special delivery)
- Duty
- Value-added tax
- Export forwarding fee
- Document handling fee
- Storage fees
- Container inspection fees
- Customs clearance
- Messenger fees
- Buying commission
- Interest fees
- Hazardous material surcharge
- State sales or other taxes or fees within that state that might be applicable for that product or business operation

There are a multitude of incremental costs that are involved in executing a successful global trade.

Failure to calculate these costs can create unnecessary problems for the importer and the exporter. Additionally, in both matrixes, the cost of travel, research and development, engineering, and technical expertise lent to accomplish the offshore manufacturing or business development might not necessarily be factored into the cost of goods that are purchased but in fact will affect the bottom line.

Foreign travel is expensive and could add up to hundreds of thousands or even millions of dollars each year. The incremental costs add up. They can range from 3% to as much as 200% of the purchase price, depending on the product and other variables.

4.3 INTEGRATING DOMESTIC SUPPLY CHAIN REQUIREMENTS

It is very important to access the costs to move the goods from inbound gateways (ports, airports, border crossings, etc.) to the final destination or the point of use. Depending on product details and final locations, the domestic transportation costs could be the largest component of the total LC. In addition, if deconsolidation, storage, assembly, further processing, or warehousing is required, this would also add to the cost. Additional costs to be considered are repacking, remarking, or relabeling that may be done before entry into the US market.

The gateway of entry and its proximity to the final destination or the point of use are also critical. This becomes a factor in the transport routing of the goods. Choosing the most suitable carrier and port of entry can make a big difference in LCs.

Many companies will locate facilities to accommodate the best gateways that can favorably reduce costs. For example, in the United States, many companies have transferred plants to the Southeast (such as North and South Carolina, Georgia, and Florida) to take advantage of the ease of inland transportation from the ocean ports of Charleston, Savannah, and Jacksonville. Although other factors affect site selection, if a company brings goods from overseas, the inland supply chain costs must be counted.

Import and export companies must execute an LC analysis, taking the following steps:

- Match the provided reference matrix samples to the supply chain and apply the unique and proprietary details, such as the logistics, purchasing components, and import duties and taxes, to create an LC supply chain matrix for the organization.
- Companies with global operations may have several matrixes.
- Learn what the international communication terms (INCOTerms) are and how the options will affect responsibilities, liabilities, and landed costing.
- Learn transfer pricing issues for companies with intercompany sales.
- Learn the Harmonized Tariff and Schedule B codes to maximize compliance capabilities and competitive options.
- Develop relationships with qualified service providers, such as customhouse brokers, freight forwarders, international domestic carriers, third-party service entities, banks, accounting and legal firms, and consultants who specialize in global supply chain operations.
- Learn the basics of bonded warehouses and foreign trade zones and how these can affect LCs positively and offer competitive advantage in global supply chains.
- Understand how trade laws are designed and implemented—Mercosur, North American Free Trade Agreement (NAFTA), Central American Free Trade Agreement (CAFTA), Israeli Free Trade Agreement, and Generalized System for Preferences.
- Learn all the government agencies that can affect the supply chain. Establish operating profiles and contacts at these agencies.
- Develop technology options that can reduce the various hidden costs of operating globally.

4.3.1 Demand Planning and Domestic Distribution

It is imperative for purchasing and sourcing managers to coordinate their decision making with those personnel who are responsible for inventory and distribution management.

The ultimate goal of the supply chain is to reduce the LCs, the inventory balances, and the domestic final mile delivery expenses.

That goal can only be reached with successful *demand planning* and a coordination between those who buy in a company and those who have to deliver.

There are numerous technology solutions that can be *stand-alone or bolt-ons* to main frame operating systems that will allow the bridge between those who buy and those who deliver.

4.4 CASE STUDY

4.4.1 LCs

A company must analyze the total costs in importing goods into the United States, including the costs that are incurred once in the country. A profile of these costs is as follows:

Stereo Speakers from Beijing to Chicago	
Unit cost: ex-works factory	$61.00 USD ($18,300)
Inland freight: 40' container (300 units)	$1200.00
Ocean freight	$3100.00
Export handling	$220.00
Export clearance charges	$94.50
Import clearance	$125.00
Duties and taxes	$955.50
Other clearances	$70.00
Inland to Chicago	$755.00
Warehousing (60 days)	$122.00
Inland to customers	$246.00
Total LC (300 units)	**$25,188.00**
Per unit	**$83.96**

The company can now dissect the costs, affecting any one line, and determine ways to reduce inbound supply chain costs. For example, if the company chose the West Coast to enter goods and warehouse them, it could reduce the inland freight costs by $600.00 ($755.00 less $155.00 for local haulage). That would reduce the total cost by 2%. The company could negotiate with a West Coast customhouse broker to store the goods for 60 days at no charge to save another 1%.

If the company can reduce the ocean freight costs by 10%, it will save another 1.2%. So, by manipulating the costs, the company could save almost 5%. More serious negotiations could result in even more savings.

Consider another example: suppose that a company finds a supplier in Mexico who can manufacture a similar product at the same ex-works price as the supplier in China. Obviously, this is an oversimplification, but for a sample business model, it works well.

The product would then enter under the NAFTA duty-free regulations, and the freight costs would be reduced by 35%. The savings would be approximately 11%–13%.

There are many options and variations that a supply chain manager can manipulate to influence the LC and obtain a competitive advantage. The supply chain manager must know what the best options are, what the variable risks are, and how to provide the most cost-effective options for the company.

4.5 REDUCING LCs

Over the past 30 years, I have observed well over 1000 corporations develop offshore manufacturing and build successful supply chains. Many experienced significant learning curves.

The following suggestions have worked to minimize learning curve issues:

- *Be patient in the decision-making process.* Take considerable time to make conclusive decisions. Do the proper research and obtain as much information as possible.

  Do not let competitive pressures force hasty choices that the company may regret later.
- *Utilize external support services.* Consultants who specialize in developing foreign market and manufacturing options can prove invaluable here.
- *Align with quality service providers, for example, freight forwarders, customhouse brokers, third-party providers, ocean and air carriers, integrated carriers, bankers, attorneys, consultants, accounting firms, and training services.* Engage providers that have personnel with

years of experience and can provide quality advice and counsel in areas that will affect the supply chain.

- *Do beta testing, when feasible, before making long-term decisions.* Allow time for testing how a foreign manufacturer and other supply chain partners will perform.
- *Ensure that contracts have escape clauses and performance guidelines.*
- *When feasible, have all of the supply chain partners invest in the supply chain with capital expenditures, particularly the manufacturer, to ensure a more secure and longer-term commitment.*

4.6 SOURCING FROM CHINA

China is one of the fastest-growing areas in third-party manufacturing for US companies. Since 2000, China has moved from fifth to second place in America's top trading partners, and as we approach 2017, this will rise to number 1.

China has offered inexpensive labor and a desire to take on every challenge. It has steadily increased its skill sets and capabilities to produce technology-driven products as well as the simplest of one-piece plastic toys.

China has vast industrial resources and an unlimited supply of inexpensive labor. It is free from most of the environmental, human resource, and developmental regulations that hamper companies manufacturing in the United States and most Western countries.

Although China is one nation, it is very much regionalized politically and in its business agendas. The majority of the regions have a favorable mind-set toward business with the West and afford ease of manufacturing development.

However, there are problems:

- It has not yet met the Western standards of a free democracy and more positive dealings with human rights issues.

- It has been unable to federalize the local governments and thus struggles to act in unison on major issues.
- Although China has been successful in its initiatives to slow population growth, it still has many people living in poverty and in underprivileged circumstances.

  China has had the greatest success in moving the most people in the history of our planet from poverty to the middle class and to be the wealthiest in the world.
- Growth in new business development has stressed the infrastructure of energy resources, communication systems, and transportation.
- Political issues between China and Taiwan create tension between China and the United States.

  The most recent issues in the South China Sea have raised serious concerns among all Pacific nations.
- Many developing countries are offering competitive business practices to lure business to their country and away from China. India, Pakistan, and Vietnam have taken bold steps to compete with China in luring investment in resources, plants, and fixed investments from the West and the United States. For example, India touts a more skilled, technically capable work force. India spends a considerable amount educating its work force to attract nonindustrial business development and more skilled-labor jobs.
- Proprietary rights are not protected to a satisfactory level to most Western companies.

Even with these problems and the competitive pressures, China is a major force in attracting US manufacturing. The following section outlines actions that US companies should take to do business successfully with China.

4.6.1 Best Practices from China

4.6.1.1 Thoughts

- China is fast becoming the largest trading partner for both imports and exports, not only for the United States but also for the world.
- America's taste for inexpensive, mass-produced consumer goods has led this China charge; just go into any Wal-Mart, Target, Best Buy, or Apple Store.

- When I first entered the world of international business in the mid-1970s, President Richard Nixon had just opened the doors for the United States to China, and no one has ever looked back.
- The economic ties between the United States and China have grown every year and created one of the largest, strongest, and most resilient business partnerships that the modern world has ever dealt with. And, the future holds even greater strategic alignment, cooperation, and growth.
- This economic alignment transcends the political dichotomy that exists between the two nations. The politics of the United States and China are almost 180-degrees separate from one another. It is the strength of the economic ties that shadows over the political posturing, the differences, and the *instability* that often raises its *ugly head*.
- There are two big overwhelming challenges that face both US- and China-based businesses: (1) how to sell and buy from one another with reasonable margins of sustainability and (2) with an ability to close all the legal, cultural, and economic gaps.
- This book creates the discussion outline on these challenges and creates a focus on what strategies, tactics, and actions need be accomplished to create a blueprint for continued successful trade between the two superpowers.
- For the last three decades, imports from China have dominated the trade landscape. But, in reality, we sell a lot of goods and services into China, and this is growing exponentially.
- E-commerce for US consumer products companies is developing and expanding every day.
- The growth of the upper and middle class in China is creating a mass of disposable income, and they are buying *named* products from the world and more particularly, the United States.
- *Consumerism* is alive, well, and growing in China, and companies such as Alibaba, Amazon, Elfants, Pepsi, and Starbucks are among the hundreds of leaders in this charge.
- The author has written over 15 books in the last 20 years on international business subjects, but this book is different as it targets only one major trade lane. The relevance is that this trade lane is complex, huge, and growing intensely.

- This US/China trade lane warrants this kind of attention that is outlined in this textbook. It is filled with timely and comprehensive information flow and useful advice on how to master all the challenges.
- In the ending chapter, which creates a best-practice overview and summary for importing and exporting that can easily apply to China and can be one of the most important *tools* in your global supply chain strategy workbox.

4.6.1.2 Relationship Driven

China is one of the leading business cultures in which relationships are a driving factor for success. Relationships must be cultivated and time allowed for them to mature. Those executives with over 20 years of favorable experience in China would agree that a good relationship is the foundation for a successful joint venture or manufacturing outsource in China.

4.6.1.3 Mentality of Contract Negotiation

The contract is the starting point of the business relationship within the Chinese culture. It is not the complete picture; rather, it is where a meeting of the minds takes place. The contract is the point from which issues can still be negotiated as circumstances dictate.

This is an important consideration because it can be very frustrating when a business deal takes a turn that is not outlined in the contract. The Chinese will take the position that it is acceptable to amend the agreement because circumstances have changed and that is now warranted; however, the US company may think that the Chinese are not honoring the original agreement. In the Chinese business culture, it is acceptable to make the change. In the US culture, both parties would review the change and come to a new agreement.

4.6.1.4 Short-Term and Performance Driven

Make sure that the agreements progress in small steps before they are extended into longer-term, more permanent agreements. Ensure success by defining specific understandings, wordings, and performance-driven guidelines that must be met.

4.6.1.5 Control the INCOTerms

A company should purchase on INCOTerms that favor its managing the freight from a point of origin or a point of export to the United States. This gives the company control over the logistics, which will have numerous benefits, such as the following:

- Typically better freight rates
- Tighter control over inbound logistics and status of inbound freight
- Control over the import process: valuation, documentation, classification, etc.
- Better supply chain control over the entire inbound process

4.6.2 Terms of Sale: INCOTerms Considerations

In attempting to understand who should control the terms of sale and what the parameters are in the decision-making process, several critical factors must be reviewed.

The INCOTerms, published by the International Chamber of Commerce, advises on and provides the definitions for the terms of international trade. They include cost, insurance, and freight (CIF); free on board (FoB); free alongside ship (FAS); and all the acronyms for potential terms of sale that the US exporter needs to understand to conduct a successful international trading. An exporter can obtain a copy of the INCOTerms booklet, which should be part of every exporter's library, from the International Chamber of Commerce Publishing Corporation, Inc., 1212 Avenue of the Americas, New York, NY 10036 or at http://www.iccbooks.com.

4.6.2.1 Overview: Sales Terms

The various terms of sale have significant consequences regarding the responsibilities, liabilities, costs, and profits or losses confronting both the importer and exporter. The INCOTerms are European in foundation, reflecting a different mind-set. The terms combine documentary and transactional requirements for passage of title and payment terms. There are many hidden costs that are involved in international trade that the INCOTerms help to define. The exporter should be aware that the terms of sale directly affect costs and could affect an exporter's competitive advantage. The more responsibility assumed, the higher the price. For example, the price might be $4500 from the plant dock, $4800 to the US port of export, and $5800 when delivered to the customer's door in Oslo, Norway.

The INCOTerms advise who is responsible for arranging the transportation services, the freight charges, insurance, and other logistics. Freight forwarders, banks, carriers, and experienced shippers are the best resource for figuring out what they are all about.

4.6.2.2 Name the Terms and the Point of Shipment

When using the terms, a point of destination or a site must be named. For example, if you were selling FoB, the question is, FoB at what point? According to the definition of the terms, once the goods are loaded on board the transportation conveyance, the title passes to the buyer. But, does this occur at the plant or at the port?

If you sell an FoB plant, the title will pass once the freight has been loaded on board the inland conveyance. This means that the buyer will arrange to pay for the inland transportation. He or she will also assume responsibility for loss or damage to the freight during transit.

Choosing to sell an FoB port of loading requires that the exporter arrange for the inland freight. He or she will then assume all transit liabilities until the freight is transferred to the international carrier. If it is an ocean shipment, the risk transfers once the freight passes the rail of the vessel, illustrating the extent of the definition of the terms.

If you had an international transaction in France that called for a CIF sale with a named point, such as Paris, and the shipment was by air, the exporter would be responsible for arranging the transportation. The shipper would assume all transit liabilities and provide marine insurance up to the point of pickup from the Paris airport. In such a case, the exporter has taken on a great deal of responsibility and, with it, an equal amount of risk. This is when the exporter needs to be a good traffic manager and/or have a quality freight forwarder. The marine insurance, the underwriter, and the claims systems must all be in place to deal with the potential losses in an international transaction.

4.6.2.3 Terms of Payment

At the time that the export sale is being consummated, the terms of payment need to be decided, as this will have a great effect on the decision making for the terms of sale. Assume, for example, that you complete the transaction with all the i's dotted and t's crossed, with the terms of sale as FoB/NY. The shipment is made with the terms of sale calling for a payment from your buyer in Paris in 60 days. The shipment arrives missing 3 of 10 pieces. They represent approximately $12,000 of the total invoice value, for which your buyer discounts your bill. You argue that the risk passed in New York; therefore, the insuring responsibility, with a clean bill of lading, was with the buyer from the time the freight was received on the international conveyance.

The buyer argues that the shipment showed up short and that under no circumstances, if the US exporter is to keep the account, would he contribute to the loss, holding the exporter fully responsible. According to this scenario, whereas the terms of sale appeared to offer less exposure to the exporter, the terms of payment that allowed 60 days provided greater exposure. The position of the importer was both unreasonable and incorrect, but it is a common path when the buyer holds the advantage of not yet having paid for the freight.

Without the contingency insurance of unpaid vendor protection, the exporter may have to sue to collect at the cost of losing a customer, unnecessary aggravation, and great expense.

4.6.2.4 Additional Considerations

A very general conclusion that can be drawn is that in most export situations, the exporter should control the terms of sale as well as the terms of payment. Every factor must be considered in this evaluation, such as, but not limited to, the following:

- Price and payment terms
- Competitive pressures
- Forwarder and carrier options
- Opportunities for loss and damage
- Previous experience with buyer
- City and country of destination
- Customs clearance in buyer's country
- Current economic and political situation in buyer's country

An additional consideration in controlling the terms of sale offers the exporter short- and long-term options for maintaining competitiveness. If you choose to sell on terms where all the basic shipping, documentation, insurance, and freight choices are in your control, then you have the ability to affect the CIF costs. You are not forced to accept a particular insurance company whose marine rates may be higher than you can obtain in the open market. If you are free to choose steamship lines, you have the option to look at possible nonconference carriers that might offer lower shipping costs. Each variable must be evaluated. Controlling the option to evaluate will afford the more competitive choices that will work to the exporter's advantage.

Another important consideration in determining the terms of sale is to look at the pitfalls of attempting a door-to-door sale, if required to do so, particularly in certain countries where customs law and practice work to the disadvantage of the exporter.

As the importer of record in door-to-door sales, you assume certain liabilities in the import country that you might want to reconsider.

In certain countries, such as Mexico (though this situation is changing), US exporters have found it preferable to sell the FoB port of entry, such as Laredo, in lieu of a CIF sale point of destination. Mexican customs (their trade and practice) have afforded the importer a better opportunity to arrange clearance than with the exporter's agent. This is also true in other countries such as, but not limited to, Thailand and Algeria. Each situation must be carefully evaluated on its own merits. The exporter's freight forwarder's local relationship with foreign clearance agents plays a vital role in this regard.

The current political and economic situation in the buyer's country is critical. Take the situation in certain parts of the new Eastern Europe. While there is a big demand for US products, payment is difficult at best. In order to make the sale, the US exporter may not be able to sell completely on secured terms but may be willing to sell on a collect or sight draft basis. This arrangement might meet the need of the importer and reduce some of the exporter's exposure.

The key word is reduce, not eliminate. The exporter will need to make arrangements through the freight forwarder or the carrier not to release the freight until the payment is made to the local representation. Good communication and tight monetary controls will be critical to the successful execution of this option.

Equally important is attention to the minutia of transactional detail for the passage of title and payment terms. Although the title may be transfered, the responsibility, particularly fiscal responsibility, may not end.

Quality marine insurance affords protection to the exporter in all situations. The marine insurance contract should have features that protect the exporter regardless of who is responsible to insure and where the title passes. Unpaid vendor or contingency insurance can be part of any successful export program. It will afford the exporter full transportation insurance in cases where they are not responsible for insurance but may be exposed to payment or contract terms.

It is also critical when letters of credit are used for international transactions that the term of the sale conform to INCO practice as well as the Uniform Customs and Practice 500 for the payment terms.

The bottom line is that the exporter must evaluate many issues in determining the best terms of sale for a particular export transaction. In any case, the exporter should negotiate a controlling INCOTerm that minimizes risk and cost in the transaction.

4.6.2.5 Lead Times

It is important to tighten the controls over the production lead times. Give as much leeway as possible to allow for various situations to occur that will not seriously affect the supply chain scheduling.

Many inconsistencies exist in China manufacturing. Some can be influenced and controlled, but others cannot. Energy flow and transportation can experience disruption. Weather extremes can prohibit consistent scheduling. Chinese management can lose sight of the US scheduling demands.

4.6.2.6 Additional Incremental Costs

A reasonable plan is to allocate 3%–5% additional inbound logistics costs than budgeted, because the normal day-to-day disruptions in the inbound supply chain from China dictate this from a historical and practical perspective.

Demurrage, air freight over ocean freight, rush shipments, port delays in Long Beach, fuel and security surcharges, and so on are but a few of the additional costs that are consistently experienced in the inbound supply chain from China.

4.6.2.7 Assists

They are monies that must be added to invoices that are declared to CBP on goods and merchandise from overseas, when the company as the purchaser provided *assists* to the foreign manufacturer in the form of tools, dyes, equipment, wherewithal, and so on.

CBP regulations define how much additional money must be declared to CBP for assisting the foreign manufacturer in producing a product that will enter the United States.

This is an often-missed area of CBP regulations that results in fines and penalties. Assists are covered in more detail in Chapter 5.

4.6.2.8 Customs–Trade Partnership against Terrorism Certifiable

The Customs–Trade Partnership Against Terrorism (C-TPAT) is a program of voluntary participation for US companies to partner with CBP to define how the company's inbound supply chain works. The C-TPAT is covered in more detail within numerous chapters and in the appendix.

As part of this process, key overseas suppliers are scrutinized for their security guidelines, for example, perimeter fencing, secure facilities, screening practices, and personnel.

It is imperative that US companies screen their suppliers in this regard to determine their C-TPAT-certifiable capability; eventually, it is likely that the CBP will allow goods to enter the United States only from C-TPAT-approved suppliers.

4.6.2.9 Proprietary Rights Management

China can be a difficult place to work with respect to proprietary rights matters. US companies are vulnerable to Chinese companies in protection against the control of patents, trademarks, formulizations, product specifications, logos, and other proprietary rights matters. Although a good legal counsel can help, there is danger in this area. Control over the manufacturing process, along with strong relationships, is the best way to manage this concern.

The need to develop a strong legal capability is critical but not a final solution as the intellectual property rights (IPR) issue is almost impossible to contract away in China.

IPR issues need to be tackled on a number of fronts:

- Obtain "top-notch" legal advisory
- Develop strong working relationships
- Take ownership of the manufacturing process, when and if feasible
- Set aggressive product enhancement and innovation schedules to be ahead of "gray-market" pirates
- Leverage agreements where you have controlling interests

4.6.2.10 Financial Management

Arranging the transfer of funds to meet financial obligations should be done in the most cost-effective manner. Letters of credit are passé and are costly to all parties. Open accounts via wire transfers are the best option in the long term. Obligations to pay should be performance driven, allowing time to inspect, experiment, adjust, and ensure that the product meets the specifications before payment is required.

4.6.2.11 Deemed Exports

Deemed exports are the Department of Commerce and Bureau of Industry and Security (BIS) procedural controls that define the transfer of capability, wherewithal, and technology to a foreign national with his or her intent to use this information outside the United States. This is a very serious issue, particularly in regard to China, and the BIS monitors this very closely. Failure to conform to these regulations can result in fines, penalties, and loss of import and export privileges. It is also important to note that in certain situations, criminal exposure exists in this regard. Deemed exports are discussed in more detail in Chapter 5, Section 5.11.21.

4.6.2.12 Exchange Rates

For the most part, the Chinese currency has been relatively stable in relation to US and other Western currencies in the past few years. Some financial analysts advise of a potential long-term problem in China in the stability of the currency against their imbalance of trade, as they continually import to a much greater extent.

4.6.2.13 Price Options

Many companies have found better options to China in assessing LC by manufacturing in Mexico, taking advantage of NAFTA and lower freight costs, or in the use of foreign trade zones, with tax and duty advantages.

This is discussed in more detail in Section 4.9.

4.6.2.14 Spread of Risk in Purchasing Decisions

Many companies have found themselves too dependent on Chinese manufacturing and have begun to spread the risk by finding alternative manufacturing sources. This is discussed further in various chapters as a proactive risk management strategy.

4.7 TRANSPORTATION AND LOGISTICS

Many companies managing inbound supply chains are significantly dependent on transportation providers. This provides access to expertise that can have a very favorable effect on the LCs, providing capability to balance cost and performance.

Some companies experience a horrific learning curve before finding service providers that meet their expectations. Managing the providers therefore becomes an important skill set for inbound supply chain and purchasing personnel. Providers can make or break the supply chain and can often make the difference in running a successful foreign sourcing and inbound logistics program.

Companies such as Panalpina, Schenkers, United Parcel Service, Expeditors, Danzas, Federal Express, and BDP have grown to become key players in global supply chain management.

It is important to choose wisely not only the company but also the office that services the company's account and the personnel who manage customer service needs. Although the provider may have hundreds or even thousands of employees, a company is likely to interface with only a handful of them.

There are midsized service providers like Armac, Apex, Dart, Scarbrough International, and Sparx, all of which ever experience, tenure, quality personnel, and a global reach but are structured to provide more intimate and personal levels of service to all of their clients.

The suggested guidelines and areas of scrutiny are as follows:

- Geographic expertise
- Transit strength
- Stability of personnel
- Quality of management and operations personnel
- Likelihood for merger or acquisition
- Fees and rates
- Technology capability, particularly in *purchase order (PO) management* and *electronic data interchange (EDI)* transfer of data
- Tracking proactiveness
- Scope of capability
- In-house compliance facility
- External education and training component

- Consulting division and access to expertise
- Access to senior management
- Size and importance of company's account to their organization
- Review of references
- Payment terms
- Documentation, operations, procedures, and systems for detail
- Transparency of infrastructure and operation
- Banking, letters of credit (LCs), and draft wherewithal

4.7.1 Bureau of Industry and Security Freight Forwarder Guidance

SERVICE PROVIDERS AND THE *ELECTRONIC EXPORT INFORMATION (EEI)* IN ROUTED TRANSACTIONS

The Export Administration Regulations (EAR) place legal responsibility on all the people who have the information, authority, or functions that are relevant to carrying out export transactions that are subject to the EAR. Forwarding agents may have compliance responsibilities under the EAR, even when their actions are dependent on the information or instructions that are given by those who use their services. However, hiring a forwarding agent or other agents (hereafter *agent*) to perform various tasks does not necessarily relieve a party of its compliance responsibilities.

The BIS published amendments to the EAR affecting relevant sections to the EAR, including Section 748.5, regarding parties to a transaction, Part 758 on export clearance, and relevant definitions in Part 772.

The primary responsibility for compliance with the EAR falls on the *principal parties in interest (PPIs)* in a transaction. Generally, the PPIs in an export transaction are the US seller and the foreign buyer.

In a *routed export transaction*, in which the foreign PPI authorizes a US agent to facilitate the export of items from the United States, the USPPI may obtain from the foreign PPI a writing in which the foreign PPI expressly assumes responsibility for determining the licensing requirements and obtaining authorization for the export. In this case, the US agent acting for the foreign PPI is the *exporter* under the EAR and is responsible for determining the licensing authority and obtaining the appropriate license or other authorization for the export.

An agent representing the foreign PPI in this type of routed export transaction must obtain a power of attorney or other written authorization in order to act on its behalf.

In a routed export transaction, if the USPPI does not obtain from the foreign PPI the writing that was described above, then the USPPI is the exporter and must determine the licensing authority and obtain the appropriate license or other authorization.

In a routed export transaction in which the foreign PPI assumes responsibility for determining the appropriate authorization for the export, the EAR requires the USPPI to furnish the foreign PPI and its agent, upon request, with the correct Export Control Classification Number (ECCN) or sufficient technical information to determine the ECCN. In addition, the USPPI must provide the foreign PPI and its agent with any information that it knows will affect the determination of license authority.

In a transaction that is not a routed export transaction, if the USPPI authorizes an agent to prepare and file the export declaration on its behalf, the USPPI is the exporter under the EAR and is required to

- *Provide the agent with the information that is necessary to complete the EEI,*
- *Authorize the agent to complete the EEI by power of attorney or other written authorization, or by signing the authorization block on the EEI, and*
- *Maintain documentation to support the information that is provided to the agent for completing the EEI.*

If authorized by either the US or foreign PPI, the agent is responsible for

- *Preparing the EEI based on the information that is received from the USPPI,*
- *Maintaining documentation to support the information that is reported on the export declaration, and*
- *Upon request, providing the USPPI with a copy of the EEI that is filed by the agent.*

Agents are responsible for the representations that they make by signing an export declaration. Moreover, no person may proceed with any transaction knowing that a violation has occurred, is about to occur, or is intended to occur in connection with it. It is the agent's responsibility to understand its obligations.

Agents, especially those acting as the exporter, should understand the *know-your-customer* guidance and red flags that are found in Supplement No. 1 to Part 732 of the EAR. Agents and exporters should decide whether there are red flags, inquire about them, and ensure that suspicious circumstances are not ignored.

Both the agent and the PPI who has hired him or her are responsible for the correctness of each entry that is made on an EEI. Good faith reliance on information obtained from the PPI can help protect an agent, but the careless use of preprinted *no-license-required* forms or unsupported entries can get an agent into trouble.

An agent should avoid making commodity classifications for which it lacks technical expertise and should obtain support documentation for ECCNs and other material.

This places additional burden on the *provider or forwarder*; therefore, supply chain executives must make sure that they can handle these responsibilities.

4.7.2 Managing Peak-Season Demands

Almost every year, we see peak seasons from November to February, particularly on freight inbound from Asia to North America.

In 2015–2016, there was no peak season, which was an unanticipated aberration.

The peak season places a serious excessive demand on carriers, where ships vie for space allocation on steamships where there is no sufficient capacity for the volume increase.

This stresses the entire inbound supply chain and where traffic managers become more *gray haired*.

Air freight becomes an option, but then it becomes overloaded, and even movements by air are backed up.

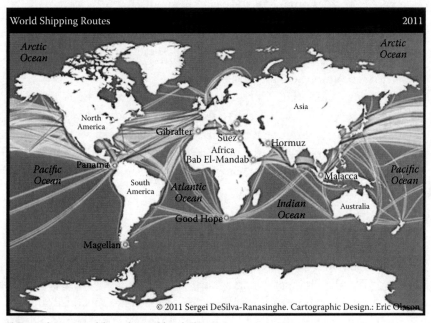

Shipping lanes to and from the world and China

The problems are both anticipated with peak-season surcharges (PSSs), or the problems can be budgeted and unanticipated with other factors such as the port strike in 2014–2015 in the West Coast, which backed up freight in as much as 120–180 days.

Many companies, as a result of the port strike and peak-season issues, have engaged aggressive strategies to lessen the unfavorable impact on their global inbound supply lines.

The author's professional recommendations are as follows:

1. *Develop a "partnership" mind-set with the carriers.*

    Carriers charge GRIs (general rate increases) and peak season surcharges (PSSs) based upon demand. Most shippers negotiate very low freight rates based upon off-season demand, not contemplating the carrier's issues during high-demand/peak-season time frames.

    As a consultant, we have been successful in working with our clients in negotiating freight agreements with carriers that allow the carrier higher pricing during high-demand seasonal variations.

    This approach affords the best opportunity for the shipper to forge a partnership relationship with the carrier that acknowledges the carrier's issues during peak-season demand.

    Pricing that allows the carrier to receive more revenue during peak season creates a better relationship, and the favorable consequence that affords that the importer's freight will move consistently throughout the year and peak season.

    The mistake that both shippers and carriers make is that they negotiate these very attractive rating agreements that work well for eight months of the year, but fail during peak season.

    That failure is almost guaranteed by how air and ocean freight contracts are negotiated, which is to drive the base price as low as possible, not contemplating the demand issues that the carrier faces during peak season.

2. *Develop the option to negotiate a competitive rate, but one that allows for*

    - Either a higher annualized rate, throughout the year or
    - GRIs/PSS increases during peak season. (These can be capped.)

    This compromises the options to have freight moved throughout the regular season and peak season and at a price that is workable for the carriers.

3. *Work with carriers in planning and booking orders out three to six weeks, when there is a better likelihood to obtain the space requirements that will be honored.*

4. *Work with service providers in negotiating with all the carrier options:*

- Coloaded space
- Non-vessel operating common carrier (NVOCC)
- Direct carrier contracts
- Freight forwarder contracts

Sometimes, the best strategy is to combine several of these options to leverage freight opportunity.

5. *Coordinate less expensive "air freight" options as a backup when ocean freight does not move timely.*
6. *Lead the drive to find alternative supply chain solutions.* One example is the ocean/air combination by moving freight from China and Southeast Asia by ocean to Dubai or Sri Lanka, then to the United States by air an at an agreed competitive per-kilo rate.

7. *Make sure that all the peripheral charges like GRIs, PSSs, demurrage, and bunker fuel are clearly identified, how these charges apply, and if they can be negotiated "out."*

4.8 MANAGING SERVICE PROVIDERS: FREIGHT FORWARDERS, CUSTOMHOUSE BROKERS, AND CARRIERS

Considerable time should be spent managing providers and carriers. It is a critical function of the inbound supply chain. The following points can assist with managing this responsibility:

- Treat them as partners.
- Be transparent.

- Set up systems to make sure that they are fully aware of the company's needs and expectations.
- Develop good relationships.
- Gain access to senior management personnel.
- Include technology solutions wherever possible.
- Negotiate—pricing is relative, subjective, and variable.
- Hold them to high standards.
- Have them provide annual stewardship reports that outline what they have accomplished in the past year and an outline for the future.
- Put the contracts out for bid every two to four years. Keep them honest. If they are doing well, give them an advantage in the request for quote process, but make sure that they compete to keep the business.
- Make sure that compliance and security are built into the relationship.
- Seek providers that can be more comprehensive in their ability to handle the company's inbound supply chain, providing service for a wide range of needs. This will maximize the company's clout for the best service and price. This allows a consolidation of capabilities, increasing the ease of handling and communications and the ability to negotiate competitive freight pricing.

LUFTHANSA GERMAN AIRLINES SETTLES CHARGES RELATED TO UNLICENSED EXPORTS

The US Department of Commerce recently announced that Lufthansa German Airlines of Atlanta, Georgia, will pay an $18,000 civil penalty to settle charges that it violated the EAR in connection with an unlicensed export and an attempted unlicensed export to an entity in India on the BIS's Entity List.

The BIS charged that between January 6 and 15, 1999, Lufthansa aided and abetted an unlicensed export and attempted the export of Cobalt-57, iron foil, and potassium ferrocyanide to the Department of Atomic Energy in India, an organization on the BIS's Entity List, without the required Department of Commerce licenses. The BIS further charged that in connection with the attempted export, Lufthansa stored the items with knowledge that a violation of the EAR would occur.

The Entity List is a compilation of end users who have been determined to present an unacceptable risk of diversion to the development of weapons of mass destruction or their means of delivery.

Most exports to end users on the Entity List require licenses from the Department of Commerce.

"This case highlights the responsibility of international freight forwarders and carriers to ensure that they do not facilitate prohibited export transactions for their clients," said Wendy Wysong, the acting assistant secretary of commerce for export enforcement.

Acting Assistant Secretary Wysong commended the Boston Field Office for its efforts in this investigation.

The Department of Commerce administers and enforces export controls for reasons of national security, foreign policy, nonproliferation, antiterrorism, and short supply through the EAR. Criminal prosecution and administrative sanctions can be imposed for the violations of those regulations.

Although there is always concern about concentrating too much in one area, in the past few years, many companies have gained certain efficiencies in this way.

4.9 THIRD-PARTY LOGISTICS

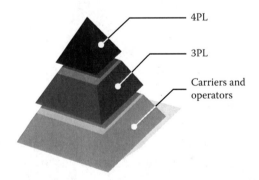

Many companies have found certain benefits in outsourcing their logistics needs. The concept is that the company's core business is manufacturing, assembly, distribution, or engineering, and so on and that the company chooses to concentrate on that rather than master other skill sets for its logistic needs.

Third-party logistics is a growing global supply chain option. Many providers offer third-party services. Basically, the principal company, in lieu of hiring logistics expertise, outsources the requirements to a third-party provider. Financial officers like the option because it moves expense from payroll to a *cost of goods sold* column, which usually changes the financial picture favorably. Operations management likes the option because it usually fills a need and provides a solution.

There are several reasons to consider third-party logistics, as follows:

- Provides access to immediate expertise.
- Usually is less expensive than staffing.
- May provide access to third-party providers' technology capabilities.
- Provides reliable personnel and logistics solutions.
- May have relationships with carriers that afford access to less expensive freight costs.
- Provides access to their infrastructure, personnel, and capabilities.
- Can sometimes terminate relationships with them more easily than with employees.
- Often will place managers and staffing on site, providing access to their wherewithal in the company's office.

Just as there are reasons to consider third-party logistics, there are of course negative aspects to consider, as follows:

- May be more expensive than staffing.
- Sometimes makes change more bureaucratic.
- Promises may be made to get the business, but they cannot be accomplished.

In evaluating third-party logistics, a company should consider the following:

- Make sure that the capabilities are there.
- Make sure that the deliverables can be accomplished.
- Interview the personnel who will be on site before entering into a final agreement.
- Make sure that their personnel have the skill sets that are required. It makes no sense to enter into an agreement and obtain personnel who are less qualified than those whom the company already possess.
- Have both financial rewards and consequences based on performance.
- Have ease of contract termination if the relationship does not work out.

- If the third party is arranging for carriers, have those freight bills paid directly by the company rather than allow them control of the company's financial dealings.
- Make sure that company management knows their senior management team, to help work out problems at the highest level, when necessary.

Regardless of the benefits and disadvantages, there is a growing trend to outsource logistics, and many companies have reaped the benefits, resulting in a better-run inbound supply chain.

CBP inspecting inbound freight

4.9.1 Free Trade Agreements

Free trade agreements (FTAs) provide various advantages to North American companies in how they manage their purchasing and sourcing options:

- They offer sanctuary countries where we have agreements that reduce the duty and tax rates or, in some cases, completely eliminate them.
- They provide closer *near-sourcing* locations for manufacturing.
- A closer location may mean less lead time.
- A closer location will lead to less costly international freight costs.
- Better influence and control over the manufacturing process.
- Potentially better legal influence and control over IPR issues.

There are over a dozen FTAs favoring companies that are located in North America.

NAFTA by far is our largest and most successful FTA. But a more comprehensive list includes the following:

- Israel: Israel–US Free Trade Agreement (incl. Palestinian Authority; 1985)
- North American Free Trade Agreement (NAFTA; incl. Canada and Mexico; 1994)
- Jordan: Jordan–US Free Trade Agreement (2001)
- Australia: Australia–US Free Trade Agreement (2004)
- Chile: Chile–US Free Trade Agreement (2004)
- Singapore: Singapore–US Free Trade Agreement (2004)
- Bahrain: Bahrain–US Free Trade Agreement (2006)
- Morocco: Morocco–US Free Trade Agreement (2006)
- Oman: Oman–US Free Trade Agreement (2006)
- Peru: Peru–US Trade Promotion Agreement (2007)
- Dominican Republic–Central America Free Trade Agreement (DR-CAFTA; incl. Costa Rica, El Salvador, Guatemala, Honduras, Nicaragua, and the Dominican Republic; 2005)
- Panama: Panama–US Trade Promotion Agreement (2012)
- Colombia: US–Colombia Free Trade Agreement (2012)
- South Korea: US–Republic of Korea Free Trade Agreement (2012)

There is a new proposed agreement that has been moving forward that is called the Trans-Pacific Partnership (TPP):

> The *TPP* is a trade agreement among 12 Pacific Rim countries concerning a variety of matters of economic policy, which was reached on October 5, 2015 after seven years of negotiations.
>
> The agreement's stated goal had been to "promote economic growth; support the creation and retention of jobs; enhance innovation, productivity and competitiveness; raise living standards; reduce poverty in our countries; and promote transparency, good governance, and enhanced labor and environmental protections."
>
> Among other things, the TPP agreement contains measures to lower trade barriers, such as tariffs, and establish an investor–state dispute settlement mechanism (but states can opt out from tobacco-related measures).
>
> The US government has considered the TPP as the companion agreement to the proposed Transatlantic Trade and Investment Partnership, a broadly similar agreement between the United States and the European Union.

The TPP has been fiercely debated by the president and Congress of the United States, and its final outcome has not yet been fully determined.

Most trade advocates are proponents of the agreement with the belief that trade will grow. Opponents are concerned about the loss of jobs and domestic-based manufacturing.

The author ultimately believes that the TPP will be enacted in some form and will have the same benefits and consequences of NAFTA, which every study points to a favorable outcome for all North Americans.

4.9.2 NAFTA

NAFTA has been an advantage for all the companies that are located in North America and has become a significant near-sourcing option for US-based companies operating in tandem with the *maquiladora* program in Mexico.

In Mexico, a *maquiladora* (Spanish pronunciation: [makila'ðora]) or *maquila* (IPA: [ma'kila]) is a manufacturing operation in Mexico, where factories import certain material and equipment on a duty- and tariff-free basis for assembly, processing, or manufacturing and then export the assembled, processed, and/or finished product.

4.9.2.1 *Examples of Companies Operating in* Maquiladoras *in Mexico*

- 3 Day Blinds
- 20th Century Plastics
- Acer Peripherals
- Bali Company, Inc.
- Bayer Corporation/Medsep
- BMW
- Canon Business Machines
- Casio Manufacturing
- Chrysler
- Daewoo
- Eastman Kodak/Verbatim
- Eberhard Faber
- Eli Lilly Corporation
- Ericsson
- Fisher–Price
- Ford
- Foster Grant Corporation
- General Electric Company
- GM
- Hasbro
- Hewlett–Packard
- Hitachi Home Electronics
- Honda
- Honeywell, Inc.
- Hughes Aircraft
- Hyundai Precision America
- IBM
- JVC
- Matsushita
- Mattel
- Maxell Corporation
- Mercedes–Benz
- Mitsubishi Electronics Corporation
- Motorola
- Nissan
- Philips
- Pioneer Speakers
- Samsonite Corporation
- Samsung
- Sanyo North America
- Sony Electronics
- Tiffany
- Toshiba
- VW
- Xerox
- Zenith

A *maquiladora* plant in Mexico

The border areas engaged in the *maquiladora* program

The flags of NAFTA: United States, Canada, and Mexico

4.9.3 NAFTA Objectives

The objectives of this agreement, as elaborated more specifically through its principles and rules, including national treatment, most-favored-nation treatment, and transparency, are to

- Eliminate barriers to trade in, and facilitate the cross-border movement of goods and services between the territories of the parties;

- Promote conditions of fair competition in the free trade area;
- Increase substantially investment opportunities in the territories of the parties;
- Provide adequate and effective protection and enforcement of IPR in each party's territory;
- Create effective procedures for the implementation and application of this agreement, for its joint administration, and for the resolution of disputes; and
- Establish a framework for further trilateral, regional, and multilateral cooperation to expand and enhance the benefits of this agreement.

The US exports to Canada and Mexico support more than three million American jobs, and the US trade with NAFTA partners has unlocked opportunity for millions of Americans by supporting made-in-America jobs and exports.

The United States' two largest export markets, Canada and Mexico, buy more made-in-America goods and services than any other countries in the world. Since NAFTA's implementation, US states like Illinois, Ohio, Michigan, and many others have seen a surge in exports across North American borders.

4.9.3.1 Some Facts on NAFTA and...

4.9.3.1.1 American Jobs

For over 30 out of the 50 states, Canada or Mexico ranks as the first or second largest export market. Many American small business exporters' first foreign customers are in Canada or Mexico, and under NAFTA, the US trade with Canada and Mexico has supported over 140,000 small- and medium-sized businesses.

4.9.3.1.2 Manufacturing

Since its entry into force, the US manufacturing exports to NAFTA have increased by 258%, and the United States maintains a growing manufacturing trade surplus with Canada and Mexico. American exports of computer and electronic products, furniture, paper, and fabricated metals have all more than tripled since NAFTA's implementation.

4.9.3.1.3 TPP

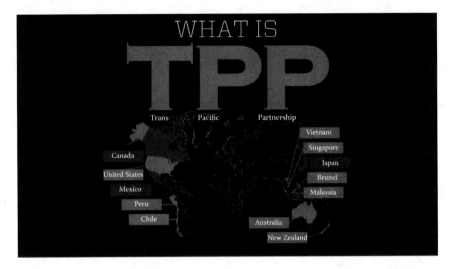

The TPP allows us to bring NAFTA into the twenty-first century for the benefit of working families in America. Following the great progress in US trade policy since NAFTA was implemented, the TPP will help the United States address environmental challenges like wildlife trafficking and illegal fishing, respond to new developments in global trade, such as the growth of the digital economy, and reinforce the US commitment to upholding cutting-edge labor and environmental standards to level the playing field for American workers.

4.9.3.1.4 Trade Balance

For services and many categories of goods, the United States maintains a trade surplus with NAFTA countries. The largest factor affecting the trade balance with NAFTA countries is the importation of fossil fuels and their by-products. If those products are excluded, there is no deficit. In fact, the United States has a large and growing trade surplus in goods, including agriculture and manufactured goods, as well as in services.

NAFTA imports have increased the competitiveness of American businesses. Nearly 60% of US total goods imports from Canada and Mexico are used in the production of made-in-America goods and services.

4.9.4 Successful Tips on Managing All FTAs and NAFTA

- Work with experts who have a working knowledge of the trade agreements.

  In the case of NAFTA, agents along the border present significant sources of knowledge and skill set in goods crossing the US/Mexican border.
- Work with transportation providers that have offices or agents locally at the border and in the interior of Mexico.
- Learn the basic regulation that impacts sales, purchasing, and logistics for goods moving across the borders.
- Learn the documentation and regulatory requirements, particularly the rules of origin.
- NAFTA can provide numerous near-sourcing advantages. All purchasing and sourcing managers should know their options in Mexico and leverage these for economic benefit.

  View the partial list of the numerous companies that are taking advantage of this free trade agreement, outlined in Section 4.9.2.1.

  NAFTA and all FTAs can be a big advantage in global supply chain competitiveness, an opportunity that is not to be passed by in most circumstances.

5

Post 9/11 and the Effects on Global Purchasing

5.1 INTRODUCTION

This chapter will focus on the impact of the unfortunate events of 9/11 and the impact on import regulations and inbound global supply chains.

A company that sources overseas cannot be successful till it meets all the import regulations that impact global trade.

The day of September 11, 2001, will live in infamy, and its impact on global trade will be felt for decades to come.

5.2 SUPPLY CHAIN SECURITY, COMPLIANCE, AND ITS EFFECT ON GLOBAL PURCHASING

While it has been over 15 years since the tragic events of 9/11, supply chain security continues to weave itself into the fabric of international business. Customs and Border Protection (CBP) implemented a layered approach to global security, beginning with the foreign port of loading, encompassing the transmission of cargo manifest data, advanced security filing, and partnering with foreign governments and other US government (USG) agencies. Recent developments include the advancement of mutual recognition of foreign security programs such as the authorized economic operator, Business Alliance for Secure Commerce, and the inclusion of exporters in the Customs–Trade Partnership Against Terrorism (C-TPAT) program.

At the same time, trade compliance continues to be a technical and integral part of the global supply chain and now includes global security as regulations have been enacted to ensure compliance with security measures. Technology continues to integrate itself into the supply chain, and the USG is keeping up with those changes. The year 2015 saw the initial implementation of the US CBP unveiling of the Automated Commercial Environment (ACE) as its operating platform. For example, the International Trade Data System (ITDS) incorporates the single-window concept to allow businesses to submit import and export data that are required by CBP and partner government agencies (PGAs).

While this measure creates a single window for businesses, this same window will provide the government with the capability of streamlining data that are received from many government agencies and compare these data for consistency and accurate reporting, leading to safer shipments and raising the compliance bar for importers.

5.3 SUPPLY CHAIN SECURITY

Compliance, security, and risk assessment have become key words in the vocabulary of every logistics, purchasing, import and export, and transportation management professional in the United States as well as their global trading partners, vendors, and service providers. The US CBP continues to manage and develop strategies to secure the US borders and protect the supply chain from terrorists and other aggressive threats.

5.3.1 Container Security Initiative

Following the events of 9/11, the decision was made to push the borders of the United States outward and to deter the risk for terrorism in the supply chain. The Container Security Initiative (CSI) was established and stations the US CBP officers in foreign locations to work with their foreign government counterparts in identifying and inspecting containers in foreign ports that pose a potential risk for terrorism. This is done through the use of intelligence information. These containers are evaluated and prescreened prior to shipment. This is usually done at the port of departure through the use of large-scale x-ray machines and radiation detectors.

The CSI is currently operating in 58 ports around the world and accounts for the prescreening of over 80% of all ocean-containerized cargo that is imported into the United States. This program demonstrates the successful collaboration and partnership outlook of supply chain security of the United States and its foreign partner governments.

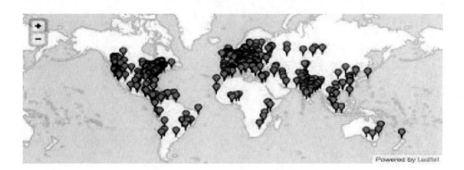

5.3.2 Advanced Manifest Regulations

Carriers create a manifest listing of the goods that are loaded on the vessel, truck, rail, or plane by the bill of lading number. The manifest lists the details of the goods including the shipper, the consignee, the pieces, the weights, the description, and whether they are dangerous or not.

The Bureau of Customs and Border Protection requires carriers to provide information on cargo entering the United States prior to arrival. This enables CBP to target shipments for security examination. This information is required to be filed electronically through the Automated Manifest System (AMS). While the required information to be filed is based on the mode of transportation, the information minimally includes the origin port/airport, the destination port/airport, the shipper, the consignee, the manifest quantity, and the weights and measures. The time frames for transmitting this information vary by mode of transport as reflected on the chart.

Electronic information for air cargo is required in advance of arrival and must be received from the inbound air carrier and, if applicable, an approved party. Failure to provide this information timely will result in a penalty of $5000.00.

While CBP has established its time frame for receiving the advanced manifest information, the carriers establish shorter time frames for transmitting this information to ensure that they are in compliance with CBP regulations to avoid penalties.

Inbound—Transmission Received by CBP in AMS	
Vessel	24 hours (before loading at foreign port) for nonbulk shipments
	24 hours before arrival for bulk shipments
Air	4 hours before *wheels up* from the North American Free Trade Agreement (NAFTA) (Canada and Mexico) and Central and South America above the equator
Rail	2 hours before arrival in United States
Truck	1 hour before arrival for non-Free and Secure Trade (FAST) participants
	30 minutes before arrival for FAST participants

5.4 C-TPAT PROGRAM

The C-TPAT program seeks to safeguard the world's vibrant trade industry from terrorists, maintaining the economic health of the United States and its neighbors. At present, there are approximately 10,678 certified partners that have been accepted into the program. These include US importers, US and Canadian highway carriers, rail and sea carriers, US Customs brokers, marine port authority/terminal operators, freight consolidators, ocean transportation intermediaries and nonoperating common carriers, and Mexican and Canadian manufacturers. These companies account for over 54% of the value of what is imported into the United States.

By extending the US zone of security to the point of origin, the C-TPAT allows for better risk assessment and targeting, freeing CBP to allocate its inspection resources to more questionable shipments. C-TPAT members are considered low risk and are therefore less likely to be examined. This designation is based on a company's past compliance history and security profile and the validation of a sample international supply chain.

CBP has numerous mutual recognition arrangements with other countries. The goal of these arrangements is to link the various international industry partnership programs so that together, they create a unified and sustainable security posture that can assist in securing and facilitating global cargo trade.

The goal of aligning partnership programs is to create a system whereby all the participants in an international trade transaction are approved by the customs function as observing specified standards in the secure handling of goods and relevant information. The C-TPAT signed its first mutual recognition arrangement with New Zealand in June 2007 and, since that time, has signed similar arrangements with South Korea, Japan, Jordan, Canada, the European Union (EU), Taiwan, Israel, Mexico, and Singapore.

In 2015, the C-TPAT program was expanded to include exporters. Exporters follow much of the same requirements for importers in documenting how they do business with their foreign customers, choose their service providers, and monitor shipments. For many exporters, participation in the C-TPAT program has become a significant marketing strategy for doing business, particularly with those partners that are located in countries that are participating in a mutual recognition arrangement with the United States.

The benefits of C-TPAT participation include the following:

- Reduced compliance exams and reduced number of inspections.
- Reduced waiting time for cargo to be examined.
- If cargo is selected for exam, it will receive priority and be moved to the front of the exam line.
- Decreased transportation times.
- Assignment of CBP supply chain security specialist.

- Access to FAST lanes at Mexico and Canada borders.
- Invitation to participate in C-TPAT training seminars that are offered by CBP.
- Incorporation of security practices into existing logistical management methods.
- Greater supply chain integrity.
- Reduced freight surcharges such as exam fees and demurrage.
- Ability to comply with C-TPAT customer requirements.
- Lower insurance costs.
- Reduced incidences of theft/loss of inventory.
- Mutual recognition as CBP has signed mutual recognition arrangements with its top trading partners including China, Canada, Mexico, Japan, and the EU. This allows freight exported to move faster through participating countries' customs more quickly.
- When another event occurs that closes the borders, C-TPAT member shipments will be prioritized when the borders reopen.
- Participation in the C-TPAT program provides mitigation of fines and penalties.
- Five to eight times fewer exams than non-CTPAT importers.

5.5 FAST

The FAST is a commercial clearance program for known low-risk shipments entering the United States from Canada and Mexico. Participation in FAST requires that every link in the supply chain, from the manufacturer to the carrier to the driver to the importer, is certified in the C-TPAT program. The key benefits of FAST enrollment are as follows:

- Access to dedicated lanes for greater speed and efficiency in processing transborder shipments
- Reduced number of inspections resulting in reduced delays at the border
- Priority, front-of-the-line processing for CBP inspections

5.6 FIVE-STEP RISK ASSESSMENT

In the evolution of the C-TPAT program, as supply chain security specialists performed on-site validations in the United States and overseas, it was recognized that many importers were not maintaining their initial high level of enthusiasm and the management of their security program. An analysis by CBP in 2013 indicated that 22% of importers did not have a risk assessment process that effectively addressed their international supply chains.

CBP introduced the five-step risk assessment guideline to assist companies in developing their own risk assessment process:

1. *Map cargo flow and identify business partners*

   Mapping out the entire supply chain allows the importers to highlight when and where cargo is most vulnerable so that they can take action. It is important to analyze all the parties who are involved in a shipment from the point of origin to the final destination to verify that none have been overlooked, such as foreign inland drayage providers or other agents handling paperwork.

2. *Conduct a threat assessment*

   The threat assessment is an evaluation of all possible threats to the supply chain and must be based on quantitative evidence. Evidence from trusted open-sourced websites and local, state, and federal authorities can be a great resource to identify regional threats. The threat assessment should be conducted for all regions in the supply chain and should focus on these key items: (a) terrorism, (b) contraband smuggling, (c) human smuggling, (d) organized crime, and (e) any other conditions in a country or region that may foster such threats. Not all countries and regions pose the same threat, and as a result, it might be determined that low-risk countries do not require analysis under steps 3 and 4.

3. *Conduct a vulnerability assessment*

   The vulnerability assessment should be of all the business partners and service providers throughout the supply chain. Vulnerability should be rated as high, medium, or low. When warranted by medium- or high-level threats, a vulnerability assessment is a further evaluation of suppliers' compliance with the C-TPAT minimum security criteria. Such criteria include the following categories: (a) business partner requirements, (b) securing instruments of international traffic, (c) procedural security, (d) physical security, (e) physical access controls, (f) personnel security, (g) security and threat awareness training, and (h) information technology security. Examples of ways in which a vulnerability assessment can be conducted include a security questionnaire, an on-site assessment, a review of cycle times with transit points, or an annual business review.

4. *Prepare an action plan*

When deficiencies or vulnerabilities are discovered in any part of the supply chain, a corrective action plan must be established with service providers to identify the areas of improvement. The next steps are to prioritize the deficiencies, nominate who is responsible, and establish documentation for dates of completion and verification.

5. *Document how the risk assessment was conducted*

Written procedures must reflect the policies and processes in place for international risk assessments. Ownership within the company must be assigned for responsibility of duties. Other things that need to be documented are the dates and frequency of assessments, as well as training and follow-up procedures. The five-step risk assessment is not inclusive of every scenario or threat that exists. However, it is intended to show the level of planning and effort that is needed to adequately address threats and vulnerabilities.

5.7 IMPORTER SECURITY FILING

In 2010, CBP introduced the Importer Security Filing (ISF) rule. ISF requires the importers to electronically submit in advance cargo information to CBP not later than 24 hours prior to the loading of ocean freight aboard a vessel that is destined to the United States. The importer or their agent, such as a customs broker or a freight forwarder, is required to file the following data elements:

- Seller
- Buyer
- Ship to party
- Importer of record number/foreign trade zone applicant identification number
- Consignee numbers
- Manufacturer (or supplier)
- Country of origin
- Harmonized tariff number
- Container stuffing location (required 24 hours prior to ship's arrival at a US port)
- Consolidator (required 24 hours prior to ship's arrival at a US port)

The penalty for inaccurate, incomplete, or untimely filing of information is $5000 with a maximum of $10,000 per shipment. In addition to the penalty, importers may find themselves subject to additional inspections and subsequent delays if the ISF is not properly filed. Additionally, noncompliant cargo could be subject to *do-not-load* orders at origin. Through the ACE Web portal, importers can access their ISF report card to monitor and manage their ISF compliance.

5.8 AIR CARGO ADVANCED SCREENING

Similar to the ISF for ocean freight, CBP has been developing a similar program for air freight shipments. The Air Cargo Advanced Screening (ACAS) program would require the transmission of advance electronic information for air cargo. This information would be required to be filed 4 hours prior to arrival in the United States and/or not later than the time of departure of the aircraft depending on the location.

As of this writing, ACAS is currently in test mode with voluntarily participants working with customs to pilot the program and determine the best way to effectively target, identify, and mitigate risk in the air cargo environment. The ACAS program will probably see fruition by 2017 as it will be a slow integration into the supply chain.

5.9 PRIOR NOTICE TO FOOD AND DRUG ADMINISTRATION

In 2002, Congress passed the Bioterrorism Act (BTA) as part of its ongoing effort to combat terrorism and to prevent the contamination of foods that are imported into the United States. About 20% of imports into the United States are food and food products. The BTA requires that the Food and Drug Administration (FDA) receive prior notice before all food, for humans and animals, is imported into the United States, allowing the FDA to effectively target shipments for import inspections. Prior notice is filed electronically.

5.10 CONSUMER PRODUCT SAFETY COMMISSION

The Consumer Product Safety Commission (CPSC) has regulatory authority over consumer products and those products that are manufactured for children. Importers for these types of products must be aware of the regulatory requirements prior to import to ensure that the goods will be allowed entry into the United States as well as to prevent the costs and bad publicity of a public recall. Manufacturers and importers of general-use products and children's products for which consumer product safety rules apply must certify that their products comply with all the applicable rules.

In some instances, third-party testing laboratories may be required. Due to the wide range of products that fall under the scope of the CPSC, manufacturers and importers should consult the CPSC website for the requirements that are specific to their product.

5.11 CONSOLIDATED SCREENING LIST FOR DENIED PARTIES

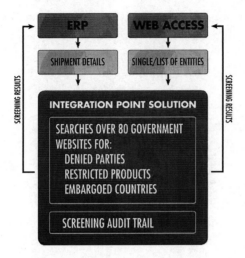

5.11.1 Integrated Solutions Provide Technology for DPL Screening

There is no escaping the importance of exercising due diligence in the supply chain. Knowing our supply chain partners, whether they are manufacturers, suppliers, agents, consolidators, truckers, etc., is key to demonstrating reasonable care and working toward a secure supply chain.

The Bureau of Industry and Security (BIS) maintains a listing of companies and individuals who have been found to have violated export regulations, treasury regulations, and state regulations. Prior to entering into business agreements with any supply chain partner, companies should screen their business partners through these lists. Any match should be investigated further to ensure that the supply chain partner is not a party who is considered a bad actor. The specific lists to be screened may be found in Section 5.10.3.

5.11.2 Import Management Overview

All companies in the United States are required to comply with the government agencies regulating their businesses, whether they are on the federal level such as the Department of Transportation, Occupational Safety and

Health Administration (OSHA), or the Internal Revenue Service, or local authorities. Those companies that import and export must also comply with the various USG agencies regulating the inbound/outbound supply chain.

In order to successfully manage compliance in the supply chain, importers and exporters must develop expertise and understand their regulatory responsibilities. Noncompliance with import and export regulations will likely result in clearance delays and additional charges such as demurrage and may even include government seizure and penalties.

5.11.3 Importer of Record

CBP is a revenue-generating agency. CBP was always part of the Department of Treasury along with the Internal Revenue Service. When the Department of Homeland Security was formed, CBP as an agency moved from one department to the other. CBP is charged with protecting the revenue of the United States. This is an important concept for importers to understand so that they act responsibly and prudently in their import activity.

The importer of record is the party who is responsible for the statements and affirmations that are provided to customs in the entry process. While many importers use a third-party licensed customs broker to actually process the customs entry, the importer remains the responsible party. The entry declarations made minimally include the description, tariff classification, values, and country of origin and statements of use.

Many importers also fail to realize that the release of goods from customs and the receipt of the delivery of goods are not the end of the clearance process. Following customs clearance, CBP has 314 days to review all the entry declarations that are made during the entry process. This time frame is called the liquidation period. During the liquidation period, CBP may ask for additional information regarding the imported items to ascertain the correctness of the information that is provided at the time of entry.

CBP does not permit the importers to distance themselves from the import process by expecting the customs broker to respond to any requests for information. In fact, CBP requires the customs broker to act in a compliant manner in the import process as well. In the event that CBP finds that the importer and the customs broker did not act in a compliant manner, CBP may fine both parties.

It is the legal requirement of importers to know the CBP rules and regulations and to supervise and control their customs broker.

5.11.4 Reasonable Care

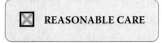

Reasonable care is a degree of care that an ordinary person would exercise in the normal course of business. For importers, it is the degree of care that importers or their agent uses in the process of entering merchandise into the commerce of the United States. The ability of an importer to demonstrate that he or she exercised reasonable care in the case of a violation will serve as a mitigating factor and likely not result in liquidated damages being assessed but only the loss of revenue (if any) plus interest.

Importers must be able to demonstrate supervision and control, exercising reasonable care and due diligence over the import process. The import process must be strategically set up to include these additional elements in the import process and not just get the goods from overseas point A to domestic point B as soon as possible and as cheaply as possible. Failure to include due diligence will certainly result in supply chain issues.

The following guidelines must be applied to assist in meeting reasonable care:

- Consult with qualified experts, such as customs brokers, consultants, and attorneys specializing in CBP law.
- Seek guidance from CBP through the formal binding ruling program.
- If using a broker, provide him or her with full and complete information that is sufficient for the broker to make a proper entry (import declaration) or provide advice on how to make an entry.
- Obtain analysis from accredited laboratories to determine the technical qualities of imported merchandise.

- Use in-house employees who have experience and knowledge of CBP regulations and procedures.
- Follow binding rulings that are received from CBP.
- Ensure that products are legally marked with the country of origin to indicate to the ultimate purchaser the origin of imported products.
- Do not classify or value identical merchandise in different ways.
- Notify CBP when receiving different treatment for the same goods at different entries or different ports.
- Examine entries (Import Declaration CF 3461) that are prepared by the broker to determine the accuracy in classification and valuation.

5.11.5 Ultimate Consignee

On most import transactions, the importer of record and the ultimate consignee are the same. The opinion of CBP is that the ultimate consignee caused the import to occur and is one of the responsible parties to the import transaction. Therefore, he or she can be held accountable for regulatory requirements even if he or she is not the importer of record.

An example of this is where a foreign manufacturer uses Federal Express (FedEx) to deliver a shipment door to door with all the charges being billed to the FedEx account of the foreign manufacturer. In this instance, CBP recognizes that FedEx is not the actual purchaser and did not cause the import.

CBP requires that if a buyer causes the import, he or she must have the usual records that are required to import. This includes the bill of lading, entry documents, purchase order, and invoice.

5.11.6 Power of Attorney

The power of attorney (PoA) is a key component of global trade documentation for both importers and exporters who exercise due diligence.

The customs broker is required to have a PoA in order to handle the import on behalf of the importer. One way of managing the import process and exercising supervision and control over the import process is for the importer to manage the number of customs brokers who are conducting customs business on their behalf.

Importers should exercise control using the PoA to include the time frame for which the PoA is valid and not leave it open ended. They may even add that any changes or subbing out of customs broker activities is not permitted without the written consent of the importer.

The PoA is established for the protection of the importer of record to control brokers, and this is an important compliance tool that also enable importers to demonstrate how they control the import process.

All powers of attorney should be dated with a date of expiration not to exceed an initial period of 30 days for renewal, pending proven performance. Once the importer is satisfied with the broker's performance, powers of attorney should not be issued for a period that exceeds one year.

Importers should perform extensive reviews of all brokerage services to critique the internal expertise being applied to each entry. Broker reviews should be done minimally on a yearly basis, if not more often, as a way to manage the performance of customs brokers. Any broker who falls below the importer's standards of compliance should have his or her PoA revoked by a letter of revocation that is sent to the CBP port director at the port of entry by the importer.

5.11.7 Invoices

Invoices must be in English and must include the following:

- Probable port of entry
- Name and address of importer of record
- Name and address of ultimate consignee if known at the time of import and if different from the importer of record
- Name and address of the manufacturer and shipper
- Description of merchandise, including the name that each item is known
- Unit price of the merchandise
- Currency of sale
- Country of origin for each item
- Statement of use in the United States (if applicable)

- Discounts from prices and rebates that are offered between the buyer and the seller
- Values of assists including tools, molds, dies, and engineering work (performed outside the United States) and provided to the manufacturer to assist in producing the imported items
- Packing list
- Endorsement by the person who prepared the invoice

The acquiring company should request a sample entry package and purchase order as well as copies of the correspondence on a typical import shipment to review whether invoices appear to be in line with the transaction prior to performing a full import review.

5.11.8 Recordkeeping

Recordkeeping is a significant area of scrutiny in CBP audits and can lead to serious fines and penalties when the recordkeeping requirements are not followed correctly. CBP regulations state that all importers must establish proper record retention procedures to ensure that all the records are maintained for five years from the date of entry. It is very important for importers to be aware of all the records that they are required to maintain. The records that must be kept include any records that substantiate the facts in the entry declaration, including payments to foreign vendors, contracts, and agreements.

For those importers whose products are subject to other government agency clearances, those government agency recordkeeping requirements must also be followed.

Many importers rely on their customs broker to maintain their records. However, the legal requirement is for the importers to keep their own records. Additionally, the customs broker may not have certain records such as payments to a foreign vendor in their files. Another reason not to rely on the customs broker to maintain documents is if the relationship between the importer and the customs broker is terminated through a change in corporate management, or a broker error, or if the broker goes out of business, the importer will not have access to those records. Records are required to be kept by the importer, and establishing a recordkeeping system and auditing those records on a periodic basis are a demonstration of reasonable care in the import process.

Typical documents required to be kept include the following:

- Purchase inquiries
- Purchase verifications
- Purchase negotiations between the buyer and seller of imported merchandise
- Purchase order communications
- Commercial invoices
- Packing list information
- Special customs declarations and certifications
- Customs Import Declaration (CBP 3461)
- Customs Entry Summary (CBP 7501)
- All communication records between the customs broker and import compliance and traffic department in reference to each import transaction
- Supervisory communication detailing supervision and control of import decisions between the importer and the broker, freight forwarder, consultants, and attorneys
- All records of communication that are received from CBP
- All records of communication relating to any statements or acts that are made by CBP
- Notice of liquidations of communication records
- Communication records detailing receipt of merchandise into the importer's establishments or designated receiving stations
- Communication records detailing the disposition of the merchandise after receipt and distribution
- Records indicating actual proof of purchase of imported goods

- Records indicating contract of carriage agreements, air waybills (AWBs), and bills of lading
- Records indicating the exact amount of prepaid international freight and/or insurance that is contained in the import sales transaction

5.11.9 Valuation

It is the importer's responsibility to ensure that the proper values are fully disclosed to CBP.

Many importers make the common-practice error of relying on the commercial invoice as the value for the goods. However, the commercial invoice may not represent the true price that is paid or payable for an import shipment. Incorrect valuation determinations may lead to fines and penalties against the importer of record.

For CBP purposes, the value of the goods is based on the price that is paid or payable to bring the goods to the foreign port/airport of loading overseas, which is commonly called the free-on-board/free-carrier foreign port value.

Keeping in mind that CBP has the period of liquidation to review any value declarations, the importer must exercise reasonable care that the value stated at the time of entry is the correct value. The customs broker does not have knowledge of all the facts that are associated with the import, and unless the customs broker is asking additional questions regarding the commercial invoice, the importer must make certain that he or she is controlling the value declarations that are made to CBP.

5.11.10 Assists

The import valuation declaration process has many components that require specific attention to purchasing and sourcing details that are included within the scope of proper value reporting practices. Many importers are not aware of these specific responsibilities of compliant reporting through the formal declaration process of imported articles. An example of a common-practice error in the valuation declaration process is the omission of proper reporting of assist values. Assists are defined as any materials, such as dies, molds, tools, and machinery, that are provided from the buyer of imported merchandise to the seller of imported merchandise at a reduced cost or free of charge.

Import shipments that contain an assist must be accompanied by a proper commercial invoice that itemizes the value and existence of an assist as an invoice requirement. There are some exemptions from an assist declaration, including the design work, engineering work, and research and development fees that are undertaken in the United States that will not be treated as an assist.

5.11.11 Drawback

Drawback is a privilege that is granted by CBP that allows an importer to collect 99% of duties that are previously paid by exporting the merchandise from the United States or destroying the imported goods that are under CBP supervision.

There are three types of drawback:

1. *Unused merchandise drawback*: a 99% refund of duties that are paid on imported merchandise that is exported in the same condition as when imported and remains unused in the United States. The importer may submit a drawback claim within three years from the date of importation.
2. *Rejected merchandise drawback*: a 99% refund on imported merchandise that does not conform to the importer's standards of approval or the standards of any government agency. The importer may submit a drawback claim for three years from the date of importation.
3. *Manufacturing drawback*: a 99% refund of duties that are paid on imported merchandise that is further processed or manufactured in the United States and subsequently exported. CBP will allow a 99% refund of duties that are paid on the imported merchandise for up to five years from the date of importation.

Unless a company is given prior permission otherwise, all merchandise must be examined by CBP before export to qualify for the drawback privilege. A filer notifies CBP of the intent to file a drawback claim in reference to an export by filing a Notice of Intent. The importer must allow at least five working days before the export of the merchandise. CBP will notify the drawback claimant of the intent to examine or waive the examination.

5.11.12 Harmonized Tariff Classification

All merchandise entering the United States must be properly identified through the assignation of a Harmonized Tariff Classification number. CBP requires that all merchandise be identified by a commodity classification number that is referenced in the Harmonized Tariff Schedule of the United States (HTSUS). Merchandise entering the commerce of the United States requires specific identification to afford CBP and other government agencies an opportunity to make the proper affirmation of release into the commerce of the United States, utilizing commodity-specific controls.

Many importers rely on their customs brokers to determine the Harmonized Tariff Schedule (HTS) codes on their behalf. This practice is noncompliant and may result in penalties to the importer for lack of reasonable care. The HTS should be determined by the importer, and the importer may ask the customs broker for assistance with the classification as the customs broker is considered a customs expert. However, the HTS determination is ultimately the responsibility of the importer. The importer should manage the tariff classification process through training its employees on the general rules of interpretation and proper classification principles.

Importers should create a classification database for their products. The HTS number can then be added to the purchase order and be used from the beginning of the import transaction to be included on the commercial invoice that is created by the supplier and be carried through the import process. This practice will demonstrate reasonable care in the import process.

5.11.13 Country of Origin Marking

It is an import requirement that goods are marked with the country of origin as to indicate to the ultimate purchaser the specific country of origin of the product. The criteria for country of origin may also play a role in the applicability of preferential tariff treatment and corresponding rates of duty.

The country of origin is also seen to be of importance in global security. This is crucial in assessing risk should an alert be issued on products from a particular place of origin. Goods not properly marked are subject to delays and marking duties.

The inclusion of marking instructions in a purchase agreement demonstrates reasonable care in the import entry process.

5.11.14 Payment of Duties and Taxes

Many importers use customs brokers to pay their duties and taxes. This is a very common practice. It should be noted that while the importer may pay the broker the monies to submit to CBP on their behalf, if the broker does not pay CBP, the importer will still be held liable for payment of duties.

Every importer is required to have a bond in order to clear customs. The first condition of a bond is to pay duties, fees, and taxes on a timely basis. Payment may be made directly by the importer or the broker via a check or electronic payment (Automated Clearing House [ACH]).

In a CBP audit, the importer will be asked how he or she manages the duty payment process. It is unacceptable to simply state that the broker pays the duty. A system of accountability must be implemented to ensure timely payment, and the importer must understand how the payment is being managed. Copies of the final ACH statement copy will serve as proof of payment as well as a copy of the check.

5.11.15 ITDS

Importing and exporting involve over 48 different government agencies that require nearly 200 different forms in order to process a shipment. The prior system requires a lot of paper and information to be entered in multiple electronic systems. The ITDS will eliminate redundancy and operational costs and facilitates more efficient processing of imports and exports. As of this writing, the implementation for other government agencies participating in ITDS is staggered over 2016.

5.11.16 ACE

The ACE is the system through which the single window of ITDS will be realized. It is the primary system that is used by the international trade community to submit import and export data and communicate with CBP and other PGAs. The ACE will be used by CBP and PGAs to collect, track, and process required trade information to determine the admissibility of shipments.

As of this writing, the US CBP is transitioning its cargo release and entry summary processing to a paperless environment. Through use of the document image system (DIS), filers can submit supporting documentation to the government during the import process and for export manifests. This process allows for timely receipt of documentation as opposed to hard copy paper.

Supporting documentation for PGAs, CBP, and remote location filing (RLF) documents and CBP forms 28, 29, and 4647 may all be submitted through the DIS and ACE.

For exporters, the ACE will allow them to obtain their own filer reports directly through the ACE system as opposed to submitting a formal written request to the US Census Bureau. This will enable exporters to better supervise their export activity on a timelier basis.

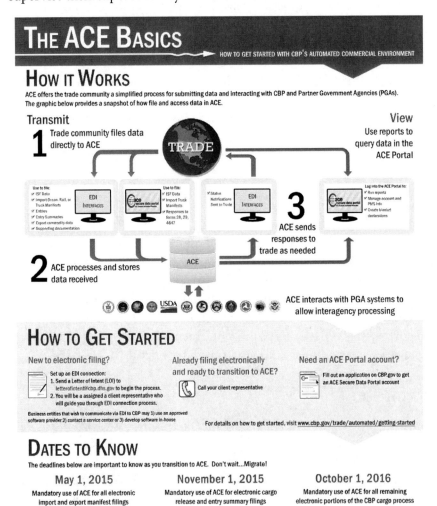

5.11.17 Centers of Excellence and Expertise

CBP has established the Centers of Excellence and Expertise to operate as an organizational structure for postrelease trade activities. These centers operate within an industry sector and from a national perspective. Some of these trade functions include (a) entry summary processing; (b) decisions and activities regarding packing, the country of origin marking, merchandise sampling, trademarks, classification, appraisement, and the rules of origin; and (c) the processing of liquidations, protests, and petitions.

CBP has 10 centers operating in a virtual environment, strategically managed as follows:

1. Agriculture and prepared products: Miami
2. Apparel, footwear, and textiles: San Francisco
3. Automotive and aerospace: Detroit
4. Base metals: Chicago
5. Consumer products and mass merchandising: Atlanta
6. Electronics: Los Angeles
7. Industrial and manufacturing materials: Buffalo
8. Machinery: Laredo
9. Petroleum, natural gas, and minerals: Houston
10. Pharmaceuticals, health, and chemicals: New York

Centers serve as a centralized source for trade inquiries for resolving issues. While centers are industry focused, they are also account based, meaning once an importer has been assigned to a center, that center will handle the postrelease trade activity for all imports regardless of the tariff classification.

5.11.18 Globally Harmonized System of Classification and Labeling of Chemicals

The Globally Harmonized System of Classification and Labeling of Chemicals (GHS) became effective in 2015. This rule requires all manufacturers and importers to comply with the new label requirements and safety data sheet (SDS) formats. The OSHA revised its Hazard Communication Standard in 2012 to require employers to adhere to the elements of the GHS, setting deadlines for worker training and for the labels and SDSs; along with new requirements for information, the labels must include signal words, hazard statements, pictograms, and more.

5.11.19 Export Compliance

In the United States, there are several government agencies that are involved in the export process. Within the Department of Commerce, there is the BIS and the Census Bureau. The Office of Foreign Assets Control (OFAC) is part of the Department of Treasury. Companies that deal with items on the United States Munitions List (USML) will also fall under the jurisdiction of the Department of State, Office of Defense Trade Controls. Homeland Security's Bureau of Customs and Border Protection is also involved in the enforcement of export regulations.

The Export Administration Regulations (EAR) are the rules by which the BIS regulates and controls the export of goods from the United States. The EAR also control certain activities such as the transfer of information to foreign nationals or engaging in restrictive trade boycotts that are not sanctioned by the United States. Companies that export from the United States are required to comply with these regulations and must have a process for managing their exports and international activities such as an Export Management and Compliance Program (EMCP). The EMCP becomes the game plan for staying compliant and avoiding export violations.

BIS/DOC: the lead agency for export controls

5.11.20 Electronic Export Information

The Census Bureau is the agency that is responsible for the collection of export data. The Electronic Export Information (EEI) is required for export shipments that have a value above $2500 per HTS line item. For licensed items, the EEI is required regardless of the value of the shipment.

The Foreign Trade Regulations (FTR) outline the requirements for filing the EEI including exceptions to filing. For example, the EEI is not required for exports to Canada.

The information required to be filed as part of the EEI includes the following:

- US principal party in interest (USPPI) name and identification number
- Date of export
- Ultimate consignee
- US state of origin
- Country of ultimate destination
- Method of transportation
- Conveyance/carrier name
- Carrier identification code
- Port of export
- Related party indicator
- Domestic or foreign origin indicator
- Commodity classification number
- Commodity description
- Shipping weight
- Value
- Export information code
- Shipment reference number
- Hazardous material indicator
- Routed export transaction indicator
- Conditional data elements as required

Incorrect data transmitted on the EEI can lead to potential delays if the information does not appear valid or CBP holds the shipment because the incorrect HTS/Schedule B number is transmitted.

There are two types of export transactions: (1) standard export transactions and (2) routed export transactions. Compliance with the FTR depends on the type of export transaction and the roles of the players within those transactions.

In a standard export transaction, the USPPI is the party in the United States that is responsible for compliance with export regulations and the correct filing of the EEI. The USPPI will choose their own freight forwarder and supervise the export process. The EEI may be filed by the USPPI or their freight forwarder. The freight forwarder must have written authorization (WA) from the USPPI to file the EEI on their behalf. The USPPI must provide the freight forwarder with the information that is needed to file the EEI timely and accurately.

In a routed export transaction, the foreign principal party in interest (FPPI) chooses the freight forwarder. The USPPI and the FPPI have specific requirements under the FTR that they must follow.

The USPPI must provide the customer's (FPPI's) freight forwarder with the data elements that are necessary for the freight forwarder to file the EEI. The freight forwarder must obtain WA from the FPPI to file the EEI on their behalf. The interesting part of this is that the USPPI is still listed on the EEI, but the authorization for filing the EEI on a routed export comes from the FPPI.

Upon request by the USPPI, the freight forwarder must provide the USPPI with a copy of the FPPI's WA and a copy of the filed EEI data elements that are provided by the USPPI in a routed export transaction.

If the USPPI wants to file the EEI in a routed export, the USPPI must obtain WA to file the EEI from the FPPI.

In either a standard export transaction or a routed export transaction, the USPPI must maintain records for five years from the date of export.

5.11.20.1 Responsibility of Prepairing and Filing the EEI— Exporter, Shipper, or Freight Forwarder

5.11.20.1.1 Who Is Responsible for Filing the EEI: The Shipper or the Freight Forwarder?

According to the US Census Bureau, in a standard export transaction, it is the USPPI's responsibility to prepare the EEI. However, the USPPI can give the freight forwarder a PoA or WA allowing them to prepare and file the EEI on their behalf.

In a routed export transaction, however, the FPPI must provide a PoA or a WA to prepare the EEI to either the USPPI or a US authorized agent. For more information on standard versus routed export transactions, please see Section 30.3 of the FTR (15 Code of Federal Regulations [CFR] Part 30).

The Internal Transaction Number (ITN) or the exemption citation must be provided by the EEI filer to the carrier when the goods are presented for export. The carrier is responsible for providing the ITN or the exemption citation to the US CBP. CBP officers will verify that the ITN or the exemption citations are clearly stated on export documents and provided to the carrier(s) within the prescribed time frames.

- *Vessel cargo*—If the manifest is required, the filing citation(s) must be reported by the carrier on the manifest (CBP Form 1302A). For those few carriers filing export manifests via the Automated Export System/Vessel Transportation Module, the filing citation must be placed in Marks and Numbers data element.
- *Truck cargo*—Carriers must provide the filing citation(s) to CBP officers upon request. It is acceptable for these citations to be placed on the bill of lading (freight or PRO bill) or other commercial loading documents. Drivers must provide documentation that clearly identifies the carrier and all the respective filing citations.
- *Air cargo (including express couriers)*—The filing citation(s) along with the associated AWB number and shipper/consignee information must be clearly *marked* (and visible) on the air cargo manifest, which must be filed with the general declaration.
- *Rail cargo*—The filing citation(s) must be reported for rail at the shipment level. Many rail carriers require this information prior to the loading of the goods. The FTR require the filing of the EEI not later than 2 hours prior to the time that the train arrives at the US border to go foreign.

The time frame varies according to the method of transportation for predeparture filing. For State Department USML shipments, refer to the International Traffic Arms Regulations (ITAR) (22 CFR 120–130), section 123.22.b.1. See §30.4.

For *non-USML* shipments, file the EEI as follows:

For Non-USML	
Vessel cargo	*24 hours prior to loading cargo on the vessel at the US port where the cargo is laden*
Air cargo	*2 hours prior to the scheduled departure time of the aircraft*
Truck cargo	*1 hour prior to the arrival of the truck at the US border to go foreign*
Rail cargo	*2 hours prior to the time that the train arrives at the US border to go foreign*
Mail	*2 hours prior to the departure of exporting carrier*
Pipeline	*Within four calendar days following the end of the month*

For *USML* shipments, file the EEI as follows:

For USML	
Vessel cargo	*24 hours prior to loading cargo* on the vessel at the US port where the cargo is laden
Rail cargo	*24 hours prior to the time that the train arrives* at the US border to go foreign
Truck cargo	*8 hours prior to the arrival of the truck* at the US border to go foreign
Air cargo	*8 hours prior to the scheduled departure time* of the aircraft

If the shipment is accompanying a purchaser (i.e., a pleasure boat that is being sailed out of the US waters by a buyer or commercial goods that are purchased in the United States and hand-carried out), the USPPI should contact the port where the goods will be leaving the United States for instructions on where to submit the proof of filing citation or exemption legend.

The ITN's exemption citations or in-bond numbers for postal shipments in excess of $2500 per Schedule B number should be filed within the post office.

5.11.21 BIS

The BIS administers the EAR and regulates the exports of most commercial items from the United States. These items are referred to as dual-use items. Items that are controlled for export may require authorization from the BIS prior to export.

Items that are controlled for export are listed on the Commerce Control List (CCL). The specific products described on the CCL are designated by an Export Control Classification Number (ECCN). The ECCN is broken down into 10 categories as follows:

1. Nuclear materials, facilities, and equipment
2. Materials, chemicals, microorganisms, and toxins
3. Materials processing
4. Electronics
5. Computers
6. Telecommunications and information security
7. Sensors and lasers
8. Navigation and avionics
9. Marine
10. Propulsion systems, space vehicles, and related equipment

Proper classification of the item to be exported is essential to determine the licensing requirements under the EAR. In many cases, the assistance of company product designers and engineers is required because the information used to ascertain the correct classification is specific and technical. If exporters have difficulty classifying a product, they can turn to outside sources such as consultants or the BIS.

In the classification process, a product will be found to be either on the list or not. In the case of an item that is found on the list, the exporter must review the destination country to determine whether a license is required to ship to the country. The Commerce Country Chart is a matrix of reasons for control that is tied to the destination country and is contained within the EAR. If, after review of the Commerce Country Chart, a license is found to be necessary, the exporter must review the transaction to determine if a license exception is available. A license exception may be used in lieu of a license, provided that the exporter performs the balance of the due diligence in the export transaction. This information is reported to the Census Bureau and the BIS on export as part of the EEI transmission.

If, after a review of the Commerce Country Chart and a review of the transaction, a license is found to be required before export, the exporter can apply for a license. This can be done electronically through the BIS website via the Simplified Network Application Process (SNAP).

If, after review of the CCL, a product is not found to be on the list, the product may be shipped under no-license-required (NLR) status, provided that the exporter has performed the other required responsibilities before export.

5.12 THE CORE ELEMENTS OF AN EFFECTIVE EMCP

- *Management commitment*: Senior management must establish written export compliance standards for the organization, commit sufficient resources for the export compliance program, and ensure that appropriate senior organizational official(s) are designated with the overall responsibility for the export compliance program to ensure adherence to export control laws and regulations.
- *Continuous risk assessment of the export program.*
- *Formal written export management and compliance program*: Effective implementation and adherence to written policies and operational procedures.
- *Ongoing compliance training and awareness.*
- *Pre-/postexport compliance security and screening*: Screening of employees, contractors, customers, products, and transactions and implementation of compliance safeguards throughout the export life cycle including product development, jurisdiction, classification, sales, license decisions, supply chain, servicing channels, and post-shipment activity.
- *Adherence to recordkeeping regulatory requirements.*
- *Internal and external compliance monitoring and periodic audits.*
- *Maintaining a program for handling compliance problems, including reporting export violations.*
- *Completing appropriate corrective actions in response to export violations.*

5.13 RED FLAG INDICATORS

5.13.1 Things to Look for in Export Transactions

Use this as a checklist to discover possible violations of the EAR. You may also wish to visit http://www.bis.doc.gov/index.php/compliance-a-training /export-management-a-compliance/freight-forwarder-guidance/23-com pliance-a-training/47-know-your-customer-guidance, which provides the *Know Your Customer Guidance.*

- The customer or its address is similar to one of the parties who are found on the Commerce Department's (BIS's) list of denied persons.
- The customer or the purchasing agent is reluctant to offer information about the end use of the item.
- The product's capabilities do not fit the buyer's line of business, such as an order for sophisticated computers for a small bakery.
- The item ordered is incompatible with the technical level of the country to which it is being shipped, such as semiconductor manufacturing equipment being shipped to a country that has no electronics industry.
- The customer is willing to pay cash for a very expensive item when the terms of sale would normally call for financing.
- The customer has little or no business background.
- The customer is unfamiliar with the product's performance characteristics but still wants the product.
- Routine installation, training, or maintenance services are declined by the customer.
- Delivery dates are vague, or deliveries are planned for out-of-the-way destinations.
- A freight forwarding firm is listed as the product's final destination.
- The shipping route is abnormal for the product and destination.
- Packaging is inconsistent with the stated method of shipment or destination.
- When questioned, the buyer is evasive and especially unclear about whether the purchased product is for domestic use, for export, or for reexport.

5.13.2 Denied Party Screening

Companies engaged in exporting and importing must exercise various levels of due diligence. They must be aware of who the end user of the product is and who the parties to the transaction are. This requires the screening of all the parties in the transaction. In the event that an exporter is uncomfortable with an export transaction or cannot ascertain answers to the end user and end-use questions, he or she should not move ahead with the export as the transaction may be detrimental to national security.

All the parties to the export transaction should be screened through the following lists.

5.13.2.1 Department of Commerce–BIS

- *Denied Persons List (DPL)*—Individuals and entities that have been denied export privileges. Any dealings with a party on this list that would violate the terms of its denial order are prohibited.
- *Unverified List*—End users whom BIS has been unable to verify in prior transactions. The presence of a party on this list in a transaction is a *red flag* that should be resolved before proceeding with the transaction.
- *Entity List*—Parties whose presence in a transaction can trigger a license requirement that is supplemental to those elsewhere in the EAR. The list specifies the license requirements and policies that apply to each listed party.

5.13.2.2 Department of State–Bureau of International Security and Nonproliferation

- *Nonproliferation sanctions*—Parties who have been sanctioned under various statutes. The linked Web page is updated as appropriate, but the Federal Register is the only official and complete listing of non-proliferation sanction determinations.

5.13.2.3 Department of State–Directorate of Defense Trade Controls

Arms Export Control Act (AECA) Debarred List—Entities and individuals who are prohibited from participating directly or indirectly in the export of defense articles, including technical data and defense services. Pursuant to the AECA and the ITAR, the AECA Debarred List includes persons who are convicted in court of violating or conspiring to violate the AECA and subject to *statutory debarment* or persons who are established to have violated the AECA in an administrative proceeding and subject to *administrative debarment*.

5.13.2.4 Department of the Treasury–OFAC

- *Specially Designated Nationals (SDNs) List*—Parties who may be prohibited from export transactions based on OFAC's regulations. The EAR require a license for exports or reexports to any party in any entry on this list that contains any of the suffixes "SDGT," "SDT," "FTO," "IRAQ2," or "NPWMD."
- *Foreign Sanctions Evaders (FSEs) List*—Foreign individuals and entities that are determined to have violated, attempted to violate, conspired to violate, or caused a violation of US sanctions on Syria or Iran, as well as foreign persons who have facilitated deceptive transactions for or on behalf of persons who are subject to US sanctions. Transactions by US persons or within the United States involving FSEs are prohibited.
- *Sectoral Sanctions Identification (SSI) List*—Individuals operating in sectors of the Russian economy with whom US persons are prohibited from transacting in, providing financing for, or dealing in debt with a maturity of longer than 90 days.
- *Palestinian Legislative Council (PLC) List*—Individuals of the PLC who were elected on the party slate of Hamas, or any other foreign terrorist organization (FTO), specially designated terrorist (SDT), or specially designated global terrorist.
- *The List of Foreign Financial Institutions Subject to Part 561 (the Part 561 List)*—The Part 561 List includes the names of foreign financial institutions that are subject to sanctions, certain prohibitions, or strict conditions before a US company may do business with them.
- *Non-SDN Iranian Sanctions Act List (NS-ISA)*—The NS-ISA List includes persons who are determined to have made certain investments in Iran's energy sector or to have engaged in certain activities relating to Iran's refined petroleum sector. Their names do not appear on the SDNs or Blocked Persons List, and their properties and/or interests in properties are not blocked, pursuant to this action.

5.13.3 Compliance with Antiboycott Regulations

Antiboycott regulations prohibit US companies from participating in foreign boycotts that the United States does not sanction. The effect of these regulations is to prevent US companies from being used to implement the foreign policies of other countries that run counter to US policy.

The antiboycott regulations of the EAR apply to all US persons, defined to include individuals and companies that are located in the United States and their foreign affiliates. These regulations pertain to exports, imports, financing, forwarding, shipping, and other transactions that may occur offshore.

Antiboycott regulations prohibit the following:

- Agreements to refuse or actual refusal to do business with Israel or blacklisted companies
- Agreements to discriminate against other persons based on race, religion, sex, national origin, or nationality
- Agreements to furnish information about business relations with Israel or blacklisted companies
- Agreements to furnish information about the race, religion, gender, or national origin of another person
- Implementing letters of credit containing prohibited boycott terms or conditions

If a company receives a purchase order or document containing boycott language, they need to consider if the language in the document is prohibited and reportable. Prohibited language will require the company to obtain a clean document with the boycott language removed. Reporting is required and can be done electronically.

5.13.4 OFAC

Within the Department of the Treasury is the OFAC, which administers and enforces economic and trade sanctions based on US foreign policy and national security goals. These sanctions are targeted against foreign countries, terrorists, international narcotics traffickers, and those who are engaged in activities that are related to the proliferation of weapons of mass destruction. Many of these sanctions are based on the United Nations and other international mandates, are multilateral in scope, and involve close cooperation with allied governments.

Under these sanctions, US companies are prohibited from trading or engaging in financial transactions with individuals, companies, and countries on the sanctions list unless the company has received specific authorization to engage in the transaction.

All US persons must comply with OFAC regulations, including all US citizens and permanent resident aliens, regardless of where they are located, all persons and entities within the United States, all US incorporated entities, and their foreign subsidiaries.

5.13.5 ITAR

The Department of State manages export control over military items through the AECA. This act authorizes the president to control the export and import of defense articles and defense services. License or approval may be granted only to the US companies that are registered with Defense Trade Controls for the export of such items.

Through Export Control Reform, the ITAR has been significantly overhauled. Many items have moved from the USML to the CCL. The USML has moved to a positive list and is much more specific than it was previously. As of this writing, there are still a few categories remaining that have not undergone overhaul but are pending review.

5.13.6 Import/Export Compliance Management

The core elements of an effective compliance management are the same for all companies regardless of the commodities and services that they are shipping and providing. There may be additional steps that must be taken for those companies that are engaged in commodities that are controlled for export due to the type of commodity or fall under another government agency requirement for imports.

The basic elements of any company's compliance management must include the following elements in order to be effective:

- Senior management commitment
- Identification of risks based on commodities and types of transactions
- Formal written manual
- Training and awareness
- Knowledge of valuation concepts
- Screening of business partners, customers, financial institutions, and supply chain partners
- Recordkeeping requirements
- Periodic auditing and monitoring
- System for reporting violations and handling compliance issues
- System for implementing corrective actions where a compliance issue is indicated
- Partnering with knowledgeable and compliant service providers

5.13.7 Internal Auditing

Importers and exporters should perform internal audits based on the risks within their supply chain. CBP and the BIS both offer guidance on managing internal audits. The following documents can be the start of creating a template for managing the internal audit process.

FOCUSED ASSESSMENT
PREASSESSMENT SURVEY QUESTIONNAIRE

The purpose of this document is to obtain information from the importers about their import operations over compliance with CBP laws and regulations. The contents of the preassessment survey questionnaire (PASQ) will be tailored based on the auditors' analysis, the importer's import activity, and the audit team's initial assessment of the potential risks for each of the audit areas that were identified in the preliminary assessment of risk (PAR). Auditors may adapt or modify this document as needed or may develop alternate formats. Auditors may also request copies of documentation in conjunction with the PASQ.

PREASSESSMENT SURVEY QUESTIONNAIRE
INSTRUCTIONS TO THE IMPORTER FOR COMPLETING THE PASQ Please respond to all the questions. The information you provide will assist us in focusing on the specific risks that are relative to your imported merchandise and the processes/procedures that are used to mitigate the risk of being noncompliant with CBP laws and regulations. In addition, your responses will help us to identify the individuals who are responsible for performing the procedures and the types of documentation that will be available for us to review. The audit team will review your responses and prepare supplemental questions that will be discussed with your personnel to further our understanding of your processes and procedures. This PASQ file is a Word document that may be filled in with your responses and returned to the auditors, either as a Word or a portable document format (pdf) file. We request that your *complete response* be provided to us by [insert date] so that we may prepare our questions prior to the entrance conference.
POINT OF CONTACT INFORMATION
Name(s) of the person(s) preparing the form: *If there are multiple preparers, you may identify a single person who can be contacted to obtain clarification of the responses.*
Title(s):
Phone number(s):
E-mail address(es):
Section 1—Information about [name of importer]'s organization and policy and procedures pertaining to CBP activities

1.1	Describe the company's mission statement, code of ethics/conduct, and objectives.

1.1.1	How are the mission statement, the code of ethics/conduct, and the company's objectives disseminated within the organization?
1.2	Who is responsible for assessing the risks in achieving the company's objectives? *Indicate if there is a subgroup or individual who is responsible for assessing the risk for being noncompliant with CBP laws and regulations.*
1.2.1	Describe how the risk assessment is accomplished. *Indicate, for example, when/how often the risk assessment is performed, what information is used, and what thresholds/tolerances the company considers to be acceptable.*
1.2.2	When was the last risk assessment that was performed? *Describe any significant changes that were made as a result of the risk assessment.*
1.3	Who, within your company, has the overall responsibility for ensuring compliance with CBP laws and regulations?
	• *Indicate if there is an import function or department, and describe the chain of command (e.g., identify who they report to).* • *Alternately, your company may entrust compliance to a customs broker, a customs consultant, or other outside agent. Identify them, and indicate who within your company (i.e., individuals or groups) is/are responsible for interacting with the broker, consultant, or other outside agent (i.e., providing information to them and monitoring their work).*
1.3.1	If there is an import function or department, provide the following information:
	• How is it staffed? *Indicate if an individual is assigned as the manager, and the number of employees who report to them.* • How long has the manager been assigned to his or her position? • What are the responsibilities of the manager, and how is he or she accountable? *Indicate if he or she is responsible for providing weekly activity reports and describe any performance measures.*
1.3.2	If compliance has been entrusted to a customs broker, a customs consultant, or other outside agent (i.e., no import department per se), provide the following information:
	• How long has the company engaged the current broker, consultant, or other outside agent? • Describe the processes that are used to communicate information and to monitor his or her work. *Indicate if there is a written contract or agreement.*
1.4	Who is responsible for developing and maintaining the written policies and procedures that are used to ensure compliance with CBP laws and regulations?
	• How often are the written policies and procedures updated?

Section 2—Information about the valuation of imported merchandise	
2.1	What basis of appraisement is used for the value of imported merchandise?
2.2	Who is responsible for transacting with the foreign vendors? *Identify all the individuals or groups/departments that are responsible.*
2.2.1	Describe how transactions are negotiated with foreign vendors. *Describe all the processes that are used and the conditions that apply.*
2.2.2	Describe the terms of sale that are used. *If there are different terms of sale, explain the conditions when each is used.*
2.2.3	If applicable, describe the terms/conditions when discounts or rebates are made.
2.2.4	If applicable, describe any additional expenses such as management fees or engineering services that are separately billed by the foreign vendors.
2.2.5	What documentation shows the terms of sale and prices (e.g., contracts, distribution and other similar agreements, invoices, purchase orders, bills of lading, proof of payment, correspondence between the parties, and company reports or catalogs/brochures)?
2.3	Describe the accounting procedures for recording purchases and payments.
	• What accounts are used to record *purchases* of foreign merchandise? *Identify or provide a list of vendor codes.*
	• What accounts are used to record *payments* that are made to foreign vendors? *Explain the methods of payment that are used (e.g., wire transfer, letters of credit).*
2.4	If applicable, what accounting data/reports are provided to the import function or department? *Indicate how often data/reports are provided (e.g., quarterly reports of price adjustments for purchases from foreign vendors).*
For risk pertaining to related-party transactions	
2.5	Describe the nature of the relationship between your company and the related foreign vendor/seller. *Indicate if your company is the exclusive US importer.*
2.5.1	Describe any financial arrangements (e.g., loans, financial assistance, and expense reimbursement) between your company and the foreign vendor/seller.

2.5.2	If applicable, explain the terms and conditions of goods that are sold to your company on consignment.
2.5.3	Describe how the prices between your company and the foreign vendor/seller/manufacturer are determined. *Identify all the sources of data that are used, and explain the accounting methodology or computational formulas where appropriate. If the transaction value is used, indicate if your company supports circumstances of sale or test values. If applicable, provide the following information:*
	• Describe when price adjustments are made.
	• Identify any additional expenses such as management fees or engineering services that are separately billed to your company.
2.5.4	Explain how transactions are accounted for. *Indicate if your company maintains its own accounting books and records.*
2.5.4.1	What intercompany accounts are used?
For risk pertaining to statutory additions	
2.6	*Assists*
2.6.1	If applicable, describe the type of assists that are provided to the foreign vendors for free or at a reduced cost (e.g., tooling, hangtags, art, or design work).
2.6.2	Who decides (or determines) that the assists will be provided? *Identify all the individuals or groups/departments that are involved in the decision.*
	• When is it decided that the assists will be provided?
	• What accounts are used to record the costs of the assists?
2.6.3	Describe the procedures that are used to ensure that the costs of the assists are included in the values that are declared to CBP. *Indicate who decides how the actual cost of the assist will be apportioned to the imported items, and explain how the apportioned cost is tracked.*
2.7	*Packing*
2.7.1	If applicable, describe the type of packing (i.e., labor or materials), containers (exclusive of instruments of international traffic), and coverings of whatever nature that is separately paid to the vendor to put the imported merchandise in condition ready for shipment to the United States.

2.7.2	Who decides (or determines) that the cost of packing will be separately charged? *Identify all the individuals or groups/departments that are involved in the decision.*
	• When is it decided that the cost of packing will be separately charged? • What accounts are used to record the costs of packing, containers, and coverings?
2.7.3	Describe the procedures that are used to ensure that the cost of the packing is included in the values that are declared to CBP.
2.8	*Commissions*
2.8.1	If applicable, describe the terms of sale with foreign vendors that require your company to separately pay for *selling agent* commissions. *Identify the vendors.*
2.8.2	Who decides (or determines) that the *selling agent* commissions will be paid directly to the intermediary?
	• When is it decided that the *selling agent* commissions will be paid directly to the intermediary? • What accounts are used to record the payment of these commissions?
2.8.3	Describe the procedures that are used to ensure that these commissions are included in the values that are declared to CBP.
2.9	*Royalty and License Fees*
2.9.1	If applicable, describe the terms of sale with foreign vendors that require your company to pay, directly or indirectly, any royalty or license fee that is related to the imported merchandise as a condition of the sale of the imported merchandise for exportation to the United States. *Identify the vendors.*
2.9.2	Who decides (or determines) that royalty or license fees will be paid as a condition of the sale?
	• When is it decided that royalty or license fees will be paid as a condition of the sale? • What accounts are used to record the payment of the royalty or license fees that are related to imported merchandise?
2.9.3	What procedures ensure that royalty or license fees are included in the values declared to CBP?

2.10	*Proceeds of Any Subsequent Resale, Disposal, or Use*
2.10.1	If applicable, describe any agreements with the foreign vendors where the proceeds of any subsequent resale, disposal, or use of the imported merchandise accrue directly or indirectly to the foreign vendor. *Identify the vendors.*
2.10.2	Who decides (or determines) that the proceeds of any subsequent resale, disposal, or use of the imported merchandise will accrue directly or indirectly to the foreign vendor? <ul><li>When is it decided that the proceeds of any subsequent resale, disposal, or use of the imported merchandise will accrue directly or indirectly to the foreign vendor?</li><li>What accounts are used to record the payment of these proceeds?</li></ul>
2.10.3	Describe the procedures that are used to ensure that the proceeds of any subsequent resale, disposal, or use of the imported merchandise accruing directly or indirectly to the foreign vendor are included in the values that are declared to CBP.
Section 3—Information about the classification of imported merchandise	
3.1	Who is responsible for determining how imported merchandise is classified? *Identify all the individuals or groups that are responsible.*
3.1.1	What records and other information (e.g., product specifications, engineering drawings, physical items, laboratory analyses) are used to determine the classification of merchandise?
3.2	Does your company have a classification database?
3.2.1	If there is a classification database, do you archive previous versions of it? *Indicate how long the previous versions are retained.*
3.2.2	If there is a classification database, is a copy provided to the broker? *Indicate how it is provided to him or her.*
3.2.3	If there is a classification database, what procedures ensure that the information in the database is accurate?
Section 4—Information about special classification provisions HTSUS 9801	
4.1	Describe the type of merchandise that is imported under HTSUS 9801.
4.2	Who decides (or determines) that products of the United States will be returned after having been exported? *Identify all the individuals or groups/departments that are involved in the process.*

	• When is it determined that the products will be returned after having been exported? • What documentation/records are maintained for the exported items?
4.3	Describe the procedures that ensure that the exported items have not been advanced in value or improved in condition by any manufacturing process or other means while abroad.
4.4	Describe the procedures that ensure that drawback has not been claimed for the exported items.
Section 5—Information about special classification provisions HTSUS 9802	
5.1	Describe the type of merchandise that is imported under HTSUS 9802.
5.2	What documentation/records are maintained for the exported items?
5.3	**For items that are imported under HTSUS 9802.00.40/9802.00.50:** What documentation/records support the cost or value of the repair?
5.4	Describe the procedures or means (e.g., unique identifiers) that are used to ensure that the articles exported for repair or alterations are the same articles being reimported.
5.5	**For items that are imported under HTSUS 9802.00.40/9802.00.50:** Describe the procedures that ensure that the foreign operation (e.g., repair or alteration process) does not result in the exported item becoming a commercially different article with new properties and characteristics.
5.6	Describe the procedures that ensure that drawback has not been claimed for the exported items.
Section 6—Information about Generalized System of Preferences/Free Trade Agreement	
6.1	If applicable, identify the name and manufacturers identification (MID) number for all of the foreign vendors from whom items are imported under the Generalized System of Preference/Free Trade Agreement (GSP/FTA).
6.2	Describe any agreements with unrelated foreign vendors. *Indicate if the unrelated vendors are required to provide cost and production records to CBP or are legally prevented from releasing the records.*
6.3	Describe the procedures that are used to ensure that the origin of articles that are imported under the GSP (or FTA) is wholly the growth, product, or manufacture of the beneficiary developing country (BDC) (or FTA country)? *Identify who performs the procedures and when/how often the procedures are performed.*

6.3.1	What documentation/records are verified? *Indicate if copies of the documentation/records are retained on file or may be obtained upon request.*
6.4	Describe the procedures that are used to ensure the cost or value of the material that is produced in the BDC (or FTA country), plus the direct processing cost, is not less than 35% of the appraised value of the articles at the time of entry into the United States. *Identify all the individuals/groups that perform the procedures and when/how often the procedures are performed.*
6.4.1	What documentation/records are verified? *Indicate if copies of the documentation/records are retained on file or may be obtained upon request.*
6.5	What documentation is maintained on file showing that the articles are shipped directly from the BDC (or FTA country) to the United States without passing through the territory of any other country, or if passing through the territory of any other country, that the articles did not enter the retail commerce of the other country?
Section 7—Information about NAFTA	
7.1	Who is responsible for maintaining the certificates of origin from NAFTA vendors?
7.2	Describe the procedures that are used to ensure that imported items are eligible for NAFTA.
Section 8—Information about antidumping/countervailing duties (AD/CVD)	
8.1	Who decides (or determines) that items may be subject to AD/CVD? *Indicate when and how often items are reviewed.*
8.1.1	What information is used to determine whether items may be subject to AD/CVD? *Identify all the individuals or groups/departments that provide information as well as the documentation/records that are used.*
8.2	Describe the procedures that are used to ensure that the correct (true) country of origin is identified for items that are subject to AD/CVD.
8.3	Describe the procedures that are used to ensure that the correct AD/CVD case numbers are identified on the entry.

Section 9—Information about Intellectual Property Rights	
9.1	Identify all imported items for which your company has authorizations from the holders of intellectual property rights (IPR) such as trade names, trademarks, or copyrights. *Describe the item, and indicate the type of IPR.*
9.2	Who decides (or determines) that an imported item may have IPR belonging to other entities? *Indicate when and how often items are reviewed.* • When is it decided that an imported item may have IPR belonging to other entities? • What information is used to determine that the items have IPR belonging to other entities? *Identify all the individuals or groups/departments that provide information as well as the documentation/records that are used.*
9.3	Describe the procedures that are used to ensure that there is a valid authorization/agreement between your company and the owner of the trade name, trademark, copyright, or patent prior to the importation of the items?
9.4	What accounts are used to record royalties, proceeds, and indirect payments that are related to the use of the IPR?

REQUEST FOR DOCUMENTATION

DATE OF REQUEST:

RESPONSE DUE:

SUBJECT: *When submitted in conjunction with the PASQ, the subject matter may be "Information about the organization and policies and procedures relative to compliance with CBP laws and regulations."*

Item No.	Description of Documentation
1	A copy of the organizational chart, if there is one.
2	A copy of the written policies and procedures that are used to ensure compliance with CBP laws and regulations (e.g., an import compliance manual).
3	A copy of the general ledger (GL) working trial balance for the period ending [xxxx] and the description of the accounts that are used.
4	A copy of written accounting procedures for recording purchases and the payments.

5.13.8 From CBP Informed Compliance Publication: Reasonable Care

5.13.8.1 *General Questions for All Transactions*

1. If you have not retained an expert to assist you in complying with customs requirements, do you have access to the customs regulations (Title 19 of the CFR), the HTSUS, and the general public outreach (GPO) publication *Customs Bulletin and Decisions*? Do you have access to the Customs Internet Website, Customs Bulletin Board, or

other research services to permit you to establish reliable procedures and facilitate compliance with customs laws and regulations?

2. Has a responsible and knowledgeable individual within your organization reviewed the customs documentation that you or an expert prepared to ensure that it is full, complete, and accurate? If that documentation was prepared outside your own organization, do you have a reliable system in place to ensure that you receive copies of the information as submitted to the US CBP, that the information is reviewed for accuracy, and that the US CBP is timely apprised of any needed corrections?

3. If you employ an expert to assist you in complying with customs requirements, have you discussed your importations in advance with him or her, and have you provided him or her with full, complete, and accurate information about the import transactions?

4. Are identical transactions or merchandise handled differently at different ports or US CBP offices within the same port? If so, have you brought this to the attention of the appropriate US CBP officials?

5.13.9 Questions Arranged by Topic

5.13.9.1 Merchandise Description and Tariff Classification

Basic question: Do you know or have you established a reliable procedure or program to ensure that you know what you ordered, where it was made, and what it is made of?

1. Have you provided or established reliable procedures to ensure that you provide a complete and accurate description of your merchandise to the US CBP in accordance with 19 U.S.C. 1481? (Also, see 19 CFR 141.87 and 19 CFR 141.89 for special merchandise description requirements.)

2. Have you provided or established reliable procedures to ensure that you provide a correct tariff classification of your merchandise to the US CBP in accordance with 19 U.S.C. 1484?

3. Have you obtained a customs *ruling* regarding the description of the merchandise or its tariff classification (see 19 CFR Part 177), and if so, have you established reliable procedures to ensure that you have followed the ruling and brought it to the US CBP's attention?

4. Where the merchandise description or tariff classification information is not immediately available, have you established a reliable procedure for providing that information, and is the procedure being followed?

5. Have you participated in a customs preclassification of your merchandise relating to proper merchandise description and classification?

6. Have you consulted the tariff schedules, customs informed compliance publications, court cases, and/or customs rulings to assist you in describing and classifying the merchandise?

7. Have you consulted with a customs *expert* (e.g., lawyer, customs broker, accountant, or customs consultant) to assist in the description and/or classification of the merchandise?

8. If you are claiming a conditionally free or special tariff classification/provision for your merchandise (e.g., GSP, HTS Item 9802, NAFTA), how have you verified that the merchandise qualifies for such status? Have you obtained or developed reliable procedures to obtain any required or necessary documentation to support the claim? If making a NAFTA preference claim, do you already have a NAFTA certificate of origin in your possession?

9. Is the nature of your merchandise, such as a laboratory analysis or other specialized procedures, utilizing proper descriptions and classifications?

10. Have you developed a reliable program or procedure to maintain and produce any required customs entry documentation and supporting information?

5.13.9.2 *Valuation*

Basic questions: Do you know or have you established reliable procedures to know the price that is actually paid or payable for your merchandise? Do you know the terms of sale; whether there will be rebates, tie-ins, indirect costs, or additional payments; whether assists were provided, and whether there are commissions or royalties that were paid? Are the amounts actual or estimated? Are you and the supplier related parties?

1. Have you provided or established reliable procedures to provide the US CBP with a proper declared value for your merchandise in accordance with 19 U.S.C. 1484 and 19 U.S.C. 1401a?

2. Have you obtained a customs *ruling* regarding the valuation of the merchandise (see 19 CFR Part 177), and if so, have you established reliable procedures to ensure that you have followed the ruling and brought it to the US CBP's attention?

3. Have you consulted the customs valuation laws and regulations, *Customs Valuation Encyclopedia,* customs informed compliance publications, court cases, and customs rulings to assist you in valuing merchandise?

4. Have you consulted with a customs *expert* (e.g., lawyer, accountant, customs broker, customs consultant) to assist in the valuation of the merchandise?

5. If you purchased the merchandise from a *related* seller, have you established procedures to ensure that you have reported that fact upon entry and taken measures or established reliable procedures to ensure that the value reported to the US CBP meets one of the *related-party* tests?

6. Have you taken measures or established reliable procedures to ensure that all of the legally required costs or payments associated with the imported merchandise have been reported to the US CBP (e.g., assists, all commissions, indirect payments or rebates, royalties)?

7. If you are declaring a value based on a transaction in which you were/are not the buyer, have you substantiated that the transaction is a bona fide sale at arm's length and that the merchandise was clearly destined to the United States at the time of sale?

8. If you are claiming a conditionally free or special tariff classification/provision for your merchandise (e.g., GSP, HTS Item 9802, NAFTA), have you established a reliable system or program to ensure that you reported the required value information and obtained any required or necessary documentation to support the claim?

9. Have you established a reliable program or procedure to produce any required entry documentation and supporting information?

5.13.9.3 Country of Origin/Marking/Quota

Basic question: Have you taken reliable measures to ascertain the correct country of origin for the imported merchandise?

1. Have you established reliable procedures to ensure that you report the correct country of origin on customs entry documents?

2. Have you established reliable procedures to verify or ensure that the merchandise is properly marked upon entry with the correct country of origin (if required) in accordance with 19 U.S.C. 1304 and any other applicable special marking requirement (watches, gold, textile labeling, etc.)?

3. Have you obtained a customs *ruling* regarding the proper marking and country of origin of the merchandise (see 19 CFR Part 177), and if so, have you established reliable procedures to ensure that you followed the ruling and brought it to the US CBP's attention?

4. Have you consulted with a customs *expert* (e.g., lawyer, accountant, customs broker, customs consultant) regarding the correct country of origin/proper marking of your merchandise?

5. Have you taken reliable and adequate measures to communicate the customs country of origin marking requirements to your foreign supplier prior to importation of your merchandise?

6. If you are claiming a change in the origin of the merchandise or claiming that the goods are of US origin, have you taken the required measures to substantiate your claim? (e.g., Do you have US milling certificates or manufacturer's affidavits attesting to the production in the United States?)

7. If you are importing textiles or apparel, have you developed reliable procedures to ensure that you have ascertained the correct country of origin in accordance with 19 U.S.C. 3592 (Section 334, Pub. Law 103–465) and assured yourself that no illegal transshipment or false or fraudulent practices were involved?

8. Do you know how your goods are made from raw materials to finished goods, who made these goods, and where they are made?

9. Have you checked with the US CBP and developed a reliable procedure or system to ensure that the quota category is correct?

10. Have you checked or developed reliable procedures to check the Status Report on Current Import Quotas (Restraint Levels) that is issued by the US CBP to determine if your goods are subject to a quota category that has part categories?

11. Have you taken reliable measures to ensure that you have obtained the correct visas for your goods if they are subject to visa categories?

12. In the case of textile articles, have you prepared or developed a reliable program to prepare the proper country declaration for each entry, i.e., a single-country declaration (if wholly obtained/produced) or a multicountry declaration (if the raw materials from one country were produced into goods in a second)?

13. Have you established a reliable maintenance program or procedure to ensure that you can produce any required entry documentation and supporting information, including any required certificates of origin?

5.13.9.4 IPR

Basic question: Have you determined or established a reliable procedure to permit you to determine whether your merchandise or its packaging bear or use any trademarks or copyrighted matter or are patented and, if so, that you have a legal right to import those items into, and/or use those items in, the United States?

1. If you are importing goods or packaging bearing a trademark that is registered in the United States, have you checked or established a reliable procedure to ensure that it is genuine and not restricted from importation under the gray-market or parallel import requirements of US law (see 19 CFR 133.21), or that you have permission from the trademark holder to import such merchandise?
2. If you are importing goods or packaging that consists of, or contains, registered copyrighted material, have you checked or established a reliable procedure to ensure that it is authorized and genuine? If you are importing the sound recordings of live performances, were the recordings authorized?
3. Have you checked or developed a reliable procedure to see if your merchandise is subject to an International Trade Commission or court-ordered exclusion order?
4. Have you established a reliable procedure to ensure that you maintain and can produce any required entry documentation and supporting information?

5.13.9.5 Miscellaneous Questions

1. Have you taken measures or developed reliable procedures to ensure that your merchandise complies with other agency requirements (e.g., FDA, Environmental Protection Agency/Department of Tourism, CPSC, foreign trade commission [FTC], Agriculture) prior to or upon entry, including the procurement of any necessary licenses or permits?
2. Have you taken measures or developed reliable procedures to check to see if your goods are subject to a Commerce Department dumping or countervailing duty investigation or determination, and if so, have you complied or developed reliable procedures to ensure compliance with customs reporting requirements upon entry (e.g., 19 CFR 141.61)?

3. Is your merchandise subject to quota/visa requirements, and if so, have you provided or developed a reliable procedure to provide a correct visa for the goods upon entry?

4. Have you taken reliable measures to ensure and verify that you are filing the correct type of customs entry (e.g., temporary import bond [TIB], transportation and exportation [T&E], consumption entry, mail entry), as well as ensure that you have the right to make entry under the customs regulations?

ELEMENT 1: Management Commitment				Initials_____Date_____
	Y	N	U	Comments
Is management commitment communicated on an ongoing basis by the following? A. Company publications B. Company awareness posters C. Daily operating procedures D. Other means, e.g., bulletin boards, in meetings				
Does management issue a formal Management Commitment Statement that communicates a clear commitment to export controls?				
Is the formal statement distributed to all employees and contractors?				
Who is responsible for the distribution of the statement?				
Is there a distribution list of those who should receive the statement?				
What method of communication is used (letter, email, Intranet, etc.)?				
Does the distribution of the statement include an employee-signed receipt and a personal commitment to comply?				
Is the formal statement from current senior management communicated in a manner that is consistent with management priority correspondence?				
Does the formal statement explain why corporate commitment is important from your company's perspective?				
Does the formal statement contain a policy statement that no sales will be made contrary to the EAR?				
Does the formal statement convey the dual-use risk of the items to be exported?				

ELEMENT 1: Management Commitment				Initials_____ Date_____
	Y	**N**	**U**	**Comments**
Does the formal statement emphasize end-use/end-user prohibitions? Proliferation activities of concerns • Nuclear • Certain rocket systems and unmanned air vehicles (UAVs) • Chemical and biological weapons				
Does the formal statement contain a description of the penalties that are applied in instances of compliance failure? • Imposed by the Department of Commerce • Imposed by your company				
Does the formal statement include the name, position, and contact information, such as the e-mail address and telephone number of the person(s) to contact with questions concerning the legitimacy of a transaction or possible violations?				
What management records will be maintained to verify compliance with procedures and processes (including the formal statement)?				
Who is responsible for keeping each of the management records?				
How long must the records be retained?				
Where will the records be maintained?				
In what format will the records be retained?				
Are adequate resources (i.e., time, money, people) dedicated to the implementation and maintenance of the EMCP?				
Is management directly involved through regularly scheduled meetings with various units that are responsible for roles within the EMCP?				
Is management involved in the auditing process?				
Has management implemented a team of EMCP managers who meet frequently to review the challenges, procedures, and processes and who serve as the connection to the employees who perform the EMCP responsibilities?				

ELEMENT 1: Management Commitment				Initials_____ Date_____
	Y	N	U	Comments
Does the statement describe where employees can locate the EMCP Manual (on the company Intranet or a specific person and location of hard copies)?				
Are there written procedures to ensure a consistent, operational implementation of this element?				
Is a person designated to update this element, including the Management Commitment Statement, when management changes, or at least annually? (Note the name of the person in the comments section.)				
Who are the other employees who are held accountable for specific responsibilities under this element? For example: • Company officials charged with EMCP oversight and ongoing commitment to the program • Management team members who are responsible for connecting with all the responsible employees in the EMCP • Persons who are charged with ensuring that the EMCP is functioning as directed by management				
If the primary responsible person is unable to perform the responsibilities, is a secondary person designated to back up the primary designee? (If not, is a procedure in place to eliminate the vulnerabilities of an untrained person proceeding with tasks that might lead to violations of the EAR?)				
Do the responsible persons understand the interconnection of their roles with other EMCP processes and where they fit in the overall export compliance system?				
Is the message of management commitment conveyed in employee training through the following? • Orientation programs • Refresher training • Electronic training modules • Employee procedure manuals • Other				

ELEMENT 1: Management Commitment				Initials_____Date_____
	Y	N	U	Comments
Is management involved in EMCP training to emphasize management commitment to the program?				
Determination:				

ELEMENTS 2 and 5: Risk Assessment and Cradle-to-Grave Export Compliance Security and Screening				Initials_____ Date_____
	Y	N	U	Comments
Are there written procedures for ensuring compliance with product and country export restrictions?				
Do procedures include reexport guidelines or any special instructions?				
Is there a written procedure that describes how items are classified under ECCNs on the CCL? A. Does a technical expert within the company classify the items? B. If your company does not manufacture the item, does the manufacturer of the item classify it? C. Is there a written procedure that describes when a classification will be submitted to the BIS and who will be responsible for it? D. Is there a written procedure that describes the process for seeking commodity jurisdiction determinations?				
Is an individual designated to ensure that the product/country license determination guidance is current and updated?				
Is there a distribution procedure to ensure that all appropriate users receive the guidance and instructions for use?				
Is there a list that indicates the name of the persons who are responsible for using the guidance?				
Is a matrix or decision table for product/country license determinations used? Are the instructions provided easily understood and applied?				
Do the instructions provided specify who, when, where, and how to check each shipment against the matrix?				
Does the matrix/table display ECCNs and product descriptions?				
Appropriate shipping authorizations: (a) license required, (b) license exception (specify which), or (c) NLR?				
Does the matrix communicate license exception parameters/restrictions?				
Are license conditions and restrictions included within the matrix/table?				
Does the matrix/table cross-reference items to be exported with license exceptions that are normally available (based on item description and end destination)?				

ELEMENTS 2 and 5: Risk Assessment and Cradle-to-Grave Export Compliance Security and Screening				Initials_____ Date_____
	Y	N	U	Comments
Does the matrix/table clearly define which license exceptions are normally available for each item? (Also, clearly state which license exceptions may not be used due to general prohibitions)				
Are embargoed destinations displayed?				
Is the country information in the table up to date?				
Are item restrictions displayed? (i.e., technical parameter limitations, end-user limitations)				
Is the matrix automated? Is a person designated for updating the tool?				
Are reporting prompts built into the matrix/table?				
Are Wassenaar reports required? Does the matrix/table denote when they are required?				
Is the matrix manually implemented? If so, is a person designated to update the tool?				
Is there a *hold* function to prevent shipments from being further processed, if needed?				
Is there a procedure to distribute and verify the receipt of license conditions?				
Is there someone who is designated to distribute and follow-up with the acknowledgment verification?				
Is there a response deadline that is defined when the conditions are distributed?				
Are there written procedures to ensure that checks and safeguards are in place within the internal process flows? And are there assigned personnel who are responsible for all the checks?				
Are the order process and all linking internal flows displayed visually in a series of flow charts?				
Is there a narrative that describes the total flow process?				

ELEMENTS 2 and 5: Risk Assessment and Cradle-to-Grave Export Compliance Security and Screening				Initials_____Date_____
	Y	N	U	Comments
Are the following checks included in the internal process?				
• Preorder entry screen checks that are performed (i.e., know-your-customer red flags)				
• DPL				
• Entity List				
• Unverified List				
• SDNs List				
• Boycott language				
• Nuclear end uses				
• Certain rocket systems and UAVs' end uses				
• Chemical and biological weapons' end uses				
• Product/country licensing determination				
• Diversion risk check				
Do the order process and other linking processes include a description of administrative control over the following documents? A. Shipper's export declarations (SED)/AES records B. Shipper's Letter of Instruction (SLI) C. Airway bills (AWB) and/or bills of lading D. Invoices				
Does the procedure explain the order process and other linking processes from the receipt of order to actual shipment?				
Does the procedure include who is responsible for each screen check throughout the flow?				
Does the procedure describe when, how often, and what screening is performed?				
Are hold/cancel functions implemented?				
Does the procedure clearly indicate who has the authority to make classification decisions?				
Are supervisory or EMCP administrator sign-off procedures implemented at high-risk points?				
Does the company have an ongoing procedure for monitoring the compliance of consignees, end users, and other parties who are involved in export transactions?				
Determination:				

ELEMENTS 2 and 5: Risk Assessment and Cradle-to-Grave Export Compliance Security and Screening				Initials_____Date_____
Review orders/transactions against the DPL	Y	N	U	Comments
Is there a written procedure to ensure the screening of orders/shipments to customers covering the servicing, training, and sales of items against the DPL?				
Are the personnel/positions who are responsible for DPL screening identified (consider domestic and international designee)?				
Is there a procedure to stop orders if a customer and/or other parties are found on the DPL?				
Is there a procedure to report all the names of the customers and/or the other parties who are found on the DPL?				
Do the procedures include a process for what is used to perform the screening? And if distribution of hard copies is required, who is responsible for their update and distribution?				
Is the DPL checked against your customer base? A. Are both the customer name and the principal checked? B. Is there a method for keeping the customer base current? C. Is there a method for screening new customers?				
Is the DPL checked on a transaction-by-transaction basis? A. Is the name of the ordering party's firm and principal checked? B. Is the end user's identity available? If so, is a DPL check done on the end user? C. Is the check performed at the time that an order is accepted and/or received? D. Is the check performed at the time of shipment? E. Is the check performed against backlog orders when a new or updated DPL is published?				
Does the documentation of screen (whether hard copy or electronic signature) include the following? A. The name of individuals performing the checks. B. Dates that the screen checks are performed. C. Date of current denied person's information that is used to perform the check. D. Is the date of the DPL used to check the transaction that is documented? Is it current?				

ELEMENTS 2 and 5: Risk Assessment and Cradle-to-Grave Export Compliance Security and Screening				Initials_____Date_____
Review orders/transactions against the DPL	Y	N	U	Comments
Are other trade-related sanctions, embargoes, and debarments imposed by agencies other than the Department of Commerce checked? A. *Department of Treasury (OFAC)* 　1. SDTs? 　2. SDNs and FTOs? B. *Department of State* 　1. Trade-related sanctions (Bureau of Politico-Military Affairs)? 　2. Suspensions and debarments (Center for Defense Trade, Office of Defense Trade Controls)?				
Are domestic transactions screened against the DPL?				
Determination:				

ELEMENTS 2 and 5: Risk Assessment and Cradle-to-Grave Export Compliance Security and Screening				Initials_____Date_____
Diversion Risk Profile (DRP) **See EAR Part 732, Supplements 1 and 3**	Y	N	U	**Comments**
Are there procedures to screen orders for diversion risk red flag indicators?				
Is a checklist used based upon the red flag indicators?				
Does the written screening procedure identify the responsible individuals who perform the screen checks?				
Is the DRP considered at all the phases of the order processing system?				
Is a transaction-based DRP performed?				
Is a customer-based DRP performed?				
Is a checklist documented and maintained on file for each and every order?				
Is a checklist documented and maintained on file in the customer profile?				
Is the customer base checked at least annually against the red flag indicators or when a customer's activities change?				
General Prohibition 6—Prohibits the export/reexport of items to embargoed destinations without proper license authority. Are embargoed-destination prohibitions communicated on the product/country matrix and part of the red flag indicators?				
General Prohibition 10—Prohibits an exporter from proceeding with transactions with knowledge that a violation has occurred or is about to occur. Is there anything that is suspect regarding the legitimacy of the transactions?				
Determination:				

ELEMENTS 2 and 5: Risk Assessment and Cradle-to-Grave Export Compliance Security and Screening **Prohibited nuclear end uses/users, EAR, Section 744.2**				Initials_____Date_____
	Y	N	U	Comments
Are there written procedures for reviewing the exports and reexports of all the items that are subject to the EAR to determine, prior to exporting, whether they might be destined to be used directly or indirectly in any one or more of the prohibited nuclear activities?				
Are the personnel/positions who are responsible for ensuring the screening of customers and their activities against the prohibited end uses identified?				
Does the procedure describe when the nuclear screen should be performed?				
A. Is your nuclear screen completed on a transaction-by-transaction basis? B. Is the screen conducted against an established customer base? If yes, is there a procedure for screening each new customer before he or she is added to that customer base? C. Is the nuclear screen completed before a new customer is approved?				
Is there a list of all the employees who are responsible for performing the nuclear screening?				
Does the check include documentation with the signature/initials of the person performing the check, and the date performed, to verify the consistent operational performance of the check?				
Is the customer base checked and the check documented at least annually in the customer profiles (see EMCP guidelines, diversion risk screen)?				
Is it clear who is responsible for the annual check?				
Is there a procedure to verify that all responsible employees are performing the screening?				
Are nuclear checklists (and/or other tools) distributed to appropriate export-control personnel for easy, efficient performance of the review?				
Have export/sales personnel been instructed on how to recognize situations that may involve prohibited nuclear end-use activities?				
Does the procedure include what to do if it is known that an item is destined to a nuclear end use/end user?				
Determination:				

ELEMENTS 2 and 5: Risk Assessment and Cradle-to-Grave Export Compliance Security and Screening				Initials _____ Date _____
Rocket systems and UAVs' prohibited missile end uses/users, EAR, Section 744.3	Y	N	U	Comments
Are there written procedures for reviewing the exports and reexports of all the items that are subject to the EAR to determine, prior to exporting, whether the items are destined for a prohibited end use?				
Are the personnel/positions who are responsible for ensuring the screening of customers and their activities against the prohibited end users/users identified?				
Does the procedure describe when the missile systems and the UAV screening should be performed?				
Does the procedure include a check against the Entity List?				
If yes, is there a procedure to maintain the documented Entity List screen decisions on file to verify consistent operational review?				
A. Is your rocket/UAV screen completed on a transaction-by-transaction basis? B. Is the screen conducted against an established customer base? If yes, is there a procedure for screening each new customer before he or she is added to that customer base? C. Is the rocket/UAV screen completed before the new customer is approved?				
Does the check include documentation with the signature/initials of the person performing the check, and the date performed, to verify the consistent operational performance of the check?				
Is the customer base checked and the check documented at least annually in the customer profiles?				
Is it clear who is responsible for the annual check?				
Is there a list of all the employees who are responsible for the annual check?				
Is there a procedure to verify that all the responsible employees are performing the screening?				
Are the missile system and UAV checklists (and/or other tools) distributed to appropriate export-control personnel for easy, efficient performance of the review?				
Have export/sales personnel been instructed on how to recognize prohibited missile systems and UAVs' end-use activities?				
Does the procedure include what to do if it is known that an item is destined to a prohibited end use/user?				
Determination:				

ELEMENTS 2 and 5: Risk Assessment and Cradle-to-Grave Export Compliance Security and Screening Prohibited chemical and biological weapons (CBW) end uses/users, EAR, Section 744.4	Y	N	U	Initials_____Date _____ Comments
Are there written procedures for reviewing the exports and reexports of all the items that are subject to the EAR for license requirements, prior to exporting, if the item can be used in the design, development, production, stockpiling, or use of CBW?				
Are the personnel/positions who are responsible for ensuring the screening of customers and their activities against the prohibited end uses/users identified?				
Does the procedure describe when the CBW screen should be performed?				
A. Is your CBW screen completed on a transaction-by-transaction basis? B. Is the screen conducted against an established customer base? If yes, is there a procedure for screening each new customer before he or she is added to that customer base? C. Is your CBW screen completed before the new customer is approved?				
Does the check include documentation with the signature/initials of the person performing the check, and the date when the check is performed, to verify the consistent operational performance of the check?				
Is the customer base checked and the check documented at least annually in the customer profiles?				
Is it clear who is responsible for the annual check?				
Is there a list of all the employees who are responsible for performing CBW screening?				
Is there a procedure to verify that all the responsible employees are performing the screening?				
Are CBW checklists (and/or other tools) distributed to appropriate export-control personnel for easy, efficient performance of the review?				
Have export/sales personnel been instructed on how to recognize prohibited CBW end-use activities?				
Does the procedure include what to do if it is known that an item is destined to a prohibited end use/end user?				
Determination:				

ELEMENTS 2 and 5: Risk Assessment and Cradle-to-Grave Export Compliance Security and Screening				Initials_____Date _____
Review orders/transactions against antiboycott compliance red flags	Y	N	U	**Comments**
Is there a written procedure to screen transactions and orders/shipping documents for restrictive trade practice or boycott language that is included in Part 760 of the EAR?				
Are the personnel/positions who are responsible for performing this screen identified?				
Is the antiboycott screening performed by using a profile checklist?			–	
Does the checklist include the following? A. The firm's name? (as a *consignee*) B. Names/initials of personnel performing the screen check C. Date that the screen check is performed				
Is there a procedure to hold orders if there is a red flag during the processing of orders?				
Is a person designated to resolve red flags or report them to the BIS Office of Antiboycott Compliance?				
Have all the units that might possibly come into contact with the red flags been trained to identify the red flags?				
Are antiboycott red flags included in the training materials?				
Determination:				

ELEMENTS 2 and 5: Risk Assessment and Cradle-to-Grave Export Compliance Security and Screening **Review customers and other parties against the Entity List**	Y	N	U	Initials_____Date _____ **Comments**
Is there a written procedure to screen transactions against the Entity List to determine whether there are any license requirements, in addition to normal license requirements, for the exports or reexports of specified items to specified end users, based on the BIS's determination that there is an unacceptable risk of use in, or diversion to, prohibited proliferation activities?				
Is the screening documented, including the following? A. The firm's name B. Names/initials of individuals performing the check C. Date that the checks are performed D. Is the screen check combined and performed with another check (e.g., DPL check)				
Is the Federal Register monitored daily for the addition of new entities to the Entity List?				
If matches occur, is there a hold function that is implemented within the order processing system that stops the order until a decision is made as to license requirements?				
Determination:				

ELEMENT 3: A Formal Written EMCP	Y	N	U	Initials_____Date_____ Comments
Are there written procedures that describe how information will flow among all the elements to help ensure EMCP effectiveness and accountability?				
Is the written EMCP developed and maintained with input from all the corporate stakeholders in the export process?				
Do the written procedures clearly describe detailed step-by-step processes that employees are expected to follow? And are contingencies addressed?				
Are the written procedures reviewed for update at least annually and when major changes occur?				
Are the written and operational procedures consistent?				
Has an administrator been designated for oversight of the EMCP?				
Is there a table that identifies individuals, their positions, addresses, telephone numbers, e-mail addresses, and their respective export transaction and compliance responsibilities? Does it include all domestic sites? Does it include all international sites?				
Is a person designated as responsible for the management and maintenance of this element?				
Is a person assigned the responsibility for the distribution of information that is related to this element?				
Is a person assigned to retain the records?				
Is the length of time the records are to be retained included?				
Is the location of where the records are to be retained included?				
Is the format of the records to be retained included?				
If the primary responsible persons are unable to perform the assigned responsibilities, are secondary persons designated to back up the primary designees? Where there are no backup designees, are there procedures in place to prevent untrained/unauthorized personnel from taking action?				
Are all EMCP tasks clearly summarized in this element and consistent with detailed information in other corresponding elements?				
Does each employee designated with tasks understand the importance of his or her role that is related to the overall export compliance system?				
Do the responsible persons understand how the processes that they are responsible for connect to the *next* process? ("...and then what happens next?")				
Do all the appropriate personnel have the ability to hold a questionable transaction?				
Are the necessary systems to allow employees to perform their tasks readily available to them?				

ELEMENT 3: A Formal Written EMCP				Initials _____ Date _____
	Y	N	U	Comments
Is the training for the understanding and use of the EMCP provided on a regular basis to the necessary employees? And are the records of the training kept?				
Based on an organization chart and the assignment of tasks, does it appear that there are conflicts of interest in the chain of command and the tasks to be performed?				
Determination:				

ELEMENT 4: Training				Initials_____Date_____
	Y	N	U	Comments
Are there written procedures that describe an ongoing program of export transaction/compliance training and education?				
Do the written procedures clearly describe detailed step-by-step processes that employees are expected to follow?				
Is a qualified individual designated to conduct training and to update the training materials? (Note the name of the person in the comments section.)				
If the primary responsible person is unable to perform the responsibilities, is a secondary person designated to back up the primary designee? (If not, is a procedure in place to eliminate the vulnerabilities of an untrained person proceeding with tasks that might lead to violations of the EAR?)				
Is there a schedule to conduct training (including the date, time, and place)?				
Does the training component of the EMCP include what training materials are used (modules, videos, and manuals)?				
Are the training materials accurate, consistent, and current with the operational company policy, procedures, and processes? (If not, note what corrective actions are needed in the comments section.)				
Are attendance logs used for documentation, which includes the agenda, date, trainer, trainees, and subjects?				
Is the frequency of training defined?				
Is a list of employees/positions who should receive export control/compliance training defined?				
Are the responsible persons trained to understand the interconnection of their roles with other EMCP processes and where they fit in the overall export transaction/compliance program?				
Is the list of employees/positions to be trained consistent with other elements?				
Is a person identified and responsible for keeping the training records?				
Is the location of where these training records are to be maintained included?				
Is the format of how these training records will be maintained noted?				

ELEMENT 4: Training				Initials_____ Date_____
	Y	N	U	Comments
Do the training methods include the following?				
• Orientation for new employees				
• Formal (structured setting, agenda, modules that are used)				
• Informal (less structured basis, verbal, daily, on-the-job exchanges)				
• Circulation of written memoranda and e-mails to a small number of personnel, (usually group-specific instruction)				
• Refresher courses and update sessions that are scheduled				
• Employee desk procedure manuals				
• Backup personnel training				
Does the content of training materials include the following?				
• Organizational structure of export-related departments and functions				
• Message of management commitment—policy statement				
• The role of the EMCP administrator and key contacts				
• US export/reexport regulatory requirements				
• EMCP company operating procedures				
• The purpose and scope of export controls				
• Licenses and conditions/license exceptions and parameters				
• Regulatory changes and new requirements				
• Destination restrictions				
• Item restrictions				
• End-use and end-user prohibitions				
• How to perform and *document* screens and checklists				
• Various process flows for each element				
• New customer review procedures				
• Identification and description of noncompliance				
Determination:				

ELEMENT 6: Recordkeeping (EAR, Part 762)	Y	N	U	Initials_____Date_____ Comments
Are there written procedures to comply with recordkeeping requirements?				
Do the written procedures clearly describe detailed step-by-step processes that employees are expected to follow?				
Are all the records in each process included in the records that are maintained?				
Are the written procedures reviewed for update at least annually and when significant changes occur?				
Are the written and operational procedures consistent?				
Is there a designated employee who is responsible for the management and maintenance of this element? Is his or her name and contact information provided?				
Identify all the other employees who are held accountable for specific responsibilities under this recordkeeping element.				
Do the designated employees know who is responsible for the next action to be taken in the process?				
If the primary responsible person is unable to perform the responsibilities, is a secondary person designated to back up the primary designee?				
Where there are no backup designees, are there procedures in place to prevent untrained/unauthorized personnel from taking action?				
Do employees understand the importance of their roles that are related to the overall recordkeeping requirement?				
Do employees have the appropriate budgetary, staff, and supporting resources to perform their responsibilities?				
Do employees have access to all the appropriate systems, tools, databases, and records to perform their responsibilities and ensure compliance with recordkeeping procedures?				
Is appropriate and specific training provided regarding this element?				
Is the training included on an annual schedule of employee training?				
Have the appropriate parties who will retain the records been identified? Are their names and contact information provided?				
Has the length of time for record retention been identified?				
Have secure physical and electronic storage locations for records been identified for the retention of records?				
Have determinations been made regarding the formats that all of the different types of records will be retained in?				
Is there a list of records that are to be maintained (see guidelines and below for checklists)?				

ELEMENT 6: Recordkeeping (EAR, Part 762)	Y	N	U	Initials_____Date_____ Comments
Does the procedure include a list of records to maintain, including the following *administrative records*? • Commodity classification records. • Commodity jurisdiction letters. • Advisory opinion letters. • Copy of the EMCP. • BIS 748P, Multipurpose Application Form. • BIS 748P-A, Item Appendix. • BIS 748P-B, End-User Appendix. • BIS 711 Statement by Ultimate Consignee and Purchaser. • Electronic version BIS 748P, SNAP ACCN Number. • Accompanying attachments, riders, or conditions; international import certificates. • End-user certificates. • License Exception TSR Written Assurance. • AES Electronic Filing Authorization. • High-performance computer records. • Transmittal and acknowledgement of license condition. • Log administering control over use of export/reexport license. • Is a log maintained to ensure return or commodities that are previously exported under License Exception TMP? • Is a log maintained to ensure that License Exception LVS limits are not exceeded? • Humanitarian Donations GFT Records.				

Are there instructions for the accurate completion and filing of the following *transaction records*?
 	
A. Commercial invoices?
B. AES electronic filing authorization
    1. Description of items(s)
    2. ECCN(s)
    3. License number
    4. License exception symbols or exemptions
    5. Schedule B number(s)
C. AWBs and/or bills of lading value of shipments				

Is there conformity regarding the above documents?				
Determination:				

ELEMENT 7: Audits/Assessments				Initials_____ Date_____
	Y	N	U	Comments
Are written procedures established to verify ongoing compliance?				
Is there a qualified individual (or auditing group) who is designated to conduct internal audits?				
Is there a potential conflict of interest between the auditor and the division being audited?				
Is there a schedule for audits? Are internal reviews performed annually, every six months, quarterly, etc.?				
Is there a step-by-step description of the audit process?				
Is a standard audit module or self-assessment tool used?				
If yes, does the audit module or self-assessment tool evaluate corporate management commitment in all aspects of the audit, not just in the written policy statement element?				
If yes, does the audit module or self-assessment tool evaluate formalized, written EMCP procedures compared to operational procedures?				
If yes, does the audit module or self-assessment tool evaluate the accuracy and conformity of export transaction documents by random sampling or 100% verification?				
If yes, does the audit module or self-assessment tool evaluate whether there is a current, accurate product/license determination matrix that is consistent with the current EAR and Federal Register notices?				
If yes, does the audit module or self-assessment tool evaluate whether correct export authorizations were used for each transaction?				
If yes, does the audit module or self-assessment tool evaluate the maintenance of documents, as required in the written EMCP?				
If yes, does the audit module or self-assessment tool evaluate whether internal control screens were performed and documented, as required in the EMCP?				
If yes, does the audit module or self-assessment tool evaluate whether there are flow charts of the various processes for each element?				
If yes, does the audit module or self-assessment tool evaluate what is used to provide verification that the audits were conducted?				

ELEMENT 7: Audits/Assessments	Y	N	U	Initials_____ Date_____ Comments
If yes, does the audit module or self-assessment tool evaluate whether there is a procedure to stop/hold transactions if problems arise?				
If yes, does the audit module or self-assessment tool evaluate whether all key export-related personnel are interviewed?				
If yes, does the audit module or self-assessment tool evaluate whether there are clear, open communications between all export-related divisions?				
If yes, does the audit module or self-assessment tool evaluate whether there is daily oversight over the performance of export control checks?				
If yes, does the audit module or self-assessment tool include a sampling of the completed screens that are performed during the order processing and/or new (or annual) customer screening?				
If yes, does the audit module or self-assessment tool evaluate whether the export control procedures and the EMCP manual are consistent with EAR changes that have been published?				
If yes, does the audit module or self-assessment tool evaluate whether the company's training module and procedures are current with EAR and Federal Register notices?				
Is there a written report of each internal audit?				
Are there written results of the review?				
Is the appropriate manager notified, if action is needed?				
Are spot checks/informal self-assessments performed? Are they documented?				
Is there evidence of a conflict of interest between the reviewer and the division being reviewed?				
Are records of past audits maintained to monitor repeated deficiencies?				
Is there a *best practice* that should be shared with other divisions in the company to improve the effectiveness and efficiency of export controls and promote the consistency of procedures?				
Are other departments aware of their export control–related responsibilities, e.g., legal, human resources, information management?				
Determination:				

ELEMENTS 8 and 9: Reporting, Escalation, and Corrective Action				Initials_____Date_____
	Y	N	U	Comments
Are there internal procedures in place to notify management within the company if a party is determined to be in noncompliance? Is the contact information provided for each official in the chain?				
Do the company policy/guidelines address the accountability and consequences for noncompliant activity? Are the appropriate incentives, rewards, requirements, and penalties in place, and is an appropriate business culture of compliance being fostered to facilitate the notification of any possible noncompliance?				
Are there internal procedures in place to notify the appropriate USG officials (e.g., Export Administration's Office of Exporter Services, Export Enforcement) when noncompliance is determined?				
Has a central corporate point of contact been defined for all communications with the USG?				
Is the management chain clearly defined for voluntary self-disclosures (VSDs), and are there clear guidelines for VSDs?				
Do all employees receive export-control awareness training (including for potential deemed exports and hand-carry scenarios)? Does this training detail the reporting, escalation, and corrective action requirements?				
Is there a 24-hour mechanism for notifying compliance management of possible export violations or problems?				
Does the company have an anonymous reporting mechanism for employees?				
Do compliance guidelines provide defined criteria for when a formal internal investigation is required? If yes, are the procedures to be followed defined? Are the reporting and documentation requirements defined?				
Do compliance guidelines include the policy and procedures for follow-up reporting to management and the reporting employee? Is there a process for evaluating the lessons that are learned?				
Determination:				

5.14 USEFUL WEBSITES FOR THIS CHAPTER

http://www.cbp.gov/ace
http://www.cbp.gov/trade/ace/training-and-reference-guides
http://www.apps.cbp.gov/csms
http://www.cpb.gov/trade/automated/ace-faq
http://www.cbp.gov/aceoutreach
http://www.census.gov/foreign-trade/outreach
http://www.cpsc.gov/en/Regulations-Laws--Standards/Regulations
-Mandatory-Standards-Bans/

5.15 CORNERSTONES OF TRADE COMPLIANCE MANAGEMENT

There are five critical components of any trade compliance program:

1. Exercising due diligence, reasonable care, supervision and control, and engagement
2. Senior management involvement
3. Assessment
4. Standard operating procedures (SOPs)
5. Training

5.15.1 Exercising Due Diligence, Reasonable Care, Supervision and Control, and Engagement

Outlined in Section 5.11.3 is a discussion on due diligence and reasonable care, which is processing shipments through the application of regulatory guidelines.

Having knowledge, being trained, and applying the learnings correctly are all the attributes of being diligent and reasonable.

Supervision and control relate more to the utilization of third parties, such as freight forwarders, and recognizing that you, as the principal importer, are responsible for the work that they do on your behalf and that you have to take ownership of the responsibility to supervise their activity.

Engagement refers to proactive participation in outreach programs that keep you informed and engaged in regulations, government agencies, and activities that provide knowledge.

5.15.2 Senior Management Involvement

The government requires engagement by senior management personnel in all aspects of trade compliance, not necessarily *day to day* but certainly in awareness and in oversight.

In private companies, this is a best practice.

In public companies, this is a best practice and an *Sarbanes Oxley (SOX)* requirement.

5.15.3 Assessment

A company that imports needs to understand where it stands relative to other companies in meeting its trade compliance responsibilities.

An assessment process is an excellent way to determine where you stand and what needs to be done to make you a trade-compliant importer.

The utilization of third parties, such as Blue Tiger International (http://www.bluetigerintl.com), to handle these reviews is an excellent and preferred option.

5.15.4 SOPs

Once the assessment is accomplished, SOPs will need to be developed, which is the best method to document your adherence to due diligence and reasonable care internally and to external authorities.

5.15.5 Training

Training is a serious and necessary element of any trade compliance initiative as it assures that personnel know what the regulations are, how the regulations apply to them, and how to operate in a compliant manner.

It affords interface where knowledge is transferred and the learning attributes are gained.

6

Risk Management and Insurance

6.1 INTRODUCTION

When a company chooses to operate in foreign markets, it has various insurance exposures that it must engage. This chapter identifies the various exposures, categorizes them, and offers risk management strategies to eliminate or mitigate them.

Just as currently, a company would not build a facility without a sprinkler and alarm system to manage the risks of fire and burglary, a company should not source from overseas suppliers without building in risk management and loss control features. This chapter outlines ways to reduce risks and minimize losses in the global supply chain.

Global procurement and sourcing create great opportunity that is fraught with risk and exposure; managing that risk is a vital component of inbound global supply chains.

6.2 INSURANCE EXPOSURES

Sourcing product from overseas creates liability exposures for a company. Purchases may be made, for example, via the Internet; by having personnel travel overseas; or by investing on, entering into a joint venture or partnership with, or outsourcing to third parties.

These liability exposures are potentially no different from those that are involved in business operations in the United States—workers' compensation, benefits, product liability, property loss or damage, goods as work in process or in transit, and so on.

However, there can also be marked differences, depending, for example, on the country in which a company conducts business, the nature of the agreements and contracts, the details of the supply chain, and local laws and insurance regulations.

Most corporations have staff risk managers to handle these exposures in the United States and abroad. Most risk managers arrange insurance programs through specialized insurance brokers and companies that have the required expertise in international business.

Supply chain professionals; logistics managers; purchasing executives; import specialists; chief financial officers; and all others involved in the supply chain who are making contracts, agreeing to various inbound options, making freight and warehousing arrangements, working with international communication sales terminology (international communication [INCO] terms), and so on, need to understand that they are directly affecting the risks and exposures of the company and therefore need to be educated in this regard and work within the company's established risk management guidelines. If no guidelines exist, it is critical to establish them. Consider the following example.

A purchasing manager acquires goods from a new supplier in Thailand. He makes the purchase on free-carrier Bangkok terms, prepaid. He releases invoiced funds before receiving the merchandise and takes insurance responsibility once the carrier nominated by him in Bangkok receives the goods. Thus, the risk of loss and damage during international transit is now in the hands of the purchaser. Has marine cargo insurance been arranged? What are the terms? Are the limits enough? Is the coverage appropriate for the mode, conveyance, and actual details of the transportation process? These questions should have been reviewed in great detail and answered before the deal was finalized and the goods were shipped.

What if the policy limit is $500,000, but the value of this shipment is $780,000? Or the policy covers air freight by commercial carriers, but the goods were shipped by parcel post, which bears the low limit of $500? Or the shipment arrives, but concealed damage is found? The policy requires that evidence be shown, before a claim is paid, whether the loss has occurred from physical loss or damage from an external cause during transit. There is no way that the purchasing manager can prove this. Would the claim be honored? The reality is that a loss would occur, and probably, there would be no coverage in place to indemnify the financial exposure. Corporate personnel involved in the global supply chain need to be proactive in identifying these risks and taking steps to manage, eliminate, mitigate, or transfer to a third party.

Consider another example: a company sold $800,000 of used farm equipment to dealers in Russia. They had a two-year track record of payment, but so far, letters of credit or sight drafts had collateralized the previous transactions. The consignee in this transaction requested 60-day terms, based on prior history. The financial department approved the transaction but required an advance payment of 10% on purchase order acceptance and wire transfer of the funds. The Russian consignee complied, and the goods were shipped. The customer paid in the 60-day period in rubles through its state banking system. The US company's bank advised that the funds had not been converted to US dollars and are detained in the foreign banking system, awaiting currency convertibility.

So, the customer has paid, but because of the imbalance of trade, the Russian bank is unable to prioritize payment on this transaction.

This exposure is known as currency inconvertibility and is a serious risk in more than 100 countries that have such significant imbalances of trade that they have difficulty meeting their international financial obligations. As a result, these state banking systems prioritize payments based upon political and economic factors. They pay for priority import items such as military goods, food, and medical transactions first and then pay for other goods. In this case, the funds were eventually transferred, but it took 18 months. That was not included in the arrangements, and there were consequences to the exporter, who did not budget nor create contingences for this financial occurrence.

In a third example, a purchasing manager traveled to Bangkok to meet with some prospective outsourcing manufacturers. Over the weekend before his meetings on Monday, he went sightseeing with one of his colleagues and took a day trip into the Thai Rain Forest Preserve.

During the trip, he became seriously ill with an allergic reaction to a plant. He was transferred to a hospital in Bangkok, where his illness was stabilized.

After a week in the hospital, he was sent back to Los Angeles, accompanied by a doctor and a nurse. His wife was flown to Thailand to travel back with them. Eventually, after two weeks in a hospital in Los Angeles, he was well, and in another three weeks, he returned to work.

His medical bills and emergency transportation expenses exceed $250,000. His US hospital bills totaled $125,000 and were covered under his corporate health plan. However, the medical insurance did not cover him on business trips overseas and ceased once he bordered the plane to travel to Bangkok. In addition, his corporate workers' compensation and disability policies would not pay these expenses because they also covered only the business being conducted in the United States. This company was almost 100% domestic and had started to source product outside the United States only in the previous year. No one knew that their insurance policies had these restrictions and therefore failed to properly endorse their policies and make underwriting arrangements to extend the coverage to personnel traveling overseas. This was an expensive lesson for this executive and the company, which assumed all of the unreimbursed expenses.

These examples portray a few of the many risks and exposures that exist for companies that engage in foreign markets. Let us examine risks in greater detail.

6.3 RISK MANAGEMENT

Corporations that operate global supply chains have the same risks in their international business operations as in their domestic operations. Larger companies typically employ professional risk managers or corporate insurance directors who arrange the purchasing of commercial insurance.

These professionals have responsibilities such as the following:

- Analyze exposures that the company faces.
- Work with insurance brokers and underwriting companies.
- Develop risk retention and captive insurance programs.
- Provide financial analysis for decisions to accept, reduce, mitigate, or transfer risk.
- Manage loss control initiatives.
- Manage claims, recovery, and mitigation efforts.
- Developing corporate standard operating procedures (SOPs) for risk and insurance.
- Work with human resources personnel in employee benefits, disability, and workers' compensation issues.
- Create internal insurance manuals and communications for management and operating personnel.
- Maintain liaison with the industry to know what competitors are doing and keep abreast of the marketplace and insurance business.
- When companies engage in foreign sourcing, insurance and risk managers extend their scope into the global supply chains, learning about the exposures and developing insurance solutions. Some in this field consider the international side to be more difficult than the domestic for the following reasons:
  - More uncertainty
  - Local and foreign laws and regulations
  - Localized insurance restrictions
  - Scope of geographic, political, and economic factors that influence the risks
  - Less control over communication channels and information gathering to make the most effective risk management decisions
- Risk managers must ensure that the brokers and underwriters they engage meet the following criteria in regard to overseas exposures:
  - Have the necessary expertise in risks in the appropriate geographic areas.
  - Have a local presence in the countries of global sourcing.
  - Can manage insurance programs on a global scale.
  - Have access to legal capabilities in those foreign countries in which the supply chains operate.

- Have quality personnel in brokerage, underwriting, claims, loss control, and customer service throughout the network of countries that are involved.
- Have financial stability in the world market.

Professional risk managers have as one of their primary purchasing responsibilities finding companies with the appropriate expertise and protecting the interests of the company's global supply chain as they would the domestic operation.

The specific exposures that must be addressed are described in Sections 6.4 through 6.9.

6.4 PERSONNEL

Companies engaged in purchasing goods from overseas and developing foreign manufacturing send personnel on international business trips. Some of these trips are short term; others are prolonged. Many companies place executives in the foreign markets to lend manufacturing and production expertise; oversee operations; or assist in logistics, distribution, and so on. While overseas, these personnel are exposed to the same risks as when doing business in the United States, with the exception that the risks may be more complex.

Benefits, disability issues, workers' compensation, auto liability, and general liability are a few of the risks to accompany personnel overseas.

In certain countries, there may be a host of other exposures based on local customs, culture, and legal differences. Additionally, personnel who travel overseas are subject to kidnap and ransom exposures. Kidnappings of business personnel have occurred in Central and South America, the Middle East, and Europe, among other countries. Many times, company personnel and the general public are unaware of these occurrences because the parties involved usually decide to avoid publicity.

Although is it not well known, many corporations maintain dedicated kidnap and ransom personnel. One of the most important benefits of having a kidnap and ransom policy in place is that it provides immediate access to expertise that can assist in managing a kidnap and ransom situation.

Kidnap and ransom underwriters typically employ former Federal Bureau of Investigation, Interpol, and Central Intelligence Agency staff with the skills that are necessary to intervene with hostage takers and negotiate a favorable resolve. If an executive is taken hostage, the kidnap and ransom policy affords access to the expertise to take the next step.

If an executive traveling overseas is injured, sick, lost, or requires personal assistance, there are companies that are related to the commercial insurance industry that provide a global emergency hotline. Corporations and individuals who travel overseas can purchase access to these services.

6.5 KIDNAP AND RANSOM

When a company makes plans to locate overseas, it is important to become familiar with the risks that are associated with living and working abroad.

One of the risks, which is often overlooked, is the chance that a staff member could be kidnapped.

It is estimated since 1995 until the present that kidnappings around the world have increased by 100%.

Ransom demands can be overwhelming. More than 14 countries have recorded ransom amounts of $25 million or more in recent years. Although kidnappers usually settle for 10%–20% of the demand, in certain territories, they refuse to negotiate and use violence to achieve their aims. Most kidnappings are carried out to obtain a ransom, and in most cases, a ransom is paid. Rescues are rare, largely because the authorities in most countries recognize that the safety of the victim is paramount.

Kidnappings can occur anywhere. Insurance companies that specialize in kidnap and ransom coverage understand the challenges that are involved in living abroad. Kidnap and ransom coverage offers confidential protection should the need arise. This insurance coverage provides assistance to the family and business, including independent investigations, negotiations, arrangement and delivery of funds, and numerous other services that are vital to a safe, speedy, and satisfactory resolution. The typical kidnap and ransom policy covers the following:

- Ransom that is paid following a kidnap or threat to kill, injure, or abduct
- Hijack
- Detention
- Death or dismemberment
- Legal liability
- Crisis management team expenses

The risks in different countries vary. The expertise of the insurance brokers and underwriters who manage these exposures will assist in determining the proper protections.

Personnel traveling overseas present a serious risk to the companies that send them. Failing to properly protect them can present another liability to a company; the company must make sure that all that could have been done was in fact accomplished. Ensuring the safety of personnel is a priority in the risk management process and is in everyone's best interest.

Companies that engage in offshore manufacturing are likely to have purchasing personnel, engineers, operations personnel, and senior management travel to the countries that are involved. Often, personnel are sent abroad for extended times. The exposure is real and should be managed proactively.

6.6 PROPERTY AND LIABILITY

Companies operating in the United States have property and liability exposures in their buildings, trucks, plants, warehouses, and so on. If they operate these overseas, they have the same exposures, often with further complications. If they employ people who conduct business in foreign markets, the liability exposures follow them there. Basically, every exposure that exists in US business operations will be found in foreign operations. Combined with local culture, law, and politics, these exposures could be worsened. The host of local customs, laws, and regulations make foreign risk exposures potentially more serious.

It is the responsibility of the risk manager to ensure that supply chain personnel understand how the supply chain operates in the foreign location so that they can understand the exposures and provide the necessary insurance solutions. Companies that operate globally may have complex risks and exposures that require appropriate risk management initiatives. Some of the areas of exposures are as follows:

- Building and content coverage
- General liability
- Employment practice liability
- Employee dishonesty
- Business income protection
- Computer and data coverage
- Medical payment coverage
- Earthquake and flood coverage
- Workers' compensation
- Excess auto liability coverage
- Equipment breakdown coverage
- Transportation

6.7 CONTRACT AND BUSINESS RELATIONSHIP MANAGEMENT

Contract and business relationship management is a critical concern for corporate risk and insurance managers. Consider this example of a company that purchases goods overseas. The company purchases various components for its Pittsburgh Assembly Plant from a source in Manila, Philippines. To accomplish the component production, the US company places raw materials and certain machinery at the Manila manufacturing location, which is owned and operated by an independent third party. The material and equipment contract does not specify who bears the risk of loss or damage when the materials are in the care, custody, and control of the Philippine company.

A landslide, such as the one that occurred in February 2006, destroys the Philippine plant. The purchasing manager from the US company believes that because the goods and raw materials were in the care of the Philippine company, it is responsible for loss or damage. Local law says that if the contract is silent, liability rests with the party that owns the goods. In this case, that would be the American company.

Had the risk or insurance manager been brought into this agreement at the beginning, the following four actions could have been taken:

1. Acknowledge the risk.
2. Assume the liability and arrange contingences for the maximum potential loss.
3. Transfer the risk to a third-party insurance company.
4. Have the contract rewritten to have the foreign manufacturer assume the risk while the goods are in its care, custody, and control. In this case, the US company would want an evidence of the Philippine company's insurance policies, be a named insured party, and possibly have a difference-in-conditions (DIC) policy to protect from potential coverage shortfalls.

In another example, a US company operates with a third-party contract manufacturer in Mumbai, India. In the agreement, the US company agrees to arrange for the delivery of various assembly parts from Bombay and contracts a long-haul Indian trucking company to pick up the goods and deliver them on a weekly basis to their contract manufacturer.

On a particular shipment, the vehicle is in a horrendous accident causing loss of life and substantial property damage. The American company is sued, along with the trucking company. Although the American company was not at fault, under Indian law, similar to that in the United States, the control of the engagement of the transportation and its routing was influenced, if not directly controlled, by the American company, and it would potentially share in any negligence or punitive payments that are determined under the Indian judicial system. Did the American company contemplate this and arrange the necessary risk transfer, avoidance, or acceptance SOPs to protect itself from financial exposure?

There are literally thousands of exposures that American companies face in purchasing goods from foreign markets. The following risk management advocacy is key to protecting corporate assets:

- Insist that all supply chain personnel have contracts, agreements, and supply chain operations that are reviewed by company insurance and risk management experts.
- Ensure that resources are developed to learn the intricacies of local customs, laws, and regulations and how they relate to supply chain operations.
- Maintain close interface with legal counsel to obtain their input on all contracts and agreements.
- Ensure that all supply chain personnel are briefed in corporate risk and insurance policy guidelines, such as policies, risk retention levels, and claims and loss control policies.
- Set up regular review schedules to be updated on the changes that take place in global supply chains. Make sure that brokers and underwriters also receive this information.
- Develop excellent working relationships with all engaged parties so that when loss or damage occurs, all parties will cooperate and compromise to mutual resolve.
- Companies that import and export must be sure to have physical loss and damage exposures on goods and assets in transit. The next section takes a detailed review of these marine cargo exposures.

6.8 MARINE CARGO

Corporations that operate global supply chains will most likely have goods in transit.

Risk factors are greatly affected by the terms of sale as defined by INCOTerms, as outlined in detail in the appendix.

Because collection for loss and damage from third-party carriers and service providers is unlikely, it is prudent for importers and exporters to arrange marine cargo insurance to cover their commercial interests. Some considerations in purchasing cargo insurance are discussed in the following list:

1. *Broker and insurance company.* A company should use only experienced, reputable, and capable companies that specialize in marine insurance. For example, Roanoke Insurance, with offices in all major cities, specializes in managing marine cargo exposures and arranging the insurance of these risks. Underwriting companies, such as Cigna, American International Group, Great American, Navigators, Through Transport, and Lloyds of London, are but a few of the insurance companies that have a strong marine cargo capability.

2. *Scope of coverage.* Terms should be *all risk, warehouse to warehouse,* providing the broadest terms and coverage from the time that a company's interest begins to when it ceases.

3. *Limits.* Limits refer to the amount of loss that the insurance company would be liable for in the event of a claim. A company must make sure that its limits are adequate.

4. *Geographic limitations.* Coverage of the policy must extend to all the geographic locations that a company ships to and from and locations through which its goods pass in transit.

5. *Modes of transit.* The policy must specifically provide coverage on all the modes of transit that a company uses—air, ocean, rail, inland, parcel post, and so on.

6. *Currency.* A company must ensure that the policy will pay in the currency that the company requires, typically US dollars.

7. *Contingency or unpaid vendor coverage or DIC.* A policy must provide protection in the event that there is a conflict between the terms of sale and payment, for situations in which the company is not responsible to insure the goods but might still be at risk because it has a financial interest in the goods. This is typical when goods are sold ex-warehouse or free on board (FoB) port on exports, but a receivable is created by extending payment terms to the foreign buyer, or when a company purchases goods on a cost, insurance, and freight (CIF) basis and the supplier provides inadequate insurance. When the company tries to collect against a legitimate loss or damage, the scope of coverage is limited, and no indemnification exists. The DIC endorsements will provide coverage in these cases.

8. *Duty and taxes.* A company that imports goods will need to ensure that loss or damage claims also extend to the financial consequence that is attached to payment of duty and taxes.

9. *Terrorism Risk Insurance Act (TRIA).* After 9/11, the government implemented the Terrorism Risk Insurance Act of 2002, which was subsequently extended to December 31, 2007. Once the TRIA act was created, all exclusions and coverage endorsements for terrorism coverage became null and void. However, the TRIA applies only to acts of terrorism that occur on US soil. Under a cargo policy, the insured party has terrorism coverage for goods in the due course of transit outside of the United States under the strikes, riots, and civil commotions (SR&CC) coverage. The SR&CC endorsement in the policy states that acts of terrorism are covered under the policy. It also states that such *warlike operations* are covered in the United States. This is specific to navigators, and some other cargo underwriters issue a TRIA endorsement. Any actual coverage for losses within the United States is more than likely going to be covered under TRIA because both the government and the insurance companies share in such losses. For coverage under TRIA to take effect, the *warlike* action must be certified by the US government as an act of terrorism. Also, coverage under TRIA is to be no broader than what the insured party's policy covers. With respect to warlike actions that a terrorist may commit, policies exclude losses resulting from nuclear, radioactive contamination and any chemical, biological, biochemical, or electromagnetic weapon.

10. *War SR&CC.* Cargo policies cover the risks of war SR&CC.

6.8.1 Basic Open Cargo Policy Provisions

Cargo insurance is a negotiated instrument of risk transfer that is supposed to be eventually manuscripted to meet the insurance needs of the policy holder. The following outline provides a basic overview:

An open cargo policy can be written to cover all cargoes that are shipped by the assured in foreign trade by overseas vessels, aircraft, and foreign parcel post. Coverage is afforded while the goods are in transit from the seller's warehouse to the buyer's warehouse in due course of transit. The contract is tailor-made to fit the requirements of the individual assured's shipments and can be written to cover broad or named perils.

The basic open cargo policy includes the following: (1) the perils clause, (2) one or more average clauses, and (3) additional basic coverage clauses including general average.

6.8.1.1 Perils Clause

The majority of risks covered under this clause come within the comprehensive term *perils of the seas*—that is, loss or damage due to heavy weather, standing, collision, sinking, contact with seawater, etc. Other perils normally covered include the following:

- *Fire*—both direct and consequential damage whether from smoke or steam or efforts to extinguish a fire. (Spontaneous combustion occurring in the insured shipment is excluded unless specifically assumed by the underwriter.)
- *Assailing thieves*—forcible taking of a shipment rather than mysterious disappearance or pilferage.
- *Jettison*—voluntary dumping overboard of cargo.
- *Barratry*—fraudulent, criminal, or wrongful act of the ship's captain or crew that causes loss or damage to the ship or cargo.
- *All other like perils*—perils of the same nature as those that are specifically mentioned above, but not *all risks* in the customary usage of the term.

6.8.1.2 Average Clauses

While total losses from any of the hazards listed in the perils clause in Section 6.8.1.1 are fully recoverable up to the policy limits, partial losses (other than general average), known as *particular average*, from these same perils are recoverable only as specified by the average clause. The assured selects the average clause that is best suited to his or her circumstances. There are five principal average clauses:

1. *Free of particular average American conditions (FPAAC)*—Limits recovery on partial losses to those that are directly caused by fire, stranding, sinking, or collision of the vessel. This is currently the most limited average clause in general use.
2. *Free of particular average English conditions*—Similar to FPAAC, except that it is not necessary that the damage to cargo be a direct result of a specified peril, is being sufficient that one of these has occurred.

3. *With average if amounting to 3%*—Provides protection for partial loss from perils of the seas. The percentage is called a franchise and is the minimum amount of claim. (Example: If a shipment is insured for $1000, the recoverable partial loss would have to amount to at least $30 to be paid. The franchise is not applied to losses that are recoverable under free of particular average [FPA] conditions.)

4. *Average irrespective of percentage*—All partial losses due to perils of the seas are fully recoverable regardless of percentage. (Optionally named peril extensions—The foregoing average clauses may be extended to include additional perils depending upon the type of commodity to be insured, packaging, voyage, stowage, etc. These extensions may include theft, pilferage, nondelivery, sweat or steam in the ship's hold, fresh water leakage, breakage, etc.).

5. *All risks conditions*—This coverage insures against all risks of physical loss or damage from any external cause.

The following types of loss are not covered by all the risks from

- Loss of market or loss, damage, or deterioration arising from delay;
- Loss arising from inherent vice of goods;
- Loss or damage arising from SR&CC (This coverage may be and is usually added by endorsement.); and
- Loss or damage arising from acts of war. (This is usually covered under a companion war risk policy.)

Policies can be written with other specific exclusions or limitations. This might happen, for example, when goods or merchandise are highly susceptible to damage. Coverage may then be limited to make the risk insurable or in order to avoid the payment of high premiums. This flexibility is the major advantage of an open cargo policy.

6.8.1.3 Additional Coverage Clauses

In addition to the perils clause and the average clauses, which were already discussed, the typical open cargo policy contains the following clauses:

- *Explosion clause*—broadens coverage to include loss or damage due to explosion from any cause, other than a cause that is associated with a war risk.

- *Inchmaree clause*—provides coverage for loss or damage to cargo from bursting of boilers, breakage of shafts, or through any latent defect in the hull or machinery of the vessel or from errors in the navigation or management of the vessel by the master, mates, engineers, or pilots.
- *Fumigation clause*—provides coverage for damage to cargo that is caused by fumigation of the vessel.
- *Warehousing and forwarding packages lost in loading, etc. clause*—provides coverage for landing, warehousing, forwarding, and special charges in the event of loss or damage that is recoverable under the average terms. It also provides for payment of the insured value of any package(s) that may be totally lost in loading, transshipment, or discharge.
- *Shore clause*—provides coverage while on docks, wharves, or elsewhere on shore and/or during land transportation and includes the risks of collision, derailment, overturning or other accidents to the conveyance, fire, lightning, sprinkler leakage, cyclones, hurricanes, earthquakes, floods (meaning the rising of navigable waters), and/or the collapse or subsidence of docks or wharves.
- *Both-to-blame collision clause*—provides coverage for any amount that the cargo owner may be legally bound to pay the shipowner under the *both-to-blame* clause in the ocean bill of lading.
- *General average and salvage clause*—provides coverage for the assured's proportion of these charges that are incurred during the voyage.
- *Sue and labor clause*—provides coverage, in the event of a loss that is recoverable under the policy, for expenses that are reasonably incurred by the assured or his or her agents to protect the cargo from further harm and to assist in recovering the damaged cargo to minimize the loss.

6.8.2 Duration of Coverage

Normally, under an open cargo policy, the goods are insured from the moment that they leave the point of shipment, being at the risk of the assured, and the coverage continues in due course of transit until they are delivered to the final warehouse at the destination.

In the absence of special arrangements, this period of coverage is determined by the warehouse-to-warehouse and/or marine extension clauses. The marine extension clause extends the coverage in certain circumstances by superceding the time limitations that are imposed by the warehouse-to-warehouse clause. The marine extension clause continues coverage during the ordinary course of transit, including deviations, delays, reshipments, transshipments, or any other variations in the voyage, so long as the assured does not exercise control over such interruptions of normal transit.

6.8.3 SR&CC

SR&CC risks are covered by an optional endorsement to the open marine policy. The SR&CC endorsement covers loss or damage to the insured property that is caused by strikers; locked-out workmen; those who are taking part in labor disturbances, riots, or civil commotions; or persons acting maliciously. Cargo is also insured against vandalism, sabotage, and malicious mischief within the United States, Puerto Rico, Canada, the Canal Zone, and the Virgin Islands.

6.8.4 War Risks

An open policy insuring against war and similar risks is usually issued as a companion to the marine open policy. It covers most of the perils arising from hostilities but excludes loss or damage resulting from the hostile use of nuclear weapons.

Coverage against major war perils applies only while the cargo is aboard the overseas vessel, but coverage against damage from mines and torpedoes also applies while cargo is aboard lighters or other craft, prior to or subsequent to the ocean voyage, or at a port of transshipment. A separate premium charge is made for war risk insurance.

It is recommended that both marine and war risk coverage be obtained from the same underwriters, thus obviating disputes when the actual cause of loss is in question, as in the case of a missing vessel.

6.8.4.1 *Amount of Insurance*

The open cargo policy contains a valuation clause-a formula for determining the amount of insurance in advance of shipment. This formula can be tailored to conform to trade customs or to follow variations in the value of any commodity that is subject to price fluctuations. A common form of valuation clause reads as follows:

> Valued at amount of invoice including all charges in the invoice and including prepaid and/or advanced and/or guaranteed freight that is not included in the invoice, plus 10%.

This formula establishes the insured value and generally approximates the market or landed value at the destination. In the case of a CIF quotation, it is relatively simple to calculate the amount of insurance by increasing the CIF price by the percentage of advance. In the above example, this is 10%. In the case of a free alongside ship or FoB quotation, when the seller agrees to arrange marine insurance, it is important to add to the price that is quoted (if not already included), the cost of export packing, local cartage charges, ocean freight charges, forwarder's fees, and consular fees. The total of these items is then increased by the percentage of advance to determine the amount of insurance. It is extremely important that adequate insurance be purchased; otherwise, in the event of loss, the assured may be required to bear a portion of the loss.

6.8.4.2 *Cost of Insurance*

The loss experience developed on an assured's own account heavily influences the judgment of the underwriter in respect to the rates being offered. Cargo insurance premiums are calculated by applying a rate to each $100 of insured value. For example, a 25-cent rate on a $10,000 shipment develops a premium of $25.

It is the usual practice to issue with an open cargo policy a schedule of marine rates that can be used by the assured to quickly and conveniently calculate the cost of insurance on each shipment. He or she applies the rate that is quoted in the policy for a specific destination or point of origin and the product to be shipped to the insured value to determine the premium charge. This method is especially convenient to exporters quoting CIF prices in establishing the total cost of shipping goods to overseas destinations.

6.9 POLITICAL RISK, RECEIVABLES, AND EXPORT CREDIT

Companies that work in the global arena will have physical assets and financial outlays and receivables that can all be in harm's way. The greater our reach into foreign markets, the greater these exposures are. When a loss occurs, it is usually swift, large, and a surprise to management personnel. "How did this happen? We have been doing it this way for 10 years, and this is the first time. Who knew that this would possibly happen?"

In recent international events, for example, in Cuba, Vietnam, Nicaragua, Sudan, Iran, Iraq, Libya, and China, US interests were confiscated, nationalized, expropriated, or deprived.

The events of 9/11 led to reexamination of wording regarding terrorism in property, political risk, and marine policies to indemnify or fail to provide coverage. Many lawsuits regarding the extent of terrorism coverage in property policies are still pending years after 9/11. The US government has provided some relief and indemnification, but the extent of coverage is limited, and the tenure is uncertain.

These risks are still significant, and world events, politics, and economic woes present exposures for all companies operating in the global marketplace.

There are several types of political risks, as follows:

- Confiscation
- Currency inconvertibility
- Nationalization
- Devaluation
- Expropriation
- Unfair calling of financial guarantee and receivable protection
- Deprivation

- Trade disruptions
- War, SR&CC
- Terrorism
- Contract frustration

Various types of political risk coverage are available. In many respects, political risk insurance is similar to export credit insurance; however, there are some distinct differences between these two categories of insurance. Basically, a political risk loss results from a peril originating in a political or government eventuality, whether the consignee is a sovereign or private entity. An export credit risk, on the other hand, is typically defined as the credit exposure emanating solely from the actions or inactions of the private buyer.

The main distinction is that credit exposures emanating solely from private buyers are inherently more volatile than those that depend on the action of a governmental entity. This results in fewer insurers willing to write export credit coverage. When it is provided, a substantial volume of underwriting and credit information is required, the rates are high, and the coverage terms are restrictive.

Incidents such as on those on 9/11, the Gulf War, and the conflict in Bosnia caused many people to focus on war and terrorism coverage. Virtually all property insurance policies contain war exclusions, making it clear that damage caused by a war between two or more countries is excluded. The application of a property insurance policy to terrorist acts may not be so clear-cut, but some form of basic coverage is provided for terrorist acts by many property insurance policies. The approach used in the war exclusion of the latest Insurance Services Office, Inc. (ISO) is the commercial property form that is commonly used even in nonbureau manuscripted or specialized forms. Such policies exclude only damage from war, rebellion, revolution, civil war, or the warlike action of a military force.

Property policies containing exclusions of this nature would typically be deemed to cover damage that is caused by most terrorist acts. However, some property insurance policies also exclude damage that is caused by a hostile or warlike action of an agent of a foreign government. Under this language, an insurer might be justified in excluding coverage if the terrorist act was proven to be inflicted by an agent of a foreign government. The ISO will not pay for loss or damage that is caused directly or indirectly by any of the following:

- War and military action, including undeclared civil war
- Warlike action by a military force, including action hindering or defending against an actual or expected attack, by any government, sovereign, or other authority using military personnel or other agents
- Insurrection, rebellion, revolution, usurped power, or action that is taken by governmental authority in hindering or defending against any of these

Coverage for the excluded property damage exposures is available in the political risk insurance marketplace in the form of a war risk, civil commotion, and terrorism policy. The need for this coverage is dictated largely by the stability of the regions in which the insured's facilities are located and the scope of the war risk exclusion in the insured's property insurance policy. Of course, war risk exclusions can vary considerably among policies and must be carefully analyzed when evaluating the need for separate coverage.

Confiscation, nationalization, expropriation, and deprivation (CNE&D) are the most commonly purchased forms of political risk coverage. They are needed by organizations with assets such as refineries or manufacturing plants that are permanently located in other countries. The policies respond when these assets are taken over by governmental action, as recently occurred in Libya, Iraq, and Nicaragua and, in the more distant past, Chile, Vietnam, and Iran.

Nationalization takes place when the host government simply takes over an asset. Deprivation is said to occur when the host government interferes with the foreign entity's access to or utilization of its asset without actually taking possession of it. In either situation, the property owner can suffer a substantial financial loss. Confiscation and expropriation are similar actions; the host government takes over the foreign asset with the intent of returning it to the owner in the future. However, the time frame is usually not specified and often extends over several years, causing financial loss to the foreign-based property owner. Because of the similarities among these exposures, the best approach to structuring CNE&D coverage is to insure all four perils in a single policy. This approach minimizes the problems that could otherwise result from disputes with insurers as to whether a particular action falls into one category or another.

Another common political risk for which insurance is available is contract frustration. This entails the nonperformance or frustration of a contract with a host government entity or private buyer in a third-world country as a result of an invalid action. An invalid action is an activity that is detrimental to US interests that would be considered inappropriate or illegal in the United States. It can be further defined as an action that wrongfully invalidates an overseas transaction in such a manner that the exporter is unable to obtain payment for his or her product or recoup his or her assets.

As an example of the contract frustration exposure, assume that a US company has a contract with a third-world government to supply custom-designed parts for the construction of a factory. However, that government cancels the contract without a valid reason before the delivery of the product. In such a situation, it would be common for the firm to have spent a substantial sum on the initial design and preparation to manufacture the parts. Because the project involved a custom design, it is unlikely that another buyer for the parts could be found, and the exporter would suffer a financial loss.

Currency inconvertibility is an increasing concern for US exporters, particularly those who sell on open account or provide open terms of payment. This type of loss occurs when the insured's customer pays in local currency, and the local government is unable to exchange the local dollars into foreign currency. Examples of countries where this can be a problem are Columbia, Brazil, Nigeria, Philippines, and Mexico.

Currency inconvertibility has become a particular problem in countries that underwent a tremendous expansion in the 1960s through the year 2000 because of foreign oil sales and the growth of foreign direct investment. When oil sales began to decline in the 1980s, and the Organization of Petroleum Exporting Countries (OPEC) could not agree on pricing and sales quotas, the affected countries suffered a trade imbalance, causing more hard dollars to leave the country than were arriving. This made it difficult for the national banks of these countries to convert the local currency into the currency of other countries because the banks were not able to purchase foreign dollars, yen, Swiss francs, and so on with hard currency. In other words, the banks may not possess an adequate amount of US dollars or other currencies to make the exchange. Ultimately, what typically occurs in these situations are a rescheduling of the country's debt over a multiyear period; the implementation of strict economic controls within that country; and the involvement by various international entities, such as the International Monetary Fund, World Bank, and General Agreements on Trade and Tariff.

When insuring a trading activity in a country that commonly has problems converting its currency, underwriters will typically write the policies with a waiting period that corresponds with the time frame over which the conversion will occur. This waiting period ranges from 30 to 360 days. The purpose of the waiting period is to ensure that the coverage applies only to fortuitous loss.

An often-overlooked exposure for many companies doing business overseas is the risk of an unfair calling of a financial guarantee. This risk usually arises with large transactions that take many months or years to complete. In such a situation, it is common for the buyer to make a down payment (e.g., 15% of the contract price), followed by periodic installment payments as the project progresses. The buyer would typically require the seller to post a letter of credit or other financial guarantee against these payments, and the buyer would be able to draw down on that letter of credit in the event that something occurs that causes the supplier to default.

The unfair calling of this financial guarantee is an exposure to the exporter and the supplier, and unfair calling insurance protects the exporter against this risk.

Another exposure that companies involved in international trade often overlook is the business interruption exposure, caused not by physical damage to a plant or other facility but rather by a political event. Both importers and exporters face this loss exposure. For example, assume that a manufacturer relies on a single supplier in a third-world country to provide raw material that it imports for its US manufacturing plants. A political occurrence, such as a war, a strike, change in government, confiscation of the supplier's assets, change in politics, or change in law occurring in the source country, could disrupt the flow of that raw material into the United States. The manufacturer's ability to produce the finished product would be impaired, and a substantial financial loss may occur if an alternative source of the raw material could not be found. In a similar fashion, an exporter can experience a loss when the product is not delivered on time because of some event that is beyond the control of the exporter. Such exposures are insurable in the political risk insurance market.

It is important to understand that most executives tend to view their potential loss as the value of the physical product, failing to consider the potential loss of earnings, extra expense, loss of profits, and loss of market if a physical or political event occurs. Trade disruption coverage can provide protection for these losses.

The political risk insurance marketplace can be divided into two basic categories: (1) government markets and (2) private markets. In the United States, the principal market is the Foreign Credit Insurance Association (FCIA) (part of the Great American Insurance Company), which was authorized through the US government via the Export–Import Bank of the United States (Ex–Im Bank). With headquarters in New York City (NYC) and satellite offices throughout the United States, the FCIA provides many types of political risk coverage, as well as export credit insurance for US exporters shipping US products to approved countries. Most noncommunist countries in the world that have favorable trading status with the United States are considered approved.

In the past, the FCIA was considered bureaucratic and unresponsive to the needs of most exporters. However, in recent years, this has changed, and the FCIA has become more responsive by offering competitive and comprehensive programs, such as the bank letters of credit and new-to-export buyer programs. Ex–Im Bank is another government program with significant benefits for companies expanding into their suppliers' operations or making fixed investments in overseas markets.

The Overseas Private Investment Corporation (OPIC) was established as a development agency of the US government in 1971. OPIC helps US businesses invest overseas, fosters economic development in new and emerging markets, complements the private sector in managing the risks that are associated with foreign direct investment, and supports the US foreign policy. OPIC evaluates all project applications on the basis of their contribution to economic development to ensure a successful implementation of the organization's core developmental mission and prioritizes the allocation of scarce resources to projects on the basis of their developmental benefits. By expanding economic development in host countries, OPIC-supported projects can encourage political stability, free market reforms, and US best practices. OPIC projects also support American jobs and exports—over 264,000 new US jobs and $69 billion in exports since 1971. Because OPIC charges market-based fees for its products, it operates on a self-sustaining basis at no net cost to taxpayers.

OPIC is the other US government-sponsored market for political risk insurance. OPIC insures US nonmilitary investment exposures, such as confiscation and nationalization, in developing nations throughout the world. Its terms and conditions are broad, and the rates are as competitive as those of the FCIA. However, only assets located in nations having favorable trade relationships with the United States qualify for coverage with OPIC.

There are two drawbacks to the US government programs. First, they are subject to US diplomatic and trade policies. When the US government is following a restrictive trade policy with a particular country, the Ex–Im Bank and other government facilities tend to follow suit, thus reducing the availability of coverage or restricting coverage terms for that country. Likewise, when the government eases trade restrictions with a country, coverage availability and terms will increase.

Although this may be good politics, it sometimes restricts coverage availability for transactions with countries that, while not on favorable trade terms with the United States, might present good business opportunities and be excellent credit risks for individual businesses. For example, a number of US companies have been very successful in trading with the Soviet Union over the past few years and have been paid regularly and responsibly. Because of its unfavorable trade relationship with the United States, however, transactions with the Soviet Union are generally not eligible for most of the US government's insurance programs.

The second drawback to US government markets is that they cover only US companies and products. As an example of how this restricts availability, consider a firm that is located in NYC and is staffed by US personnel who export Canadian products into Europe on an open account basis, thus creating an exposure that could be covered by export credit insurance. This company would not be eligible to buy credit insurance from the US government facilities because the product is not manufactured in the United States.

Of course, this limitation of coverage availability is fundamental to the underlying purpose for which the Ex–Im Bank and OPIC were created: to encourage and support the exportation of US products and services. These facilities are not always profitable, but they provide an indirect means of subsidizing US business interests overseas. At this time, the US government will subsidize only the activities that directly benefit US interests, products, or services.

Most other Western nations have also established facilities that are similar to the Ex–Im Bank and OPIC to insure export sales to other countries. US companies with divisions domiciled in these nations can often access these local government programs.

The private insurance market provides coverages that are not available from the government markets, and it is not bound by the diplomatic policy of any one nation. This market is basically made up of some US-domiciled insurance companies and London markets. The principal US companies that write political risk insurance are Lloyds, Atradius, Euler Coface North America, FCIA, and American International Underwriters, but there are a handful of other insurers that occasionally write various types of political risk coverage.

Coface in NYC is an excellent risk option for companies looking for receivable and political risk protections. Their managing director, Michele Scherer, is a great resource for companies looking for credit and risk information. She can be reached at Michele_scherer@coface-USA.com or 212-560-0410.

Being commercially driven, US insurers will write insurance in areas in which there is opportunity for profit. The natural downside of this tendency is that it is difficult to obtain insurance from these insurers in countries where the possibility of loss is significant. In general, however, US insurers offer broad policies and competitive rates and are willing to write on a spread of risk basis, affording the exporter a complete program covering all overseas sales.

The London market is composed of Lloyd's of London, the Institute of London Underwriters, and other insurers. This marketplace is as competitive as its US counterpart. In addition, the London insurers are typically willing to put out more capacity and are more agreeable to manuscripting policy forms. London underwriters also have different perspectives on certain areas of the world than their US counterparts and may provide coverage in areas where US insurers are reluctant to do so.

Care should be taken in choosing an agent or broker to access the marketplace. The broker should have substantial international resources and a staff who is knowledgeable in international trade and the political risk marketplace.

For companies that manufacture overseas and have supply chains originating or completing in foreign countries, particularly in countries where strained US relations or certain political instabilities exist, there are serious potential exposures. From a historical perspective, all developing and third-world countries present risks.

6.10 TEN STEPS IN MANAGING POLITICAL RISK INSURANCE

Sections 6.10.1 through 6.10.10 discuss the 10 steps to be taken in the management of political risk insurance.

6.10.1 Selecting a Broker or Underwriter

The choice of a broker is perhaps the risk manager's most important concern because the broker is the first line of contact. Many brokers can talk around the subject of political risks, but there are few who can perform adequately in a limited insurance market. Currently, there are few options in the choice of underwriting market, but the number is increasing rapidly as more insurance companies enter the political risk arena to meet the demands of American businesses.

A properly selected broker and underwriter combination will maximize risk management effectiveness. Establishing broker or underwriter rapport will help accomplish mutual understanding, reliable service, continuity of coverage, and increased opportunities for competitive pricing.

In some markets, the broker and the underwriter are in one entity, such as what we have in Coface North America. Michelle Milone-Sherer would be an excellent contact person: contact her at Michelle_Scherer@coface-USA.com or at 212-560-0410.

6.10.2 Service Requirements

In the process of selecting a broker and an underwriter, an analysis must be made of what the corporate entity requires in the relationship. Aside from arranging the protection of assets, other services available include the following:

- Export financing
- Filing of applications
- Political risk intelligence
- Loss control and claims handling
- Contract and exposure review
- Communication of coverage to divisions, subsidiaries, etc.

The servicing area for political risk varies greatly among brokers, underwriters, and specialty consultants. Commissions and fees that affect the bottom line should reflect the services that are provided and the ultimate decision in the choice of broker and market.

6.10.3 Combining Risks

Risk managers should combine various political risk exposures under one policy. This will maximize underwriting clout in obtaining favorable terms and conditions and will help reduce premiums. Underwriters will favor a spread of risk and react positively toward being the corporation's only political risk market.

Because of the limited number of markets, minimal capacity, and the small underwriting and brokerage political risk community, it makes good risk management sense to concentrate risks into one market and not continually seek competition. Risk managers should also combine other international risks in the coverage, such as kidnap and ransom, DIC, business interruption, marine, construction all risk, and so on. Underwriters favorably view combining these insurances in a package policy because they are typically more stable and predictable than other political risks and help provide more reasons for the market to perform.

6.10.4 Communication

Because political risk insurances are unique and cannot be explained to the layperson as easily as other forms of conventional property and liability coverage, there is an absolute need to establish comprehensive communication channels between the risk manager's office and operating units such as international sales, treasury, corporate finance and credit, and legal. The following actions are recommended:

- Set up in-house seminars to educate and inform employees.
- Establish formal communication systems, including updates and weekly status reports.
- Appoint local coordinators to become familiar with the subject area and operating plan if, because of distant operating units, logistics present problems.
- Consider having brokers communicate directly with the divisional operating personnel. This might expedite information transfers and provide additional support.

However, the risk manager should always be kept informed of activity.

6.10.5 Contract Review

The typical method of providing underwriting data to the market is through questionnaires. This is an excellent starting point; however, a thorough review should always include analysis and review of the contract, terms of sale, terms of payment, and other documents relating to the exposure. This will help ensure that the proper coverage is obtained, the underwriter thoroughly understands the risks, and any questions as to intent are answered clearly. Changes can often be obtained by altering the contract wording, terms of sale, and so on, which could greatly reduce exposure and increase the underwriting ability.

6.10.6 Political Risk Intelligence

Political risk insurance focuses on economic, social, and political events. To assess the need for coverage, the exposures must be understood, and understanding the exposures requires information. There are numerous sources of international intelligence, including the US State and Commerce Departments, private information services, banks, trade associations, embassies, and the media. As part of brokerage services, qualified facilities will assist in the area of information support and provide up-to-date intelligence on world conditions.

6.10.7 Rates, Terms, and Conditions

Consider that each market's standard policy is different and that manuscripting is a necessity if proper coverage is to be provided. The exact exposure should be explicitly defined, and coverage should be tailored to meet the risk, whether it is for nationalization, currency inconvertibility, license cancellation, war, or other situations. Other areas that should be addressed are as follows:

- Deductibles and coinsurance
- Waiting period
- Rescheduling
- Warranties and exclusions
- Method of reporting of exposures
- Coverage for business interruption and protection of profits
- Loss of market and delay
- Changes or fluctuations in currency, an area for which it is becoming more difficult, if not impossible, to arrange coverage
- Currency for claims payments
- War risks

Cost, which appears to be controlled by market conditions, current economic and political situations, and the quality of presentation, is typically a significant corporate expenditure. Premiums vary greatly with each risk, and compiling checklists comparing quotas is a good method for fair evaluation.

6.10.8 Export Credit

Most political risk coverages exclude export credit. (The proximate cause of loss emanates from the private buyer.) Risks such as nonpayment and contract frustration are significant exposures when dealing with private buyers. It is important to determine whether the ultimate buyer is private or governmental because interests may be jointly held. The right time to make this determination is before the policy is secured, not after a loss has occurred.

Markets for export credit coverage are more limited than for political risk and require specific underwriting details about the creditworthiness of the buyer and the payment track record. Obtaining this insurance is often a tool for increasing foreign sales because account receivables are protected, and banks are more apt to provide lucrative export financing.

6.10.9 Loss Control

Insured parties should seek measures to minimize opportunity for loss and to entice the interest of local businesses. Such measures include the following:

- Utilization of local management, personnel, etc.
- Development of sales that require continuing support, such as providing service, maintenance, spare parts, accessories, etc.
- Development of rapport with local officials by joining business associations, trade groups, etc.
- Review of opportunities for local financing of the import or project.
- Analysis of the contract to further protect interests or secure favorable treatment from the host country.

All of these measures will help control the fate of your venture in the event of a loss.

6.10.10 Claims Procedures

Before a loss, written procedures should be developed addressing the who, what, when, where, and how of handling claims. The responsible company personnel should have the contact information for the broker's and underwriter's personnel and their home phone numbers.

Contingency plans should be developed to provide options in the event of loss so that business will stay on track with little interruption. The company should run drills and have meetings with key personnel.

Procedures should be agreed to ahead of time to arrange for arbitrators in the event of contractual and/or business disputes.

6.11 LOSS CONTROL MANAGEMENT

Most corporate insurance and risk management specialists will preach that the best approach to managing risks and exposures is loss prevention, avoidance, and proactive SOPs.

In the current building of warehouses, plants, and office buildings, a company would not construct without sprinkler and alarm systems. As a primary means of loss prevention, these systems have had a great benefit for loss of life and property mitigation. The cost–benefit analysis always airs on the side of loss prevention. A company should not build a supply chain without the same loss prevention steps in place. This does not mean putting a sprinkler system in a cargo container or an alarm on packages coming from Shanghai.

However, there are numerous loss prevention and loss control ideas that can be built into global supply chains. The following is an outline of many loss control considerations for inbound supply chains:

- *Review the packing, marking, and labeling of all goods in transit.* Build into purchase agreements minimum standards that must meet acceptable legal and transit risk standards to ensure safe and timely receipt.

- *Study the actual physical movement of inbound cargo.* Perform a risk analysis. If cargo is temporarily held in consolidation, bonded, or in foreign trade zones or warehousing, where the company as the importer has an insurable interest, ensure that there are minimum asset protections in place, for example, sprinklers, alarm systems, proper material-handling equipment, management supervision and control, security procedures, and personnel.
- In foreign locations, ensure that parties that have care, custody, and control have minimum standards in place that mimic the company's US operations risk management profiles and strategies.
- Work with the company's insurance brokers and underwriters in engaging their loss control engineers and professionals to work on your inbound supply chains in bringing their expertise and resources to the company's loss control initiatives.
- Invest in education and training programs that raise the level of information flow to management and operations personnel working in the inbound supply chain, which will result in more effective loss control strategies, execution, and implementation and a more informed work force.
- *Establish supply chain operating groups and committees from all aspects of inbound supply chain disciplines that can coordinate loss control programs.* These work well across company profit and cost centers, affording better cooperation and ultimately better internal loss prevention programs.

Loss control in global supply chains locks in the best opportunities for bottom-line success in the long term. It is better to budget known dollars initially in loss control management than operate with the potential of unknown loss, damage, and financial consequences.

7

Developing an Inbound Supply Chain Risk Management Strategy

7.1 INTRODUCTION

This chapter uses the information in Chapters 1 through 6 to build a plan of action, discussing the development of a plan to reduce risk and create the most competitive environment to make the inbound (import) supply chain work successfully.

7.2 DEVELOPING AN INBOUND SUPPLY CHAIN RISK MANAGEMENT STRATEGY

The risk management programs of a corporation should have the following primary purposes:

- Identifying exposures
- Transferring financial risk
- Mitigating potential losses through proactive loss control

When a company sources overseas, these simple issues become more complex, as identified in Chapter 1. The key is to work these primary purposes into the procurement process. As outlined in Chapter 5, the same exposures found in US operations are present in overseas operations. But, a few more exposures are unique to the global supply chain.

7.2.1 Spread of Risk

US companies tend to become overly dependent on only one or a few sources of offshore production. Vulnerability exists if this source is lost as a result of acts of God, political or economic distress, or another event. How does a company replace that primary production facility's output? Is it even possible on short notice? How long will it take to find options?

How will those options work? What will the financial consequences be? It is much better to evaluate these risks proactively and provide a spread of risk in the company's sourcing options so that there are existing, accessible options in place.

7.2.2 Applying Loss Control to Foreign Partners

A few of the areas a company should examine in the area of loss control are as follows:

- The company's US facilities are protected. Are its suppliers protected as well?
- The company has security procedures in place in all its plants. Do its overseas production sources have similar security procedures?
- Personnel screening is in place in the company's US facilities. Do its overseas vendors have a screening process in place?
- The company has packing guidelines for exports from the United States. Does the company have similar requirements or standards in place for its suppliers in China?

These questions often indicate problem areas, and these and many more issues need to be examined in these important areas. The standard operating procedures (SOPs) of a US company should be followed by its overseas partners; if the overseas partners cannot follow the SOPs by 100%, then they should follow these procedures at least to a standard that is deemed acceptable to the risk management team.

7.2.3 Engaging Foreign Partners

A company should treat its overseas vendors, factories, plants, third-party contract manufacturers, and so on as true partners in its global supply chain. Overseas entities are often accommodating in regard to the company's risk management strategies. Investing in their operations when it benefits the company is a good practice. A company can negotiate what it wants in its purchasing agreements and make these issues part of the overall deal. It can negotiate benefits to the supply chain initially.

7.2.4 Exercise Patience

It is critical that a company enter long-term agreements slowly and cautiously. It should allow time to get to know its suppliers in a reasonable testing period.

Once the initial problems have been worked out, the agreement can be extended to a longer period, up to a year or so. Once the company has become comfortable with the partner, the long-term contract can be executed.

7.2.5 Invest in the Relationship

It is critical to invest time and money in building the relationship on personal and business levels with trading partners. It will be money that is well spent in mitigating future problems and building a foundation for the most effective working relationship.

In international business, a company cannot contract out risk in total. However, the gaps can be covered in relationship building.

7.2.6 Managing the International Terms of Sale and Purchase

One of the most misunderstood foundation issues in foreign trade is international communication terms (INCOTerms). But, it is one of the most important skill sets for supply chain managers and their staff.

7.2.6.1 Rules for Any Mode(s) of Transport

7.2.6.1.1 Ex Works

Ex works (EXW) means that the seller delivers when he or she places the goods at the disposal of the buyer at the seller's premises or at another named place (i.e., works, factory, warehouse, etc.). The seller does not need to load the goods on any collecting vehicle, nor does he or she need to clear the goods for export, where such clearance is applicable.

7.2.6.1.2 Free Carrier

Free carrier (FCA) means that the seller delivers the goods to the carrier or another person who is nominated by the buyer at the seller's premises or another named place. The parties are well advised to specify as clearly as possible the point within the named place of delivery, as the risk is passed to the buyer at that point.

7.2.6.1.3 Carriage Paid to

Carriage paid to means that the seller delivers the goods to the carrier or another person who is nominated by the seller at an agreed place (if any such place is agreed between parties) and that the seller must contract for and pay the costs of carriage that are necessary to bring the goods to the named place of destination.

7.2.6.1.4 Carriage and Insurance Paid to

Carriage and insurance paid to (CIP) means that the seller delivers the goods to the carrier or another person who is nominated by the seller at an agreed place (if any such place is agreed between parties) and that the seller must contract for and pay the costs of carriage that are necessary to bring the goods to the named place of destination.

The seller also contracts for insurance cover against the buyer's risk of loss of or damage to the goods during the carriage. The buyer should note that under CIP, the seller is required to obtain insurance only on minimum cover. Should the buyer wish to have more insurance protection, he or she will need either to agree as much expressly with the seller or to make his or her own extra insurance arrangements.

7.2.6.1.5 Delivered at Terminal

Delivered at terminal means that the seller delivers when the goods, once unloaded from the arriving means of transport, are placed at the disposal of the buyer at a named terminal at the named port or place of destination.

Terminal includes a place, whether covered or not, such as a quay; a warehouse; a container yard; or a road, rail, or air cargo terminal. The seller bears all the risks that are involved in bringing the goods to and unloading them at the terminal at the named port or place of destination.

7.2.6.1.6 Delivered at Place

Delivered at place means that the seller delivers when the goods are placed at the disposal of the buyer on the arriving means of transport ready for unloading at the named place of destination. The seller bears all the risks that are involved in bringing the goods to the named place.

7.2.6.1.7 Delivered Duty Paid

Delivered duty paid means that the seller delivers the goods when they are placed at the disposal of the buyer, cleared for import on the arriving means of transport ready for unloading at the named place of destination. The seller bears all the costs and risks that are involved in bringing the goods to the place of destination and has an obligation to clear the goods not only for export but also for import, to pay any duty for both export and import and to carry out all customs formalities.

7.2.6.2 Rules for Sea and Inland Waterway Transport

7.2.6.2.1 Free Alongside Ship

Free alongside ship means that the seller delivers when the goods are placed alongside the vessel (e.g., on a quay or a barge) that is nominated by the buyer at the named port of shipment. The risk of loss of or damage to the goods is passed when the goods are alongside the ship, and the buyer bears all costs from that moment onwards.

7.2.6.2.2 Free on Board

Free on board means that the seller delivers the goods on board the vessel that is nominated by the buyer at the named port of shipment or procures the goods that were already so delivered. The risk of loss of or damage to the goods is passed when the goods are on board the vessel, and the buyer bears all costs from that moment onwards.

7.2.6.2.3 Cost and Freight

Cost and freight means that the seller delivers the goods on board the vessel or procures the goods that were already so delivered. The risk of loss of or damage to the goods is passed when the goods are on board the vessel.

The seller must contract for and pay the costs and freight that are necessary to bring the goods to the named port of destination.

7.2.6.2.4 Cost, Insurance, and Freight

Cost, insurance, and freight means that the seller delivers the goods on board the vessel or procures the goods that were already so delivered. The risk of loss of or damage to the goods is passed when the goods are on board the vessel. The seller must contract for and pay the costs and freight that are necessary to bring the goods to the named port of destination.

The seller also contracts for insurance cover against the buyer's risk of loss of or damage to the goods during the carriage. The buyer should note that under CIF, the seller is required to obtain insurance only on minimum cover. Should the buyer wish to have more insurance protection, he or she will need either to agree as much expressly with the seller or to make his or her own extra insurance arrangements.

7.3 RECOMMENDATION(S)

The primary goal of INCOTerms is to identify the point in time in an international transaction when the responsibilities and liabilities are passed between the buyer and the seller.

The biggest impact for inbound supply chains is costing and insuring liability.

We recommend purchasing utilizing EXW origin and FCA outbound gateway. This affords the following:

- Control over freight routing and costs
- Control of import clearance, which as the ultimate consignee, irrespective of INCOTerms, may make the company responsible anyway
- Better control over tracking and tracing
- Best options to control overall landed costs
- Best-practice methodology to minimize supply chain exposures
- In addition to INCOTerms in all global contracts, it is also important to clearly state intent for the following:
  - The correct INCOTerm representing the buyer's and seller's intent
  - Payment terms
  - When title will pass
  - How freight will be handled

Although INCOTerms address these issues potentially by default, the actual reality is that they may not in certain circumstances that are created by poor communications and verbal misunderstandings. It is better to address each of these issues separately by line item. The INCOTerm utilized can be a guideline but is not necessarily comprehensive. INCOTerm skill set training is an important education and training element for supply chain personnel.

There is a school of global trade that teaches INCOTerms in a very comprehensive but easy method for the students' ability to learn and utilize in their everyday business dealings: the *National Institute of World Trade* (NIWT; http://NIWT.org).

The NIWT teaches both public and in-house classes as well as work with both importers and exporters in leveraging the correct INCOTerms.

7.4 SUPPLY CHAIN SOPs

The key for a successful global supply chain is the creation, implementation, and utilization of SOPs. A quality supply chain will have written guidelines for personnel to follow. The International Organization for Standardization (ISO) 9000/1 and related initiatives were successful in standardizing procedures for overall company operations. This concept should be applied to the procurement, sourcing, and inbound supply chains that are created by offshore manufacturing.

A well-run supply chain operates in a clear, consistent pattern according to the execution of the company's operating procedures. The following points should be considered in creating SOPs:

- SOPs must be reviewed by legal personnel to determine the validity and the risk potential for lawsuits.

- SOPs should be created with input from all the related areas of the company.
- SOPs should be clear and concise.
- The benefits and consequences should be clear.

7.5 TECHNOLOGY OPTIONS

The future of international trade lies with greater utilization of technology. The execution and management of e-commerce sales, fulfillment, logistics services, and payment options through technology are discussed in this section.

Import and export transactions are now handled totally by technology. Companies not spending time, money, and resources on automating import and export operations will not last long in global trade. The efficiencies gained in import, export, and supply chain technology automation will make one company substantially more competitive than another. The guidelines and options for the use of technology in global trade are outlined in Section 7.5.1, with an emphasis on documentation, tracking, and information management. Post-9/11 regulations make mandatory certain technological solutions to revised compliance and security regulations.

One aspect of inbound supply chains relates to purchase order (PO) management systems working through an electronic data interchange (EDI)-based transactional network.

This streamlines dataflow and makes for the most efficient import operations for high-volume inbound logistics systems.

Robust *PO management* systems contain the following trademarks:

- EDI based
- End to end from the original PO to final delivery
- Transaction is passed through from origin in North America to the service providers to the vendor/supplier to the outbound carrier to the Importer Security Filing, customs clearance, and into the domestic inventory and distribution network
- Create management reports, quarterly business review (QBR), and robust reporting details

7.5.1 Competitive Advantage

US importers and exporters can gain a significant competitive advantage in global trade through the use of technology. Access to new markets, more cost-effective sales efforts, and less costly logistics are but a few of the immediate benefits.

Technology solutions need not be overly expensive. Many custom-made and off-the-shelf software programs can provide cost-effective solutions. Many software and service providers offer extensive data on overseas businesses. These resources are both government and commercial based. Information such as the following can be found using EDI or the Internet:

- Market data on overseas opportunities
- Information on potential overseas suppliers
- Names and contact data for overseas companies (compliance and security management)
- Names and contact data on resources, support services, and service providers

- Research profiles on products, services, and demographics
- Specific product and prospect opportunities

Many of these data providers, such as Trade Compass, based in Washington, DC, have become major information providers. Others, such as the Department of Commerce (DoC), Vastera, Next Link, and Dun & Bradstreet, have been providing the service a long time but have greatly expanded their individual capabilities.

Letters of credit, which are heavily used in global trade, can be transacted via automation without the need for paperwork. Wire transfers, sight drafts, and other means of documentary credit devices can now be accommodated via EDI. Many of the world's leading financial institutions have begun various initiatives independently and in conjunction with various banking service providers to establish the following:

- Common EDI means of communication
- Secure methods of protecting confidential data
- More timely, paperless transactions
- Global links between foreign firms in countries with local and international banks

Successful logistics providers now view their role as information and communication providers as well as companies that move freight. The integrated carriers, freight forwarders, customhouse brokers, ocean and air carriers, and so on who are making investments in technology will be the only ones who will survive in the coming years.

The logistics industry is enhancing its use of technology as follows:

- Developing defined EDI or Internet interfaces with customers' import and export order entry systems
- Providing linkage into warehousing, inventory management, and shipping functions
- Establishing systems for tracking freight and to deal with customer service issues
- Becoming an integral partner with its clients as an information resource
- Having programs that ease the knowledge of the preparation and execution of international documentation
- Affording access to government reporting requirements and export licensing matters

Integrated carriers such as Federal Express and United Parcel Service, along with the larger freight forwarders and air and ocean carriers, have generally taken the lead in offering various competitive products. Many logistics providers are expanding the services that they provide because technology has afforded options that are previously not available.

7.6 COMPLIANCE AND SECURITY MANAGEMENT

Global supply chains can utilize technology in managing some of the compliance and security responsibilities, such as the following:

- Documentation accuracy
- Denied parties screening (Office of Foreign Assets Control [OFAC]/ Department of State [DoS])
- Export license requirements (DoC and DoS)
- Screening of vendors and unverified parties
- Country profiling
- Documentation transfer
- Data security
- Retrieval of compliance and security information from various data banks, both private and government

These are a few of the areas in which a technology interface could assist a corporation in managing the security and compliance responsibilities. There are many software providers (see Appendix) that can provide these services. In addition, many service providers such as freight forwarders, customhouse brokers, and banks offer software solutions as part of their overall service packages.

7.6.1 International Trade Administration Enforcement and Compliance

Enforcement and Compliance (E&C) safeguards and enhances the competitive strength of US industries against unfair trade through the enforcement of US antidumping duty (AD) and countervailing duty (CVD) trade laws and ensures compliance with trade agreements that are negotiated on behalf of US industries. E&C promotes the creation and maintenance of US jobs and economic growth by supporting the negotiation of international trade agreements to open foreign markets. In addition, E&C works in close coordination with the president's Interagency Trade Enforcement Center on a variety of trade-related issues.

E&C also administers the foreign trade zone (FTZ) program, and certain sector-specific agreements and programs such as the Steel Import Monitoring and Analysis licensing program.

7.6.1.1 Services that ITA Provides

- Counsels US industries on how to petition the US government to seek relief from injurious and unfairly traded imports
- Monitors steel imports and administers the steel licensing program
- Helps US exporters and investors facing foreign trade/investment barriers
- Ensures foreign government compliance with international trade agreements
- Assists US businesses facing foreign trade remedy (AD, CVD, safeguard) actions
- Pursues subsidy enforcement and compliance activities
- Conducts AD/CVD investigations and administrative reviews to determine if imports are being sold at a less-than fair-value or benefitting from unfair subsidization
- Administers suspension agreements and other bilateral agreements
- Works with Customs and Border Protection (CBP) to ensure the enforcement of AD/CVD orders and to pursue issues of fraud and duty evasion

- Participates in and supports the negotiation of international trade and investment agreements to provide framework for fair and competitive commerce
- Levels the playing field and improves US competitiveness through the FTZ program
- Administers programs to facilitate the importation of eligible scientific instruments and apparatus, promote watches and jewelries that are manufactured in the US insular possessions, and monitor the duty-free treatment of articles that are used for the physically handicapped

7.6.1.2 ITA

E&C is made up of three offices:

1. *AD and CVD operations*
   Enforces US antidumping duty and countervailing duty laws through the conduct of investigations and reviews to remedy unfairly traded dumped and/or subsidized imports and determines the appropriate duties to offset the unfair trade practices.
2. *Policy and negotiations*
   Promotes fair and competitive trade by assisting US exporters facing foreign trade barriers, foreign subsidies, and foreign trade remedy cases; supporting the consistent administration of the AD and CVD laws (trade remedy laws); and contributing to the negotiation of improved market access and trade disciplines for US industries.
3. *FTZs*
   Encourages activity and value added at US facilities in competition with foreign alternatives by allowing delayed or reduced duty payments on foreign merchandise, as well as other savings.

7.7 FTZ BENEFITS

7.7.1 Why Companies Use FTZs

All of the benefits the FTZ program can offer to manufacturers and processors who are located in the United States are too numerous to list here. But, there a few main benefits that account for most of the companies that use the FTZ program. Those benefits are listed as follows:

- *Relief from inverted tariffs*—In certain instances, there are tariff (import duty) relationships that actually penalize companies for making their product in the United States. This occurs when a component item or raw material carries a higher duty rate than the finished product. Hence, the importer of the finished product pays a lower duty rate than a manufacturer of the same product in the United States. This gives the importer an unfair and unintended advantage over the domestic manufacturer. The FTZ program levels the playing field in these circumstances.

  For example, an FTZ user imports a motor (which carries a 4% duty rate) and uses it in the manufacture of a vacuum cleaner (which is free of duty). When the vacuum cleaner leaves the FTZ and enters the commerce of the United States, the duty rate on the motor drops from the 4% motor rate to the free vacuum cleaner rate. By participating in the FTZ program, the vacuum cleaner manufacturer has virtually eliminated duty on this component and therefore reduced the component cost by 4%.

- *Duty exemption on reexports*—Without a zone, if a manufacturer or processor imports a component or raw material into the United States, it is required to pay the import tax (duty) at the time that the component or raw material enters the country. However, an FTZ is considered to be outside the commerce of the United States and the US customs territory. So, when foreign merchandise is brought into an FTZ, no customs duty is owed until the merchandise leaves the zone and enters the commerce of the United States. Only then is the merchandise considered imported and the duty paid. If the imported merchandise is exported back out of the country, no customs duty is ever due.

- *Duty elimination on waste, scrap, and yield loss*—Again, without a zone, an importer pays the customs duty that is owed as material is brought into the United States. This is because the material is considered imported at this point. If the processor or manufacturer is conducting its operations within a zone environment, the merchandise is not considered imported, and therefore no duty is owed until it leaves the zone for shipment into the United States. To demonstrate how this would benefit a company that has scrap, waste, or yield loss from an imported component, let us look at a chemical processing plant.

  For example, a chemical plant manufacturing hydroxywidgitpropolyne, which carries a 15% duty rate, uses the raw material oxyovertaxophene, which also carries a 15% duty rate, for one of its raw materials.

Part of the production process consists of bringing the imported oxy-overtaxophene to extreme temperatures. During this process, 30% of the oxyovertaxophene is lost as heat. If a processing company not in the FTZ program imports $10 million per year of oxyovertaxophene, it will pay $1.5 million in duty as the raw material enters the United States.

If the same company utilizes the FTZ program, it does not pay duty on the oxyovertaxophene until it leaves the zone and is imported into the United States. The zone user brings the oxyovertaxophene into the zone with no duty that is owed. It then processes the oxyovertaxophene into hydroxywidgitpropolyne. Remember, during this process, 30% of the raw material is lost due to waste factors, so the $10 million in oxyovertaxophene is now worth only $7 million. Assuming that all of the end product is sold into the United States, the 15% customs duty totals only $1.05 million. This represents a savings of $450,000.

While at first glance, it might look like the FTZ program is simply benefiting an importer, it is important to remember that its competitors making the same product overseas already have the benefit of not having to pay on the yield loss in the production of their hydroxywidgitpropolyne.

• *Weekly entry savings*—On May 18, 2000, the Trade and Development Act of 2000 was passed and signed by President Bill Clinton. This act had a provision in it that allowed the use of the Weekly Entry procedure for all manufacturing and distribution in FTZs.

Weekly Entry (allowed only to FTZ users) provides economies for both customs and FTZ users. Under Weekly Entry procedures, the zone user files only one customs entry per week rather than filing one customs entry per shipment. Customs no longer has to process an entry for each and every shipment being imported into the zone, and the FTZ community no longer has to pay for the processing of each and every entry.

Companies located outside FTZs pay a 0.21% merchandise processing fee for each and every formal entry that is processed by US customs. There is a minimum $25 processing fee and a maximum $485 processing fee per entry, regardless of the duty rate on the imported merchandise. The maximum processing fee is reached for entries (shipments) with a value that is over $230,952. Companies often receive many shipments over this amount.

For example, 10 shipments per week, each with a value of over $230,952, would amount to a merchandise processing fee of $4850

($485 × 10) per week. If this number is annualized, the amount is $252,200 (52 × $4850) per year.

Companies in an FTZ may take advantage of the Weekly Entry procedure. In the case of the example above, Weekly Entry would provide for one entry per week. For example, the 10 ($230,952) shipments per week would be filed as a single shipment of $2,309,520 each week. The merchandise processing fee would amount to the maximum of $485 total for the week. If this fee is annualized utilizing Weekly Entry, it is a total of only $25,220 yearly. In this example, Weekly Entry provides a savings of $226,980 per year. Each company's savings could be significantly more or less depending on the number of shipments that are received during the year.

DEPARTMENT OF THE TREASURY
UNITED STATES CUSTOMS SERVICE

NORTH AMERICAN FREE TRADE AGREEMENT
CERTIFICATE OF ORIGIN

Please print or type

19 CFR 181.11, 181.22

1. EXPORTER NAME AND ADDRESS	2. BLANKET PERIOD (DD/MM/YY)
	FROM
TAX IDENTIFICATION NUMBER:	TO
3. PRODUCER NAME AND ADDRESS	4. IMPORTER NAME AND ADDRESS
TAX IDENTIFICATION NUMBER:	TAX IDENTIFICATION NUMBER:

5. DESCRIPTION OF GOODS(S)	6. HS TARIFF CLASSIFICATION NUMBER	7. PREFERENCE CRITERION	8. PRODUCER	9. NET COST	10. COUNTRY OF ORIGIN

I CERTIFY THAT:

• THE INFORMATION ON THIS DOCUMENT IS TRUE AND ACCURATE AND I ASSUME THE RESPONSIBILITY FOR PROVING SUCH REPRESENTATIONS. I UNDERSTAND THAT I AM LIABLE FOR ANY FALSE STATEMENTS OR MATERIAL OMISSIONS MADE ON OR IN CONNECTION WITH THIS DOCUMENT;

• I AGREE TO MAINTAIN, AND PRESENT UPON REQUEST, DOCUMENTATION NECESSARY TO SUPPORT THIS CERTIFICATE, AND TO INFORM, IN WRITING, ALL PERSONS TO WHOM THE CERTIFICATE WAS GIVEN OF ANY CHANGES THAT COULD AFFECT THE ACCURACY OR VALIDITY OF THIS CERTIFICATE;

• THE GOODS ORIGINATED IN THE TERRITORY OF ONE OR MORE OF THE PARTIES, AND COMPLY WITH THE ORIGIN REQUIREMENTS SPECIFIED FOR THOSE GOODS IN THE NORTH AMERICAN FREE TRADE AGREEMENT, AND UNLESS SPECIFICALLY EXEMPTED IN ARTICLE 411 OR ANNEX 401, THERE HAS BEEN NO FURTHER PRODUCTION OR ANY OTHER OPERATION OUTSIDE THE TERRITORIES OF THE PARTIES; AND

• THIS CERTIFICATE CONSISTS OF _____ PAGES, INCLUDING ALL ATTACHMENTS.

11.	11a. AUTHORIZED SIGNATURE	11b. COMPANY
	11c. NAME (Print or Type)	11d. TITLE
	11e. DATE (DD/MM/YY)	11f. TELEPHONE NUMBER (Voice) (Facsimile)

Customs Form 434 (121793)

• *Duty deferral*—Again, since FTZs are outside the customs territory of the United States, goods are not imported until they leave the zone. Therefore, customs duty is deferred until merchandise is imported from an FTZ into the United States. So, instead of companies having substantial monies tied up in customs duties on their inventory, they have the use of those monies for other purposes.

There are many other substantial benefits that the FTZ program has to offer to manufacturers and distributors in the United States, but the benefits listed are the key benefits that attract most companies to the FTZ program. More and more companies look globally when deciding to locate or expand a new manufacturing or processing facility. When these companies make these location and expansion decisions, they do take into account all the costs of manufacturing in a certain country. Unfortunately, there are unintended import tax penalties for many companies located in, or considering locating in, the United States. The FTZ program plays an important role in providing a level playing field when investment and production decisions are made. While the US government might incur a reduction in customs duty revenue by the use of the FTZ program, it more than makes up for it by the income tax that it gains from the jobs that are created or retained. In addition, local governments benefit from sales and property taxes.

The FTZ program has proven to be a successful trade program by consistently creating and retaining jobs and capital investment in the United States.

7.8 FEDERAL CORRUPT PRACTICES ACT

With US global supply chains expanding their scope, companies must adhere to a growing list of government security and compliance initiatives. Terrorism and corporate accounting fraud are the key topics of the new government regulations. There are many parallels between these issues, the challenges that they present, and the means to create a proactive system of checks and balances to protect the supply chain from internal and external forces. With these new challenges, however, a company cannot forget to incorporate preexisting laws into a preventive twenty-first-century supply chain compliance action plan.

One law that is particularly important in such a plan is the Foreign Corrupt Practices Act (FCPA) of 1977. The original purpose of the FCPA was to assign monetary penalties to US companies and individuals who are found guilty of bribery. This act specifically targets unlawful payments to foreign government officials, politicians, or political parties for the sole purpose of obtaining or maintaining business.

The Department of Justice (DoJ) has been the agency that is responsible for the enforcement of the FCPA and, along with the Securities and Exchange Commission (SEC), has fined numerous corporations and individuals large monetary penalties for their infractions. With Sarbanes–Oxley (SOX) regulations and Department of Homeland Security (DHS) mandates to safeguard US interests against terrorism just on the horizon, FCPA regulations may be taking a backseat on priority lists for exporters. However, not taking the proper precautions to mitigate the potential risk of exposure to FCPA violations may cause considerable problems for US companies as their growth in the overseas market continues.

Violating these laws often results in stiff fines along with possible prison time. Some corporations have found this out the hard way. In January 2005, as a result of violating FCPA laws, the biotechnology giant Monsanto, headquartered in St. Louis, Missouri, paid a $1 million fine to the DoJ and a $500,000 fine to the SEC. These penalties represent mitigated amounts because of Monsanto's prompt reporting of the discovery of misconduct and their subsequent cooperation with the investigation pertaining to the actions of their affiliate in Indonesia. In December 2004 and February 2005, GE InVision, a subsidiary of General Electric, settled its cases with the DoJ and SEC. The FCPA violations cost the company a combined total of just under $2 million. The Titan Corporation and Schering–Plough are two additional companies that were recently found guilty and fined for violations.

A US company conducting business in a foreign country must ensure that none of its employees, subsidiaries, agents, or hired contractors violate FCPA laws. Investing in a monitoring system that performs thorough screenings of all entities conducting business on behalf of the US company is highly recommended. The internal policing of this issue must begin with identifying problematic persons or entities wanting to represent the company in a foreign market. Refusal to submit written compliance to FCPA guidelines, failing to maintain sufficient books or records, requesting payments for an undisclosed third party, or having any relationship with a member of a political party should serve as red flags to exporters.

Maintaining an *out-of-sight, out-of-mind* mentality or pleading ignorance to situations will not help a company during an FCPA investigation. The concepts of maintaining awareness and establishing internal controls appear repeatedly in the SOX regulations. Applying these principles to SOPs in order to prevent FCPA violations is critical.

Establishing criteria for monitoring the supply chain in order to expose potential FCPA issues can start by requiring that all contracts include concise FCPA compliance language. Companies should insist that all payments be made via check or wire transfer, avoiding any party insisting on using offshore accounts. Another safeguard is to ensure that all applicants for foreign office positions undergo thorough background checks confirming that they do not hold public office or have close ties to a foreign government.

Awareness of corporate responsibilities has become paramount in the current post-9/11, SOX world. The government has increased its vigilance in protecting both the homeland and public confidence in the American business system. US exporters must take the necessary precautions to guard their supply chains from activities that pose risks to the United States or jeopardize the security of the company. By taking a proactive and organized approach, a corporation can build a system of checks and balances to simultaneously mitigate risks in areas of security, compliance, and accounting.

Maintaining high compliance and security standards within a global supply chain best prepares an organization to adhere to new government initiatives and protect itself against FCPA infractions and violations of other laws.

Globalization has expanded the arena of executives. They travel all over the world, making deals and committing on behalf of the company. They are involved in millions of dollars in negotiations and contracts. Now is the time for companies to ensure that their executives are aware of the FCPA and are in strict adherence. The following actions will help ensure this:

- Obtain expertise, either internally or outsourced, to assist in identifying potential FCPA exposures.
- Initiate FCPA guidelines in the SOX and supply chain compliance guidelines.

- Ensure that executives receive awareness training and develop SOPs for dealing with potential FCPA scenarios.
- Develop specific SOPs to incorporate into operating guidelines and ensure compliance.
- Issue internal communications from senior management with non-tolerance and strict penalty guidelines.
- Initiate annual audits by outside consultants, law firms, and specialists to analyze potential FCPA violations.
- Establish internal resources and call centers in the event that an executive needs assistance in dealing with a potential FCPA violation or a potential problem situation without the threat of backlash.
- Identify high-risk countries, customers, situations, etc., that may become involved in an FCPA violation and proactively mitigate these situations.
- Work with internal risk management personnel to determine insurance options and alterative loss control procedures.
- Companies that are proactive in FCPA management will avoid pitfalls and enjoy more successful international trade, with less government scrutiny and interference.

7.9 RADIO FREQUENCY IDENTIFICATION: SUPPLY CHAIN

7.9.1 Compliance and Security Tool

The long, separate paths of hyped anticipation and the actual applicability of radio frequency identification (RFID) technology are beginning to merge at last. This convergence is slowly unveiling the benefits of the long-awaited supply chain *super tool*.

RFID is beginning to make its way into mainstream use, with tangible purposes and real benefits. Wal-Mart led the field on the commercial side when in 2005, it advised its top 100 vendors that they must use RFID tags as a prerequisite for doing business with the company. Other mainstream giants such as Best Buy and Target have followed suit. The two most prohibitive obstacles in the path of RFID, (1) international standardized acceptance and (2) cost per tag, are beginning to yield to the inroads that are created by the retail superpowers. These pressures from top-level commercial entities have made integrating real benefits from RFID technology much more attainable. The military and several government agencies have been observing the progress. They have identified RFID as a potential asset to assist in national security and provide a platform to enforce tighter compliance standards for importers and exporters.

In April 2002, the US CBP introduced a government program called Customs–Trade Partnership Against Terrorism (C-TPAT). C-TPAT is a voluntary joint government and private sector program that is designed to create a standardized level of security in the international supply chains of US companies. Supply chain service providers, including ocean carriers, airlines, freight forwarders, and customs brokers, are also participants in this initiative. The C-TPAT program began with US importers disclosing a working profile of their international supply chain. All supply chain components, including manufacturers, overseas agents, and carriers, as well as the warehouses and US corporate offices themselves, are required to submit a detailed self-assessment of SOPs pertaining to supply chain compliance and security. The supply chain links use the C-TPAT security criteria that are created by CBP and the trade community as a guide. Once companies receive a confirmation of membership to C-TPAT, they must commit to maintaining a minimum level of security and compliance in order to retain membership to the program.

In March 2005, CBP announced new minimum security requirements for applicants and members of the program. The new requirements came in the form of seven-point container inspections before loading at origin and using publicly available specification (PAS) ISO 17712 security seals on ocean containers. Although the C-TPAT program has been considered very successful, gaining over 9000 members within a four-year period, the General Accounting Office (GAO) issued a critical assessment of C-TPAT in 2005. The GAO stated that the scope and methodology that CBP uses to measure its validation processes of importers are inconsistent. This inconsistency comprises the validity of the data that are compiled from the importer's C-TPAT profiles, which are collectively used to analyze the importing community's overall level of security. CBP responded to the GAO by issuing *tiered benefits* and more stringent program requirements for participants.

This back-and-forth between government watchdogs and CBP likely represents a trend for the future. Every time the program is critiqued, CBP patches the issue that caused the criticism. CBP will be open to this type of subjective influence until it is able to make the program universally mandatory instead of voluntary and include RFID technology (or an equivalent) as a requirement that an importer must adopt for C-TPAT consideration. Until CBP does this, the program will be attempting to substantiate its existence as a post-9/11 supply chain preventive measure. For this reason, CBP is monitoring the progress of RFID in mainstream acceptance.

CBP Commissioner Robert C. Bonner announced during a 2005 Customs Trade Symposium in Washington, DC, that he was ready to take the C-TPAT program to the next level, which he called *C-TPAT Plus*. C-TPAT Plus entails no inspection on arrival and immediate release for low-risk shippers who use RFID-like technology. The technology must include the ability to detect and record whether tampering has occurred with a container seal after being affixed at the point of origin. Importers who employ the RFID, or *Smart Box*, technology in their supply chain security profiles are promoted to *green lane* clearance status by CBP.

The years 2005–2016 saw US government agencies in the early stages of realizing the potential of RFID technology. In January, the DHS began testing RFID technology as part of its US-VISIT program to efficiently and correctly identify visitors at US border crossing points. Each person crossing over the border is given an RFID tag, which contains a unique serial ID number that links the visitor's photograph, fingerprints, and basic personal information to the US-VISIT database. As part of the US-VISIT initiative, all non-US visitors have digital fingerprints and photographs that are taken before entrance into the country.

The information gathered as part of US-VISIT in conjunction with RFID technology enhances and strengthens national security efforts. In addition, foreign visitors who apply for US visas are simultaneously enrolled in the US-VISIT program. As a result of this program and with the aid of RFID, the additional information made available about foreign visitors uncovered suspicious details about certain people who were previously unattainable. In cases in which the additional information raised *red flags*, 7000 visa applications were denied, and 600 people were stopped from entering the country. There have been 39 arrests that can be attributed to the additional information that is provided by this program and the RFID technology.

In August 2005, the DHS began testing another form of RFID technology by imbedding RFID chips into immigration documents at five crossing points on the Mexican and Canadian borders. CBP form I-94A carries the RFID chip and improves the efficiency and timeliness in which foreign visitors can enter and exit the country. The ultimate goal of this program is to come as close as possible to automating the CBP border crossing process. With each DHS immigration program that is described above, the personal information attained with RFID is kept to a minimum, and the foreign visitor can be tracked only within the borders of the United States.

Recently, the GAO found that the US army is failing to maintain an accurate inventory control of items that are shipped to repair contractors. The GAO noted that this lack of supervision and control places these items at risk for loss or theft. In December 2005, the GAO issued a report stating, "Although the Department of Defense (DoD) policy requires the military services to confirm receipt of all assets shipped to contractors, the army is not consistently recording shipment receipts in its inventory management system." Basing their findings on the army's 2004–2016 shipment data, the agency found that the army could not successfully reconcile shipment records with receipts for over 42% of unclassified secondary repair item shipments and 37% of the classified secondary repair items. The combined value of these items was just under $500 million.

The GAO also notes that the army lacks documentation control and fails to follow up on confirmations of receipt. Implementing basic RFID technology could assist the army with this problem in two ways. First, the army's ability to mark inventory with RFID tags would enable tighter inventory and item reconciliation controls and would upgrade the security of these goods from theft or loss. Second, converting to an RFID-controlled system would transfer a manually heavy, time-consuming process out of human hands and into the arms of automated efficiency. For this reason, among others, the DoD and the US military are testing several RFID programs with the intent of integrating the technology to improve their supply chain practices.

A.T. Kearney, a management consulting firm, recently conducted a thorough research initiative regarding the potential benefits of RFID. Their extensive study found that logistics executives from some of the world's largest importers and exporters (ranging from retail to high-tech industries) cited inventory management and container security as top issues regarding their international supply chain. The A.T. Kearney study also concluded that the RFID technology provides more than tampering alerts. RFID was actually found to provide tangible monetary savings in the form of inventory reductions and out-of-stock reductions, as well as preventing the loss of containers and theft. Other recent studies performed by Stanford University and the business systems integration consulting firm BearingPoint pointed to similar findings. All three groups pointed to key benefits and savings per container to the importer when utilizing RFID technology in the range of $400–$1800 per container shipment.

So, what are the obstacles in launching this technology? The formidable issue delaying common RFID use internationally is lack of agreement among countries and companies on a universal, standard format.

China's ultimate decision regarding its role in RFID standardization will have substantial commercial and political implications. The RFID market in China has led to meetings involving its most revered business leaders and high-ranking government officials. With China as the centerpiece, representatives from the RFID industry organization EPC Global have been working toward finding a universally acceptable standard for RFID to further its acceptance as a vital fixture of the twenty-first-century supply chain model. EPC Global has been working very closely with the ISO for the approval of universally acceptable RFID standards.

The Chinese government has been very supportive of EPC Global's efforts, and ISO approval will improve their standing. China may also receive pressure for accepting a standardized RFID platform from the commercial side. Wal-Mart is China's leading exporter of goods. Taken alone, the company represents more export volume to China than the total dollar volume of exports from Germany or Britain.

Although the company is not specifically mandating that China itself become RFID compliant, the fact that the majority of its top suppliers are China based and have moved to satisfy their client proves that Wal-Mart can single-handedly influence foreign economic policy in yet another arena, albeit indirectly. However, nationalism is strong in China, and any move by Wal-Mart will be met by a rapid response. The controversial Chinese businessman Edward Zeng, the founder and chief executive officer (CEO) of Beijing-based Sparkice, has been pushing the government of his country to adopt a China RFID standard as opposed to the more conventional and accepted EPC Global American version. Zeng has been lobbying the Ministry of Information

Industries to reject the American version in favor of the version that was developed by Sparkice. His rationale for this direction ranges from issues of national security, to nationalism, and ultimately to the fact that Zeng stands to gain substantially from China using Sparkice's proprietary IP, which would position him as the largest RFID market in the world. The standardization issue will have to pass through Beijing's ministries, committees, and commissions before a decision is made. For this reason alone, the acceptance of an RFID standard in China is not expected soon.

The current security methods for ocean containers mainly consist of disposable plastic bands and metal bolts securing the doors. These bands and bolts also have a unique identification serial information that is printed on them that represents the seal number. At the ports of entry or departure, the seal's serial number and container number are recorded manually and input into the carrier's database. There are obvious limitations to this method of container seal security. For example, the carrier cannot determine the time, date, or location of a seal or door being compromised. The inspection of the container at the pier is a manual, time-consuming endeavor. In addition, the seals do not meet the CBP Service Container Security Initiative minimum requirements. RFID technology would enhance security, the automated and instantaneous seal serial number data transfer to the carrier's database, and the immediate recordation of a breach with the seal or container door.

Another advantage of utilizing RFID is the CBP's stamp of approval recognizing compliant supply chain practice.

The pharmaceutical industry is unique to all others in its area of interest in utilizing RFID technology. Its interest is in how RFID protects the security of shipments and the ability of RFID to maintain the traceability of pharmaceutical products at a bottle, jar, or even blister package level. Pharmaceutical manufacturers want an RFID environment that would provide an efficient, cost-effective product recall management system. The prospect of guaranteed integrity of the product through the supply chain to the end user is of great interest to the industry. In the past, when a manufacturer announced the recall of a product, the response was for pharmacies and retailers to strip the product from shelves and dispose of it immediately. Although this was considered a mandatory public safety measure, it cost the industry millions of dollars. For example, suppose that a manufacturer must issue a product recall because of an irregular production event affecting 200 bottles. That manufacturer has employed RFID technology at the bottle level and can target specific units that it feels are dangerous, as opposed to destroying an entire lot when only a small percentage of the bottles are involved. Even though this technology would safeguard the products tremendously, the issue of tagging individual units as opposed to individual pallets or boxes is daunting from an expense standpoint.

Supply chain executives must continue to give this issue the attention that it deserves. Monitoring the progress of this technology is critical for corporate logistics decision makers. Staying current by building and maintaining a relevant supply chain infrastructure with current technology is an intelligent, cost-effective strategy. This approach is far less expensive than forced, expensive, reactive measures after neglectfully falling behind. It is better to be proactive than reactive, when a response might be too late or too costly. Eventually, RFID will be a function of competitive advantage.

Although the realization of full-scale international RFID acceptance is not right around the corner, it is not far away. The concept of widespread RFID integration will gain substantial credibility when a viable return on investment can be substantiated. As soon as corporate models illustrating how the efficiencies created by RFID translate into real monetary savings are published, the future of the technology will be secure.

Several government agencies and industries have taken note of the vast potential of this technology and how it can enhance national security, protect the international supply chain, and promote sizable efficiencies in inventory control and management. With support and encouragement from the diverse and influential elements of the government and private sectors, acceptance of a basic RFID environment is something to expect in years ahead. Inbound supply chain executives need to pay attention to RFID, proactively, because it is likely to become an integral part of import processes, not only to be competitive but also to meet regulatory demands.

In 2016, RFID has made progress but not nearly the gained traction that one would think that such a robust technology can offer. Cost is the main obstacle. But, a number of government agencies from all over the world and certain industry verticals are moving forward with RFID as an important *chain of custody* and *supply chain management* tool.

7.10 SOX

The fiscal landscape of American corporations changed dramatically since the accounting scandals of the past few years were made public.

When the federal government witnessed such poor corporate accounting practices and the lack of responsibility by corporate officers, they intervened with legislation. SOX regulations required very strict lines of communications and better fiscal accounting practices within public corporations.

These regulations have had a major impact on American public corporations in forcing them to create SOX operating guidelines and procedures. These extend to global supply chains. With SOX now in place, the CEO and the CFO will be held responsible. The law states that both must sign off on and can be held accountable for the following:

- All financial statements, both internal and external, such as those that are published and distributed to shareholders, the SEC, and analysts. These include quarterly and annual forecasts, 10(k) and 10(q) filings, and other statements.
- Accounting practices and SOPs.
- Certification from internal and external auditors validating that SOP documentation and practices are legal and accurate.

The company must make itself available for scrutiny by outside auditors, the SEC, and government investigators. If a wrongdoing is uncovered, company officials will be held responsible and punished.

This added scrutiny has benefits for supply chain professionals. Anne Marie Griffin, Microsoft's senior manager for global trade compliance, noted in 2004 at the summer's American Association of Exporters and Importers conference that SOX has helped with export compliance. *"There's money now; there's high visibility,"* she said. *"Our chief financial officer (CFO) comes and sees us and gets us the resources that we need, including information technology systems."*

In 2016, Kelly Raia, the vice-president (VP) of trade compliance, Apex Global, has determined that *"Trade compliance has and will continue to be a focus of our client's activities in service provider relationships, maintaining and raising the bar of compliance and security management."*

For years, CBP, the Bureau of Industry and Security (BIS), the Census Bureau, and other government agencies have required companies to submit import and export documentation that includes Entry Summary forms 7501 and 3461 (for imports); Automated Export System Electronic Export Information (EEI) (for exports); commercial and pro-forma invoices, certificate of origin, correct Harmonized Tariff System of the United States (HTSUS)/Schedule B classifications to determine duty rates and taxes, letters of credit and money transfers, applicable licenses or permits, quota documentation, and packing lists.

This documentation and related shipping and receiving SOPs authenticate a company's trustworthiness to conduct international business. It is only natural that these processes be incorporated into the SOX Act's requirements. With millions of dollars that are expended daily in this area, this will become an area for audit and prosecution. There is a dotted-line progression of the C-TPAT into the SOX arena. In December 2004, a new intelligence agency was authorized by Congress and signed into law by President George W. Bush that will have ramifications not only in compliance and security but also for applications to administer the new SOX regulations.

Companies have found that C-TPAT participation has helped with supply chain management. Many corporations are creating import and export compliance departments that usually report directly to corporate counsel or internal audit departments and have important input in supply chain, manufacturing, and risk management decisions. These professionals have become the *de facto* watchdog over the entire supply chain.

Many companies with limited staff retain consulting firms to manage their compliance programs. Not only does the consultant monitor supply chain, manufacturing, and risk management issues but also broker and service provider relationships.

Corporations are discovering the importance of a safe, competitive, and secure global supply chain. Operating within the SOX guidelines has become another skill set that must be mastered by logistics, traffic, and warehousing managers, as well as CEOs and CFOs. The success of a company's import and export operation may depend on it.

7.10.1 SOX Supply Chain Concerns

- Intercompany transfers
- Valuation
- Money transfer
- Suppliers
- C-TPAT
- Recordkeeping

In global supply chains, many of the following functions interface both directly and indirectly with SOX principals:

- *Document preparation*: Importing and exporting requires significant volumes of paper and documentation. Many of these documents are created to move freight, such as the following:
  - Invoices
  - Packing lists
  - Origin statements
  - Quality statements
  - Bills of lading
  - EEI
  - Customs declaration forms: 7501 and 3641, as well as statements of use, sales literature, product descriptions, requests for information, etc.
- *Valuation and pricing*: A company must make statements on the various communications in an international sale or purchase that determine the values that are declared to CBP and the Census Bureau.
- *Money transfer*: Money is moved around the globe to pay for purchases or accommodate other financial requirements.
- *Intercompany transfers*: This can be a problematic area, particularly with imports into the United States. Many corporations, particularly the North American subsidiaries of foreign corporations, have difficulty in dealing with two specific issues: (1) proper HTSUS classification and (2) the correct value to use for customs purposes. As discussed in Chapter 2, there are very detailed and specific guidelines for intercompany transfer accounting.

- *Vendor and supplier relationships*: The supply chain has a strong integration feature with the vendors and suppliers who link into the import and export process. There are all sorts of accounting interfaces that occur between the corporation and these vendors and suppliers. All of these would be part of the SOX responsibility.
- *SOP development*: Corporations have structured various SOPs to manage the SOX requirements. As discussed in Chapters 2 and 3, companies should create SOPs to help manage their compliance and security program. It is also a basic requirement of CBP and the BIS that SOPs or other guidelines be created within the import and export business to outline corporate responsibilities in compliance and security.

Therefore, companies must also incorporate into compliance and security the SOP responses to SOX regulatory mandates.

- *C-TPAT.* Many public corporations are becoming C-TPAT certified. They are *de facto* demonstrating to CBP how their supply chain works and affirming it to be secure. The process of C-TPAT certification involves providing significant information flow to CBP, which is considered an affidavit of circumstance or fact. This is in agreement with SOX requirements.
- *Fiduciary issues.* SOX is intended to regulate fiduciary governance in public corporations. The supply chain in international business is all about money moving globally. The fiduciary requirements in the import and export transaction mirror what SOX is designed to manage.
- *Recordkeeping.* Compliance and security in the global supply chain require the maintenance of a recordkeeping system, outlined in Chapter 5.
- *Lines of accountability and responsibility.* The main relationship between SOX and supply chains has to do with accountability and responsibility. SOX mandates that company officers and a company's internal administration make it clear that the fiduciary lines of accountability and responsibility are concise, clear, and functional to the best interests of the corporation, its employees, and stockholders and that they meet all SEC regulations.

The supply chain governance of CBP; the BIS; and the departments of state, treasury, and commerce requires the same compliance as SOX.

Although the regulations of these agencies and acts may not agree verbatim, they have the same underlying intent and concepts.

7.11 BEST PRACTICES: 10-STEP MANAGEMENT APPROACH

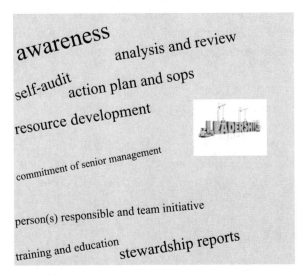

Managers of global supply chains must recognize that the operation of international supply chains has changed. New regulations in response to world conditions and increased government scrutiny require increased compliance and security. Supply chain managers need expertise for handling the new regulations relating to logistics, inventory, purchasing, and operational responsibilities.

Along with the pre-9/11 risks of global trade—political; economic; carriers; forwarders, agents, and distributors; CBP regulations; the BIS; weather; acts of God; cultural, language, and legal differences; handling; storage; terrorism; and war—there are now an array of new challenges, such as the following:

- Patriot Act
- Transportation Security Administration
- DHS
- Export Administration Act (revised)

- C-TPAT
- United States Principal Party in Interest (USPPI) for EEI filing
- Bioterrorism Act
- Reorganization of the government
- Deemed exports
- Enhanced plant and warehouse security measures
- 24-h manifest rules
- Container Security Initiative
- Focused assessments
- Importer Self-Assessment (ISA)
- Green lanes
- Personnel hiring screening
- Technology security: firewalls and spam
- Enhanced denied parties screening
- Foreign Corrupt Practices Act
- SOX issues

Corporations must manage their global supply chains in a safe, timely, and cost-effective manner but still be compliant and secure and eliminate the exposures that are faced through terrorism. This involves moving goods in the import and export supply chain in compliance with new regulations while lowering the logistics costs. The following is a 10-step guideline for achieving this:

1. *Awareness*
2. *Commitment of senior management*
3. *Analysis and review*
4. *Person(s) responsible and team initiative*
5. *Resource development*
6. *Action plan*
7. *SOPs*
8. *Training and education*
9. *Self-audit*
10. *Stewardship reports*

7.11.1 Awareness

Supply chain individuals must be aware of the current issues and how they might affect the import and export supply chain. Being reactive after the fact will result in delays, potential fines, penalties, and extra costs, typically not anticipated or budgeted.

Awareness means having a consistent inbound flow of information and developing resources to understand the issues, the most recent modifications, and the options for mitigating these matters.

Understanding how to benefit from information inflow—trade periodicals, bulletins from related agencies, and so on—is as important a skill set as knowing how to have goods cleared by customs in China or dealing with the Food and Drug Administration in the United States in importing food, pharmaceuticals, or related merchandise. That information inflow will eventually require change in some aspects of the supply chain on the part of senior management personnel.

7.11.2 Senior Management

All corporations have profit and cost centers that are managed by individuals with their personalities, egos, interpretations, and ideas on how various responsibilities should be managed.

Compliance, security, and terrorism issues cross all the boundaries of a corporation—finance, legal, customer service, operations, logistics, traffic management, inventory, purchasing, manufacturing, and even the customers and suppliers. Often, people in corporations are resistant to change.

In the discussion of issues regarding terrorism, compliance, and security with uninformed executives, there may be a natural resistance to infrastructure change recommendations that are put forth by compliance and security personnel. The support of senior management is vital in this situation. Their promotion of the compliance and security initiatives will break down the resistance and allow for constructive review and implementation. Thus, it is critical that senior management personnel are aware of the importance of regulatory compliance and the penalties for noncompliance and institute internal controls for adherence. Supply chain initiatives that carry senior management support are much more likely to be successful than those that do not.

Sample Senior Management Internal Memorandum
Importico Manufacturing, LTD
Internal memorandum

From: Edward Baxter, chief operating officer (COO)
To: All personnel
Subject: Supply Chain Compliance
Date: 3 March 2016
Since this company began to source goods overseas nine years ago, we have continually strived to be responsive to all the compliance and security regulations that are put forth by all government entities. About three months ago, Lynn Wycoff, our import logistics manager, took classes that led her to analyze just how well we were doing in comparing our supply chain to others and to accomplish some *benchmarking*.

She retained a consulting company, Blue Tiger International (BTI; http://bluetigerintl.com), that assisted her in that analysis.

We have discovered that we are doing pretty well overall but that we need to raise the bar of our compliance and security procedures for our inbound supply chain from China and India.

Lynn has been authorized to structure an internal committee representative of all the centers of management that are involved in our supply chain. This committee will work, under Lynn's supervision and our consultant, BTI, to develop SOPs and some training and education modules for all our sales, finance, and operations personnel to follow.

The bottom line is that our supply chain will not only run smooth and cost effectively, but also it will be at the highest standards of compliance and security.

While we can feel good about where we are, we can now feel even better about where we will be going.

Your cooperation and support are required to coordinate a successful initiative and are appreciated in advance.
Thank you,
Edward Baxter, COO
Cc: CEO, president, CFO, and human resources VP

For a company to move in a new direction, it must assess its current situation.

7.11.3 Analysis and Review

The process to determine the current situation of a company involves a facility review, detailed analysis, and mock audit of supply chain and operations. This is typically best accomplished by engaging an independent consultant. This will afford a third-party analysis. An outside consultant will not have agendas that conflict with personnel or career matters and will have external reference points for benchmarks.

This review will provide the blueprint for actions to improve the company's management of the effects of terrorism, compliance, and security issues. The review and scrutiny also respond to the CBP and BIS doctrines of exercising due diligence, reasonable care, supervision, and control. A facility review can also assess relationships with vendors, providers, carriers, forwarders, and brokers to ensure the strength of those links in the supply chain and add to the company's compliance and security profile. Accountable and responsible personnel should manage the reviews.

7.11.4 Responsible Personnel

One person should be responsible for managing the risks of terrorism, compliance, and security. This person can be part of any profit or cost center, as long as he or she has the skill sets that are necessary to manage the job. He or she should work with a team approach.

Individuals from all profit and cost centers and divisions should be involved. This will promote greater cooperation; personnel will feel that they have influence, they will believe that their ideas will be heard, and they can provide constructive input.

Corporations are currently creating positions in supply chain and import and export compliance and security at a faster rate than at any other time in contemporary global trade history. The NIWT, an organization based in New York, with representation throughout the United States, conducts the seminars, testing, and certification of supply chain managers (http://www.niwt.org).

This association teaches skills for personnel who have compliance and security responsibilities and offers instruction that helps companies meet the standards of due diligence, reasonable care, and internal training and education.

These responsible personnel, who may have these duties added to their job description, will eventually have to implement and effect corporate change. This is of course best accomplished by creating a plan of action.

7.11.5 Resource Development

It is imperative that supply chain management personnel develop resources to gain information. Quality information is the foundation for being informed on critical issues, which is necessary for good decision making. Good decision making is required for successful and profitable global supply chains. It is important that supply chain managers regularly read the relevant business publications and distribute information to the staff.

Along with trade periodicals and agency publications, information can be obtained from the Internet. Supply chain personnel should devote approximately 5% of their time to these types of resource materials. The best supply chain managers are well read and informed. They recognize the value that this brings into the negotiation process and have the ability to use information inflow for the corporation's advantage.

7.11.5.1 Recommended Key Websites (Additional in the Appendix)

- *BIS*: http://www.bis.doc.gov
- *International Trade Administration*: http://www.ita.gov
- *US CBP*: http://www.cbp.gov
- *OFAC*: http://www.treas.gov
- *Census Bureau*: http://www.census.gov
- *Foreign Commercial Service*: http://www.doc.gov
- *US Council for International Business (Carnets)*: http://www.uscib.org
- *Journal of Commerce*: http://www.joc.pub
- *Automated Export System*: http://www.aesdirect.gov
- *Bureau of National Affairs (nongovernmental agency)*: http://www .bna.com

7.11.5.2 Recommended Periodicals

- *American Shipper*
- *Journal of Commerce*
- *World Trade Magazine*
- *Traffic World*
- *Shipping Digest*
- *Logistics Magazine*
- *Inbound Logistics*
- *Government Security News*

7.11.5.3 Recommended Email Lists

- http://www.niwt.org
- http://www.supplychainbrain.com
- http://www.theworldacademy.com

- http://www.cscmp.org
- the_journal_of_commerce@xmr3.com
- http://www.iafis.org
- business_technology-alert@bt10.net
- news@eyefortransport.com
- http://www.logisticsmgmt.com
- http://www.importexportwizard.com
- http://www.topica.email-publisher.com
- newsdesk@exim.gov
- http://www.ncbfaa.com
- http://www.nitl.org
- http://www.amanet.org

Active participation in various organizations that interface with global supply chain issues is key to resource development. The following are a few of these organizations:

- *NCBFAA*: National Customs Brokers and Forwarders Association of America
- *CLM*: Council of Logistics Managers
- *LIEXA*: Long Island Import/Export Association
- *AFA*: Air Forwarders Association
- *TIA*: Transportation Intermediaries Association
- *FCBF*: Florida Customhouse Brokers and Forwarders Association
- *ISM*: Institute for Supply Management
- *CSCMP*: Council of Supply Chain Management Professionals

In addition, there are literally hundreds of books on the various aspects of supply chain management. These are important in building a library of core information. Some recommended books are as follows:

- *Mastering Import and Export Management*, Thomas Cook, AMACOM Books
- *Export/Import Procedures and Documentation*, Thomas E. Johnson and Donna L. Bade, AMACOM Books
- *Extending the Supply Chain: How Cutting-Edge Companies Bridge the Critical Last Mile into Customers' Homes*, Kenneth Karel Boyer, AMACOM Books

7.11.6 Action Plan

Once the analysis is completed and the lead compliance person is chosen, a plan must be developed using an Excel spreadsheet.

The action plan describes personnel responsibility and accountability and sets the agenda for the actions to be taken. It should be updated on a weekly or an agreed periodic basis. Maintaining a system will help ensure success. The action plan will eventually lead the company and the individuals in charge of compliance and security to create SOPs.

7.11.7 SOPs

SOPs are a necessary component of any supply chain and a key tool in successfully implementing consistent personnel behavior in purchasing, sourcing, and logistics.

Their importance can be outlined in the following four areas:

1. It provides a plan for all to follow and becomes the internal resource for guidance on the operation of the company's global supply chain.
2. It commits the processes to a written format that clearly outlines how a company and its personnel will function in its supply chain.
3. The SOPs become a benchmark to meet the government's requirements of due diligence and reasonable care.
4. It provides written guidelines for new personnel to follow.

In addition, public companies must be concerned with SOX regulations and fiduciary responsibilities to create financial and operating guidelines, controls, and information flow back to corporate management, to ensure the agreement between compliance and security management SOPs and SOX SOPs.

Various government websites (e.g., http://www.cbp.gov and http://www.bis.doc.gov) present guidelines and benchmarks for creating SOPs. SOPs must be easy to comprehend, comprehensive, and functional and not so restrictive that they impede basic responsibilities in transportation services.

There must be a reasonable compromise between security and compliance that meets regulatory requirements but still allows freight to be moved safely, timely, and cost effectively. A key element in creating, implementing, and ensuring compliance with appropriate SOPs is educating and training the staff.

7.11.8 Training and Education

Training in the following areas is a cornerstone for logistics and purchasing along with compliance and security programs:

- Logistics outsourcing
- Choosing freight forwarders, brokers, and vendors
- Classification
- Valuation
- Recordkeeping
- Red flag management
- Documentation
- SOP development

- Denied parties screening
- Crisis and risk avoidance
- Problem resolution
- Negotiation skill sets
- Purchasing and sourcing management

Education and training are a government benchmark for exercising due diligence and reasonable care.

Three excellent resources for education and training are as follows:

1. National Institute for World Trade (http://www.niwt.org)
2. American Management Association (http://www.ama.net.org)
3. Blue Tiger International (http://www.bluetigerintl.com)

Personnel need to undergo training and retraining every one to three years. Global business practices can change at any time. Refresher courses and continuing education programs are vital best-practice initiatives.

7.11.9 Self-Audit

The goal of the process outlined in the 10 steps is for a corporation to run its global supply chain compliantly and securely on an independent basis. This means that the company can self-audit its import and export operations and be confident that its personnel, SOPs, and operations are in compliance with post-9/11 regulations and competing cost effectively in the marketplace.

7.11.10 ISA Program

One of the many benefits of becoming a member of C-TPAT is the ISA program. In this program, once an importer demonstrates his or her ability to self-audit and self-regulate, CBP will grant it ISA status, which allows the company to regulate itself without day-to-day CBP scrutiny.

7.12 SUMMARY OF THE 10 STEPS

To gain the benefits of ISA status, a company should work through the 10 steps that are outlined in this chapter. The ultimate timing of these steps is not critical.

A company can outline an action plan that spans 1 year, 9 months, 18 months, or whatever works best for its supply chain.

Keep in mind that the government's approach is more concerned with the point of discovery, that is, the actions of the company and its executives from the time that they first become aware that they are nonsecure or noncompliant, than with what happened in the past.

This does not eliminate the consequences of prior history, but it can significantly mitigate them.

Executives have choices in supply chain management activities. If they are reactive to the regulatory climate, they will be slaves to the process, with unknown consequences and uncontrollable costs. However, if they are proactive, they can better control imports and exports and seriously reduce the costs, exposures, fines and penalties, and loss in the supply chain.

8

Closing Remarks

8.1 INTRODUCTION

Global trade is an increasing phenomenon, and it will continue to grow as we move into the second and third decades of the twenty-first century.

Along with this trend is the critical importance of global supply chain management and the impact that it has on overseas purchasing and sourcing.

Senior management in every organization, in every vertical—defense, consumer products, electronics, automotive, pharmaceutical, food, communications, and broadcast, to name a few—recognizes the following:

- The importance of the management of the supply chain on impacting on their company's overall competitiveness.
- The well-managed supply chain can reduce risk and costs in the entire company.
- The supply chain can make the difference in the bottom line and greatly impact profitability.
- The supply chain must be linked into and coordinated with other aspects of the company, particularly sourcing, purchasing, sales, business development, research and development, demand planning, inventory management, and domestic distribution.
- Trade compliance is an important factor that must be weighed into the supply chain decisions.
- Import operations must have a serious influence on all purchasing and sourcing decisions.

Inbound management is the controlling team that will impact how freight moves from the overseas supplier to last-mile delivery systems.

Investment in these people and the resources they need to perform to expectation is an important element of global supply chain and the interface with senior management.

My thoughts and recommendations are strewn throughout this book; in summary, my observations and concluding thoughts are as follows.

Over 35 years of interface with corporate executives engaged in managing the various aspects of global supply chains have led me to observe the following characteristics and practices of successful inbound supply chain managers:

- Think outside the box and are proactive in dealing with anticipated problems.
- Take the time that is necessary to align themselves with quality staffing, consultants, and professional service providers who can maximize the opportunity for the most well-run and most cost-effective operation.
- Reward for excellence staff who not only understand the big picture but also pay attention to detail.
- Comprehend the *business compromise* in two areas:
  1. Price versus service
  2. Long-term gain versus short-term benefit
- Appreciate that sometimes, service benefits can outweigh pricing considerations and that some decisions that now seem short sighted will have longer-term benefits.
- Communicate well to staff, internally throughout the organization, the government (when warranted), vendors, and providers.
- Provide good management and leadership skills.
- Negotiate well.
- Are always assessing risk and finding ways to transfer, mitigate, or eliminate it.
- Are good listeners and use information flow to make better, more informed decisions.
- Are well read and spend at least 5% of their time reviewing websites and reading trade materials and good supply chain publications.
- Belong to at least one to three professional trade organization(s) and participate on a regular basis.
- Believe that a person needs to continually improve his or her business skill sets and continues to learn and grow, both informally and formally.
- Promote education and training to all staff.
- Have the ability to be flexible as the situation warrants.

- Believe that for business professionals to be effective, they have to continually expand and grow.
- Consider responsibility a serious character trait, along with diligence, honesty, and forthrightness.

Follow these thoughts, and mastering the global purchasing, sourcing, and logistics of inbound supply chains will come easier and faster. Best of luck!

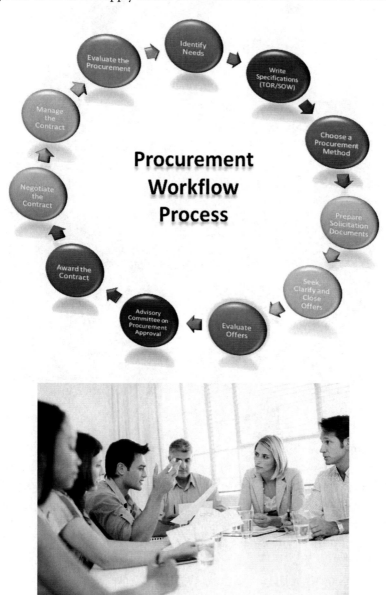

8.2 COMPLIANCE, SECURITY, AND LOGISTICS IN GLOBAL PURCHASING AND SOURCING MANAGEMENT: GOOD MANAGEMENT TRUMPS GOOD LUCK

My business is helping companies compete in world trade, and I have been engaged in this activity since 1971.

While my practice has witnessed change over the past 30 years in how global sales, customer service, and supply chains operate, there remains a basic premise that currently holds true in a post-9/11 compliance and security trading environment.

Call it *Cook's factor*; it is that those firms that are *proactive versus being reactive* in how they deal with the inevitable will do better not only in being successful but also in creating a better foundation to manage global trade-in.

The events of 9/11 and all the regulatory and purchasing environment changes in the past two decades changed how all of us think about compliance, security, and global sourcing.

For starters, it made the American government, led by various agencies like Homeland Security, Customs Border and Protection, the Bureau of Industry and Security (BIS), and the Transportation Security Administration to name a limited few, to more carefully scrutinize the global supply chains affecting trade to and from the United States.

In the past decade, it became very evident to the government that the security of supply chains needed to be prioritized and, more importantly, tightened up. Correspondingly, we have seen a host of new regulations and initiatives. There are the Patriot Act, the Export Administration Act, the Bioterrorism Act, the 24-hour Advanced Manifest Rule, focused assessments, Free and Secure Trade initiatives, and a veritable litany of acronyms like C-TPAT and FAST.

No surprise, some of these have been carefully thought out, and others were more hastily conceived in a kind of administrative *knee-jerk* response. It awaits the test of time to see if compliance with these efforts will work. But, regardless of one's opinion, these new regulations are here, and they affect how we manage our supply chains, which brings me back to Cook's factor.

Those of us engaged in supply chain activities have choices, both as individuals and as corporations, about how we want to respond. If we are *reactive* to the regulatory climate that now prevails, we will be captives to the process with unknown consequences and uncontrollable costs.

By doing only what is required, one risks being limited to minimal standards of acceptability. On the other hand, if we are proactive—if we tailor compliance programs not only to respond to explicit security considerations but also to improve the performance of supply chain processes—we will better control the destinies of our imports and exports and seriously reduce the costs, the exposures, the fines and penalties, and the ultimate loss of the supply chain becoming disabled. Amidst the extensive discussions and analyses of security compliance, there is a more fundamental question running through the conversation: do you choose to run your company by *good luck* or run it by better management? In over 30 years of helping companies compete effectively in importing and exporting, it is clear to me that protecting your supply chain in a post-9/11 world requires proactive preparation.

Those enterprises that are able to assess their situations and then proactively deal with a range of potential impending disruptions are those that do well. On the other hand, companies that seek to falsely economize by cutting corners and being blind to the real-world implications of current events by being reactive to their environments are likely doomed to uncompetitive supply chains, loss of revenue and profits in the short term, and in the long term, even the ability to operate viably.

Here are some vivid examples. Take the hundreds of companies that receive tens of thousands of dollars in fines every year for selling goods to overseas entities that are on the Department of Commerce List of Denied Parties.

They had a choice to be responsible and check the list prior to engaging in the export transaction or get caught and suffer the consequences (fines, loss of revenue, and possible loss of export privileges).

Take the hundreds of companies that are audited by Customs and Border Protection (CBP) that receive millions of dollars in fines and penalties for violating common-practice errors in valuation, recordkeeping, classification, or documentation.

They had a choice to exercise reasonable care and due diligence or suffer the consequences. Take the over 20,000 companies that are eligible to participate in custom's trade program, the Customs–Trade Partnership Against Terrorism (C-TPAT), but have not yet executed their applications.

What will happen to these companies following another terrorist attack? The borders will close for all companies but might only open for those who are C-TPAT certified (meaning those who are not rolling the dice when it comes to their supply chain).

In all fairness, the issues are not simple. I currently see a growing concern among global supply chain executives in how best to deal and manage all these post-9/11 compliance and security regulations and initiatives.

My best *guesstimate* is that a third of them have been proactive, leaving two-thirds either complacent or nonreactive at all. They rely on good luck and not on good management.

The implications for the latter two-thirds strike me as particularly dire.

Radio frequency identification (RFID) is a good example. There is a *charge* being led by many large retailers to have all vendors provide RFID capabilities that interface with their supply chain information technology capability. RFID adds significant cost to the supply chain, specifically to the product unit and the technical infrastructure, to maintain an RFID system.

Many companies are reluctant to make such an investment, particularly in the absence of viable *business models* that can show a return on investment (RoI).

We have studied this matter in the past decade and have identified numerous potential security and compliance benefits to RFID. We have also observed the government agencies (specifically CBP, Coast Guard, and Homeland Security) that are testing RFID advancements to potentially incorporate this technology into the global supply chain security.

In addition, many pharmaceutical companies now believe that RFID can assist them in product trailing and preventing tampering. *Chain-of-custody* issues are addressed in certain RFID scenarios.

In addition, cargo seal manufacturers are working with authorities to see if RFID can provide a better security seal for ocean freight 40' and 20' steamship containers. We believe that there are hidden benefits in terms of supply chain security that provide an added opportunity for RoI, which might not show up in more conventional RoI analyses.

Most professionals feel the window of opportunity to initiate proactive steps to secure that the supply chain remains open—perhaps for another two to three years. By then, however, the probability of disruption is likely and, with it, the rigid control of supply chain activity for noncompliant companies. The year 2015 has seen a lot of terrorist-related events, and authorities are anticipating this to continue into 2016.

As I travel around the country, I see more and more companies recognizing their vulnerabilities and that are primed to engage in compliant security initiatives. That is the good news as the process unfolds.

The *less good news* is that many enterprises remain uncertain on what they should do or how to begin. The National Institute of World Trade (NIWT; http://www.niwt.org) reports an increase in activity and participation in global supply chain areas where supply chain executives are seeking better resources, training, and skill set development so that they can be compliant and secure and run better import and export operations.

The various proactive steps the supply chain executives have initiated in compliance with security regulations have actually enabled their supply chains to run better, more cost effectively, and more responsibly.

Every study we have done suggests that there are certain typical steps in the security compliance process that enable the supply chain not only to be safer but also to operate better. The US government agencies engaged in managing compliance and security all require companies to exercise *due diligence and reasonable care*.

8.3 THE IMPORTANCE OF SELF-AUDIT

The ultimate goal of this whole process outlined in the eight steps is for an enterprise to run its global supply chain compliantly and securely on an independent basis. This means that the company can self-audit import and export operations and feel confident that its personnel, SOPs, and operations will run in accordance with the new millennium of compliance and security regulations.

Customs has put forth an initiative that is called the Importer Self-Assessment (ISA) program.

Upon demonstrating a capacity to self-audit and self-regulate in compliance with US CBP's standards, the firm is granted ISA status. Such status will significantly reduce the extent to which the firm will be scrutinized on a day-to-day basis by customs.

We are observing more companies creating positions in supply chain or import/export compliance and security than at any other time. To facilitate this process, the NIWT offers numerous training and educational programs in global supply chain, trade compliance, and security.

This association teaches the skill sets for personnel who have compliance and security responsibilities and offers instruction to help companies meet the standards of exercising due diligence, reasonable care, and internal training and education.

> As I travel around the country, I see more and more companies recognizing the importance of a better-run global supply chain and their vulnerabilities, and they are now primed to engage in resource development, training, and skill set development initiatives.

Additionally, good management will always win over good luck. And, successful good management always contains the following:

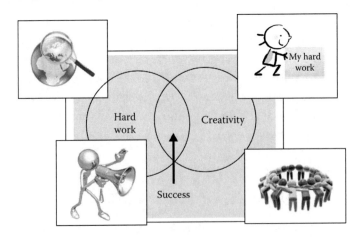

- Hard work
- Innovation and creativity
- Persistence
- Unselfishness
- Discipline
- People skills
- Team initiatives
- Pay attention to detail
- Think globally and act locally
- Great communication skills
- Having fun
- Showing that you care

This book is a good tutorial as a *starting point* and reference guide.

Credits

Kelly Raia
Travis Cook
American Management Association
Foreign-Trade Zone Corporation
Richard Furman
Federal Aviation Administration (FAA)
Transportation Intermediaries Association (TIA)
National Customs Brokers and Forwarders Association of America
Florida Customs Brokers and Forwarders Association
Wikipedia
The various US government agencies that are involved in the global supply chain management: CBP, BIS, OFAC, Departments of the Treasury, State, and Commerce/International Trade Administration (ITA)
American Shipper Magazine
Journal of Commerce
World Trade Magazine

Glossary

Abandonment: Refusing the delivery of a shipment that is so badly damaged in transit, it has little or no value.

Acceptance: An international banking instrument that is known as a time draft or bill of exchange that the drawee has accepted and is unconditionally obligated to pay at maturity.

Ad valorem: A tariff that is calculated based on a percentage of the value of the product.

Advising bank: A bank operating in the exporter's country that handles letters of credit for a foreign bank by notifying the exporter that the credit has been opened in their favor.

Agency for International Development shipments: A US government agency that was created to provide relief to developing countries that must purchase products and services through US companies. Specialized export documentation is necessary to complete the transactions.

All inclusive: A term of sale that is used to notate that *all charges are included.*

All-risk cargo insurance: A clause that is included in marine insurance policies to cover loss and damage from external causes during the course of transit within all the terms and conditions that are agreed to by the underwriters.

Allowance: Typically afforded by a consignee as a credit or deduction on a specific export transaction.

Arbitration: Wording that is included in export contracts introducing an independent third-party negotiator into the dispute resolution in lieu of litigation.

Arrival notice: Advice to a consignee on inbound freight. Sometimes referred to as a prealert. Contains details of the shipment's arrival schedule and the bill of lading data.

As is: An international term denoting that the buyer accepts the goods as is; it is a connotation that there may be something wrong with the merchandise, and the seller limits future potential liability.

Automated Broker Interface: The electronic transmission and exchange of data between a customhouse broker and CBP.

Automated Export Systems: The electronic transmission of the Shipper's Export Declaration to the Census Bureau, the Bureau of Industry and Security, and Customs and Border Protection (CBP).

Automated Manifest System: The electronic transmission of a carrier or vessel's manifest between the carrier or steamship line and CBP.

Balance of trade: The difference between a country's total imports and exports. If the exports exceed the imports, a favorable balance of trade, or trade surplus, exists; if not, a trade deficit exists.

Barter: The direct exchange of goods or services without the use of money as a medium of exchange and without third-party involvement.

Bill of lading: A document that establishes the terms of a contract between a shipper and a transportation company under which freight is to be moved between specified points for a specified charge. It is usually prepared by the shipper on forms that are issued by the carrier; it serves as a document of title, a contract of carriage, and a receipt of goods.

Bond: A form of insurance between two parties obligating a surety to pay against a performance or obligation.

Bonded warehouse: A warehouse that is authorized by customs authorities for storage of goods on which payment of duties is deferred until the goods are cleared and removed.

Breakbulk cargo: Loose cargo that is loaded directly into a conveyance's hold.

Bretton Woods Conference: A meeting under the auspices of the United Nations at Bretton Woods, NH, in 1944, that was held to develop some degree of cooperation in matters of international trade and payments and to devise a satisfactory international monetary system to be in operation after World War II. The particular objectives intended were stable exchange rates and convertibility of currencies for the development of multilateral trade. The Bretton Woods Conference established the International Monetary Fund and the World Bank.

Bunker adjustment fee: Fuel surcharge that is issued by a steamship line.

Bureau of Industry and Security: The Department of Commerce agency that is responsible for Export Administration Regulations, formerly known as the Bureau of Export Administration.

Carnet: A customs document permitting the holder to carry or send merchandise temporarily into certain foreign countries without paying duties or posting bonds.

Certificate of origin: A document that is used to certify the country of origin for a product.

Clingage: When shipping bulk liquids, it is the residue remaining inside the conveyance after discharge.

Combi: An aircraft with pallet or container capacity on its main deck and belly holds.

Commission agent: An individual, a company, or a government agent who serves as the buyer of overseas goods on behalf of another buyer.

Commodity specialist: An official who is authorized by the US Department of the Treasury to determine proper tariff and the value of imported goods.

Consignment: Delivery of merchandise from an exporter (the consignor) to an agent (the consignee) under the agreement that the agent sell the merchandise for the account of the exporter. The consignor retains the title to the goods until the consignee has sold them. The consignee sells the goods for commission and remits the net proceeds to the consignor.

Consolidator: An agent who brings together a number of shipments for one destination to qualify for preferential rates.

Cost, insurance, and freight: A system of valuing imports that includes all the costs, insurance, and freight that are involved in shipping the goods from the port of embarkation to the destination.

Countertrade: The sale of goods or services that are paid for in whole or in part by the transfer of goods or services from a foreign country.

Credit risk insurance: Insurance that is designed to cover the risks of nonpayment for delivered goods.

Currency: National form for payment medium: dollars, pesos, rubles, nairas, pounds, etc.

Distributor: A foreign agent who sells for a supplier directly and maintains an inventory of the supplier's products.

Dock receipt: A documented receipt that the shipment has been received by the steamship line.

Domestic International Sales Corporation (DISC): Established in 1971 by US legislation, DISCs were designed to help exporters by offering income tax deferrals on export earnings. DISCs were phased out in 1984.

Draft: A negotiable instrument that is presented by the buyers' bank for payment.

Drawback: Duties to be refunded by the government when previously imported goods are exported or used in the manufacture of exported products.

Dumping: Exporting or importing merchandise into a country below the costs that are incurred in production and shipment.

Duty: A tax that is imposed on imports by the customs authority of a country. Duties are generally based on the value of the goods (*ad valorem* duties), some other factor such as weight or quantity (specified duties), or a combination of value and other factors (compounded duties).

Embargo: A prohibition on imports or exports as a result of a political eventuality.

European Community (EC): The 12 nations of Europe that have combined to form the world's largest single market of more than 320 million consumers. The EC includes Belgium, Denmark, France, Greece, Ireland, Italy, Luxembourg, the Netherlands, Portugal, Spain, the United Kingdom, and West Germany.

Ex works from factory: The buyer accepts goods at the point of origin and assumes all the responsibility for the transportation of the goods that are sold. Also ex warehouse, ex mine, and ex factory as defined in INCOTerms.

Export: To send or transport goods out of a country for sale in another country. In international sales, the exporter is usually the seller or the seller's agent.

Export–Import Bank of the United States (Ex–Im Bank): Ex–Im Bank facilitates and aids the financing of exports of US goods and services through a variety of programs that are created to meet the needs of the US exporting community. The programs, which are tailored to the size of a transaction, can take the form of direct lending or loan guarantees.

Export management company: A private company that serves as the export department for several manufacturers, soliciting and transacting export business on behalf of its clients in return for a commission, salary, or retainer plus commission.

Export trading company: An organization that is designed to facilitate the export of goods and services. It can be a trade intermediary that provides export-related services to producers or can be established by the producers themselves, though typically, export trading companies do not take title to goods.

Fair trade: A concept of international trade in which some barriers are tolerable as long as they are equitable. When the barriers are eliminated, there should be reciprocal action by all parties.

Force majeure: Expressed as *acts of God*. Conditions that are found in some marine contracts exempting certain parties from liability for occurrences that are out of their control, such as earthquakes and floods.

Foreign Corrupt Practices Act of 1977: US legislation with stringent anti-bribery provisions and guidelines for recordkeeping and internal accounting control requirements for all publicly held corporations. The act makes it illegal to offer, pay, or agree to pay money or any item of value to a foreign official for the purpose of getting or retaining business.

Foreign Credit Insurance Association: An insurance program, previously government managed and underwritten, now privately held, that insures commercial and political risks for US exporters.

Foreign sales agent: An individual or company that serves as the foreign representative of a domestic supplier and seeks sales abroad for the supplier.

Forfaiting: The selling, at a discount, of a longer-term receivable or the promissory note of a buyer.

Franchising: A form of licensing by the service sector for companies that want to export their trademark, methods, or personal services.

Free alongside ship: A system of valuing imports that includes inland transportation costs that are involved in the delivery of goods to a port in the exporting country but excludes the cost of ocean shipping, insurance, and the cost of loading the merchandise on the vessel.

Free domicile: Terminology that is used for *door-to-door* deliveries.

Free on board: A system of valuing imports that includes inland transportation costs that are involved in the delivery of goods to a port in the exporting country and the cost of loading the merchandise on the vessel, but excludes the cost of ocean shipping and insurance.

Free port: An area, such as a port city, into which merchandise may legally be moved without payment of duties.

Free trade: A theoretical concept to describe international trade that is unhampered by governmental barriers such as tariffs or nontariff measures. Free trade typically favors the reduction or elimination of all tariff and nontariff barriers to trade.

Free trade zone: A port that is designated by the government of a country for the duty-free entry of any nonprohibited goods. Merchandise may be stored, displayed, or used for manufacturing within the zone and reexported without the payment of duties.

Freight all kinds: A mix of cargoes traveling as one.

General Agreement on Tariffs and Trade: A multilateral treaty to which 85 nations (or more than 80% of world trade) subscribe; it is designed to reduce trade barriers and promote trade through tariff concessions, thereby contributing to global economic growth and development.

Generalized System of Preferences (GSP): Notes duty-free/reduced tariffs on imports from the countries that are listed on the GSP list.

Harmonized Tariff System of the United States: A system of classifying products that are imported into the United States by number.

Harter Act: Legislation protecting a shipowner from certain types of claims that are due to the actions of the crew.

Hazmat: Hazardous materials that are regulated by various government agencies: Department of Transportation/Code of Federal Regulations Title 49, International Air Transportation Association, Internal Market and Consumer Protection, Coast Guard, etc. Personnel who interface with hazmat cargoes need to be certified to do so.

Hedging: A mechanism that allows an exporter to take a position in a foreign currency to protect against losses due to wide fluctuations in currency exchange rates.

Hold: The space below the deck inside an ocean-going vessel.

In bond: Transportation of merchandise under the custody of a bonded carrier.

International Air Transportation Association: The agency that regulates and promotes safe, reliable, secure, and economical air services for travelers and air freight.

Irrevocable letter of credit: A letter of credit in which the specified payment is guaranteed by the bank if all the terms and conditions are met by the drawee (buyer). *See also* revocable letter of credit.

ISO 9000: Issued in 1987 by the International Organization for Standardization, ISO 9000 is a series of five international standards that establish the requirements for the quality control systems of companies selling goods in the EC. It now includes many additional countries and companies throughout the world.

Joint venture: A business undertaking in which more than one company shares ownership and control.

Letter of credit: A document that is issued by a bank per instructions from a buyer of goods who authorizes the seller to draw a specified sum of money under specified terms, usually on the receipt by the bank of certain documents within a given period of time.

Licensing: A business arrangement in which the manufacturer of a product (or a company with proprietary rights over certain technology, trademarks, etc.) grants permission to some other group or individual to manufacture that product (or make use of that proprietary material) in return for specified royalties or other payment.

Logistics: The science of transportation covering the planning and implementation of specific strategies to move materials at a desired cost.

Mala fide: Misrepresentation or in bad faith.

Maquiladora: A tax-free program allowing the import of materials into Mexico for the manufacturing of goods for export back to the United States. Now declining in importance as a result of the North American Free Trade Agreement.

Marine insurance: Insurance covering loss or damage of goods during transit. It covers all modes of transport.

Market research: Specific intelligence about the market in which a seller proposes to sell goods or services. This information is gathered through interviews, commissioned surveys, and direct contact with potential customers or their representatives.

Marks and numbers: The references that are made in writing to identify a shipment on the exterior packing, typically referenced in the documentation.

North American Free Trade Agreement: An agreement that creates a single unified market of the United States, Canada, and Mexico.

Office of Foreign Asset Controls: The Department of the Treasury office issuing regulations on transfers/funding of money.

Open account: A trade arrangement in which goods are shipped to a foreign buyer without guarantee of payment. The obvious risk this method poses to the supplier makes it essential that the buyer's integrity be unquestioned.

Outsourcing: Transferring the location of manufacturing to a foreign location but transferring all or most control of the manufacturing process to a foreign entity.

Overseas Private Investment Corporation: A government-sponsored organization that promotes investment in plans and equipment in less developed countries by offering guarantees that are comparable to the Ex–Im Bank.

Paperless release: The electronic release of a shipment by CBP prior to hard copies being presented.

Political risk: In exporting, the risk of loss due to such causes as currency inconvertibility, government action preventing the entry of goods, expropriation, confiscation, or war.

Power of attorney: A document that authorizes a customs broker or a freight forwarder to act on the exporter's or importer's behalf on issues that are relative to customs clearance, transportation, documentation, etc.

Premium: Insurance dollars that are paid to an underwriter to accept a transfer of risk.

Prima facie: At face value.

Pro forma invoice: (1) Invoice that is prepared by the supplier to the buyer, usually as a means to secure financing. (2) Invoice that is prepared by an importer when the supplier's invoice does not meet the invoice requirements that are set forth by CBP.

Protectionism: The setting of trade barriers that is high enough to discourage foreign imports or to raise the prices sufficiently to enable relatively inefficient domestic producers to compete successfully with foreign producers.

Purchasing agent: An individual or a company that purchases goods in their own country on behalf of foreign importers, such as government agencies or large private concerns.

Remarketers: Export agents, merchants, or foreign trading companies that purchase products from an exporter to resell them under their own name.

Revocable letter of credit: A letter of credit that can be canceled or altered by the drawee (buyer) after it has been issued by the drawee's bank. Compared to an irrevocable letter of credit, which is totally binding without both parties' written agreement.

SOP: Standard operating procedure. Written guidelines on how corporate affairs are managed following consistent ideology, wording, and focus.

Sourcing: Transferring the location of manufacturing to a foreign location but maintaining all or some control over the ownership of the manufacturing process.

Tariff: A tax on imports or the rate at which imported goods are taxed.

Terminal handling charge: The fee that is assessed by a terminal for handling a shipment.

Time draft: A draft that matures in a certain number of days, either from the acceptance or date of draft.

Tracking: A forwarder's or carrier's system of recording the movement intervals of shipments from origin to final destination.

Trade acceptance: *See* acceptance.

Transfer risk: The risk that is associated with converting a local foreign currency into US dollars.

Transmittal letter: Cover communication outlining the details of an export transaction and its accompanying documentation.

Twenty-foot equivalent (TEU): Twenty-foot equivalent or the standard measure for a 20-foot ocean freight container. Two TEUs represent one 40-foot standard container.

Ullage: Measuring the amount of liquid or dry bulk freight in the hold of a vessel by measuring the height of the stow from the opening on deck.

Uniform Customs and Practice: International rules governing documentation collections.

US Agency for International Development: A US government agency that carries out assistance programs that are designed to help the people of certain lesser developed countries cultivate their human and economic resources, increase production capacities, improve the quality of human life, and promote economic or potential stability in friendly countries.

Value-added tax: An indirect tax that is assessed on the increase in the value of goods from the raw material stage to the production process to final consumption. The tax to processors or merchants is levied on the amount by which they have increased the value of items that they purchased for use or resale. This system is used in the EC.

Vigilance: Ensuring safety.

Warehouse receipt: A receipt that is given to signify that goods have been received into a warehouse.

Weight breaks: Discounts to freight charges are given as the total weight increases at various weight breaks: 50 pounds, 100 pounds, 500 pounds, etc.

Wharfage: Charges that are assessed for handling freight near a dock or pier.

With average: A marine insurance term meaning that the shipment is protected from partial damage whenever the damage exceeds an agreed percentage.

Zone: Freight tariffs are often determined by certain geographic areas that are called zones.

Appendix

- Import Regulations Reference Guide
- Guidance on Reexports
- FDA Enforcement
- Tips for New Importers and Exporters
- Managing the North American Free Trade Agreement United States/ Canada/Mexico
- Outline of Terrorism Act of 2002
- Advance Manifest Rules for Cargo Information: "2-Hour Rule," "24-Hour Rule," etc.

IMPORT REGULATIONS REFERENCE GUIDE

Bureau of Customs and Border Protection

Profile

- Established in 1789 by the second act of the First Congress and is older than the Department of the Treasury (DoT), of which it is a part.
- Principal source of revenue for the United States during its first 125 years of existence: 95%–99% of the total government revenue.
- Currently provides the nation with the secondary source of revenue, calculated at an estimated $22.1 billion to the DoT for fiscal year 2003.
- Administers the laws, executive orders, and presidential proclamations governing the importation of merchandise and baggage and the collection of duties and taxes thereon.
- The entry, clearance, and report of arrival and the unloading of vessels, vehicles, and aircraft.
- The prevention and detection of smuggling operations and the seizure of merchandise, vehicles, and vessels that are involved.
- The exclusion of entry-prohibited articles.
- The control of imports that are subject to established quotas.

- The verification of import statistics for the Bureau of Census.
- The administrative imposition and collection of penalties for violations of laws, including the granting of administrative relief under certain conditions.

Department of Homeland Security

The newly established Department of Homeland Security (DHS) has brought together 22 different government agencies under a sweeping reorganization. The US Customs Service has been incorporated into the DHS after 213 years of existence under the DoT.

While retaining the oversight of commercial processing of merchandise into the commerce of the United States and the revenue collection tasks that are associated with the collection of duties and taxes, customs will now become increasingly responsible for Homeland Security under the new name of the Bureau of Customs and Border Protection (http://www.cbp.gov).

Organizational Structure

The CBP territory of the United States consists of 50 states, the District of Columbia, and Puerto Rico. CBP is an agency under the DoT, headquartered in Washington, D.C.

Staff of the Commissioner of Customs

Assistant Commissioners

In an effort to disseminate hands-on expertise throughout, the CBP created five strategic trade centers to handle major trade issues, including fraud; antidumping; and the protection of patents, trademarks, and copyrights:

Chicago: Canada and NAFTA
Dallas/Ft. Worth: Mexico and NAFTA
Los Angeles: autos and parts
Miami: production equipment and critical equipment
New York: textile and steel

Twenty management centers oversee management functions for CBP-specific port office locations. Each port office location will have the authority to initiate a full CBP investigation or audit proceedings against any importer. CBP has increased its control and expertise throughout the United States.

The restructuring took place as of CBP fiscal year 1996 to update the CBP to look and operate like a modern private-sector organization. This restructuring abolished the management functions of 7 regional offices and 42 district offices and divided those responsibilities among the five strategic trade centers and the 20 CBP management centers.

Management Centers

Mid America: CMC/Chicago
East Texas: CMC/Houston
West Texas: CMC/El Paso
Southern California: CMC/San Diego
Mid Pacific: CMC/San Francisco
North Pacific: CMC/Portland
South Pacific: CMC/Los Angeles
South Florida: CMC/Miami
West Great Lakes: CMC/Detroit
South Texas: CMC/Laredo
Arizona: CMC/Tucson
Northwest Great Plains: CMC Seattle
New York: CMC/New York
Mid Atlantic: CMC/Baltimore
Puerto Rico/Virgin Islands: CMC/San Juan
North Florida: CMC/Tampa
North Atlantic: CMC/Boston
East Great Lakes: CMC/Buffalo
South Atlantic: CMC/Atlanta
Gulf-CMC/New Orleans

Import Regulatory Issues

- Duty rates decrease on average every year, creating a downward trend in the collection of duties and taxes.
- Anticipated revenue collection from fines and penalties associated with customs audits offset this decrease in the collection of duties and taxes.

The Modernization Act of 1993 is a congressional act that outlined and redefined current regulations and introduced new legislation in reference to the importer's responsibilities. It introduced a warning before audit enforcement for future CBP aggression toward increased compliance levels.

Phase I

- *Informed compliance.* The legal responsibility of an importer to seek formal training on import rules and regulatory issues, which will allow the importer to elevate the level of education and knowledge necessary to demonstrate reasonable care over their import transactions

Phase II

- *Enforced compliance.* The legal responsibility of CBP to enforce the rules and regulations established in the Customs Federal Regulations and defined in the Modernization Act of 1993

Focused Assessment

CBP has endorsed the focused assessment approach as a more effective means in the audit process. Rather than a detailed sampling of over 100 files per importer combined with a wide range of scrutiny that is contained in most compliance assessment audits, CBP will focus on key areas of compliance. This approach categorizes the importer as a high-risk importer or a low-risk importer.

- Valuation
- Classification
- Recordkeeping
- Internal controls and supervision
- Generalized System for Preferences (GSP) declarations
- American Goods/Repair and Return Declarations

Reasonable Care

Reasonable care is defined as the degree of care that a person of ordinary prudence would exercise in the same or similar circumstances. It is the legal responsibility of the importer and the importer's agent (customs broker) to use reasonable care in entering merchandise. It is the responsibility of CBP to fix the final classification and value. This standard was mandated by the Customs Modernization Act and passed into law on December 8, 1993.

Meeting Reasonable Care Standards

Importer

The reasonable care standards that apply to the importer are as follows:

- Consult with qualified experts such as customs brokers, consultants, and attorneys specializing in customs law.
- Seek guidance from CBP through the formal binding ruling program.
- If using a broker, the importer must provide the broker with full and complete information that is sufficient for the broker to make a proper entry (import declaration) or for the broker to provide advice on how to make an entry.
- Obtain analysis from accredited laboratories to determine the technical qualities of imported merchandise.
- Use in-house employees who have experience and knowledge of CBP regulations and procedures.
- Follow any binding rulings that are received from CBP.
- Ensure that products are legally marked with the country of origin to indicate to the ultimate purchaser the origin of imported products.
- Cannot classify own identical merchandise or value own identical merchandise in different ways.
- Must notify CBP when receiving different treatment by CBP for the same goods on different entries or different ports.
- Must examine entries (Import Declaration CF 3461) that are prepared by the broker to determine the accuracy in classification and valuation.

Penalty   The penalty for importer failure to meet reasonable care standards is domestic value or twice the duty, whichever is less. If duty free, the penalty is calculated at 20% of the value.

Broker

The reasonable care standards that apply to the broker are as follows:

- Considered an expert and thus must give competent advice.
- Must exercise due diligence to ascertain the correctness of information imparted to a client.
- Shall not knowingly impart to client false information relative to any customs business.

- Shall not withhold information from a client who is entitled to that information.
- Must establish internal procedures to limit the advice being given by qualified licensed individuals.
- Must obtain and receive directly from importer complete and accurate information sufficient to make entry or to provide proper advice.

Penalty   The penalty for a broker not meeting reasonable care standards is $30,000 per violation as provided for in 19 USC 1641 (the section of the law governing customs brokers).

Ten Steps toward Import Compliance

1. *Internal supervision and control.* Importers of record are responsible for the development and maintenance of internal standard operating procedures (SOPs), which directly relate to the customs clearance declaration process. A standardized measure must be in place to control the correctness of information being tendered to CBP and all other government agencies in relation to entering the commerce of the United States. These SOPs should monitor all the communications that are made on behalf of the importer of record in reference to all clearances, by both the broker and importer.
2. *Harmonized classification.* Importers are responsible to ensure that every harmonized number declared on the import declaration is accurate based on the guidelines that are established in the Harmonized Tariff Schedule of the United States. Importers are also responsible to know the principles of classification to monitor and control the advice that is tendered by third-party service providers such as customhouse brokers.
3. *Global security management Customs–Trade Partnership Against Terrorism (C-TPAT) participation.* A nationwide invitation has been sent to the importing community for voluntary participation in the C-TPAT. There are significant advantages to voluntary participation that will expedite the customs clearance process. Management of import supply chain security procedures is a crucial part of the participation process. Development and enhancement demonstrating control measures that effectively monitor the safeguarding of cargo entering the commerce of the United States are the goal.

4. *Commercial invoice requirements.* Commercial invoice requirements, as established in the CFR 19 Part 141.86, is a major concern for CBP. The invoice drives the international shipment and clearance procedures. Misleading, and misstatement of, facts could circumvent governing authorities and result in major devastation of domestic property and even lives. Correct import declaration reporting information is founded on the contents of the invoice. Every importer is bound by basic bond conditions under CFR 113.62 to provide complete entry and entry declaration information.

5. *Duty payment management.* Every importer's first bond condition is to pay duties, fees, and taxes on a timely basis. It is the importer's responsibility to establish and verify that all the duties, fees, and taxes are being submitted in accordance with CFR 19113.62(a).

6. *Informed compliance.* It is the responsibility of every importer, as established in the Customs Modernization Act of 1993, to meet and maintain *informed compliance* standards of increased and current education and training on industry-specific topics that are associated with the duties and responsibilities of importers of record.

7. *Record retention.* Importers of record are responsible to establish a record retention system that maintains all records relative to an import transaction for five years from the date of entry of the merchandise into the commerce of the United States.

8. *Valuation.* Importers of record are responsible to ensure that proper valuation principles are applied to each import transaction and subsequent declaration, as outlined in the CFR Pt 152. Falsely declared values corrupt trade statistics and possibly defraud the government out of revenue. Valuation verifications and the knowledge of valuation principles are crucial to safeguarding your company from unforeseen CBP penalties for misstatement of valuation facts.

9. *Country of origin marking.* Importers are responsible to ensure that all merchandise is properly marked upon entry into the United States, as referenced in the CFR 19 part 134. Documentation must also indicate the proper country of origin on all shipments.

10. *Power of attorney management.* All importers should properly manage the number of customs brokers who are conducting customs business on their behalf. It is imperative that proper control be established and maintained to ensure that only qualified persons are presenting all declarations.

REFERENCES

CBP: http://www.cbp.gov
Customs Federal Regulations CFR title 19
Harmonized Tariff Schedule of the United States 2005

Customs–Trade Partnership Against Terrorism

The Customs–Trade Partnership Against Terrorism (C-TPAT) is a joint effort by CBP and the trade community to raise the level of security that is associated with the import and export supply chain of merchandise to and from the United States.

Every importer, exporter, manufacturer, customs broker, non-vessel operating common carrier, and warehouse proprietor should join this partnership in a proactive effort to raise the bar on security standards in the United States. Some of the benefits of participations are a decrease in the delay of imported cargo because of examinations, no in-house CBP audits that are performed on C-TPAT members, and a more efficient import supply chain process.

Care should be exercised in the application process to ensure that complete statements of facts are given in the partnership questionnaire and application process.

Importers' Self-Assessment Program

A privilege is offered to C-TPAT members that contains the opportunity for an importer to perform a self-analysis of adherence to compliance standards and provide the findings to CBP for review. This process could dramatically minimize in-house CBP presence in the overall focused assessment process. Importers are encouraged to seek the professional assistance of qualified individuals to perform and/or aid in the self-assessment process.

Global Security Awareness

As a result of the events of September 11, 2001, CBP has implemented plans to increase awareness of global security issues. The realization that information was being received after merchandise had already arrived in the United States prompted several new initiatives. In December 2002,

CBP established the requirement that carriers submit a cargo manifest to CBP 24 hours before lading on the vessel in a program that is titled the 24-Hour Advanced Manifest Rule for ocean shipments, the Wheels-Up or 4-Hour Advanced Manifest Rule for air shipments, and the 2-Hour Advanced Manifest Rule for ground transportation. CBP has posted personnel at foreign ports to screen high-risk containers before they are shipped, as part of the Container Security Initiative. CBP has also invested significantly in new detection technology for increased cargo screening both abroad and in the United States.

Effective Import Compliance Management

To maintain the flow of goods into the United States, it is important to create SOPs that will reflect a focus on customs compliance and security.

Import Process Objectives

The critical import process objectives are as follows:

- Strategically planned
- Efficient
- Compliant
- Secure

Security background investigations and cargo security validations should be incorporated into the entire import supply chain process.

Container Security Initiative

The Container Security Initiative (CSI) is a program to significantly enhance the security of the world's maritime trading system. By working together, we can jointly achieve far greater security for maritime shipping than by working independently. Recognizing that trade is vital to the world economy, CBP has proposed the four-part program that is designed to achieve the objective of a more secure maritime trade environment while accommodating the need for efficiency in global commerce. A critical element in the success of this program will be the availability of advance information to perform sophisticated targeting using risk management principles.

The four core elements of the CSI are as follows:

1. Using automated information to identify and target high-risk containers
2. Prescreening those containers identified as high risk before they arrive at US ports
3. Using detection technology to quickly prescreen high-risk containers
4. Using smarter, tamper-proof containers

The CSI program is quickly being adopted by mega seaports in Asia, Europe, and elsewhere in the world. Currently, the world's top 20 seaports have joined CBP in the CSI to protect global commerce from terrorist threats. The following facts demonstrate the importance of the work of CBP in this area:

- The volume of trade moving throughout the nation's 102 seaports has nearly doubled since 1995.
- In 2001, CBP processed more than 214,000 vessels and 5.7 million sea containers.
- Approximately 90% of the world's cargo moves by container.
- Globally, over 48 million full cargo containers move between major seaports each year.
- Each year, more than 16 million containers arrive in the United States by ship, truck, and rail.
- CBP processed 25 million entries in 2001.
- More than $1.2 trillion in imported goods passed through the nation's 301 ports of entry in 2001.
- Almost half of incoming US trade (by value) arrives by ship.

Advanced Manifest Notification Programs

24-Hour Advanced Manifest Notification

The 24-Hour Advanced Manifest Rule provides CBP with a window of 24 hours "prior to the loading of a foreign vessel" to review automated manifest information to make prescreening determinations that are related to examination of merchandise.

Wheels Up or 4-Hour Advanced Notification

The Wheels Up or 4-Hour Advanced Manifest rules require that an air shipment manifest be electronically reported to CBP at the time that the flight is wheels up or at least 4 hours before the arrival of the shipments landing into the first US port of importation.

2-Hour Advanced Notification for Ground and Rail Shipments

This prearrival notification of manifest must be transmitted to CBP at least 2 hours before the arrival of a ground transportation or rail shipment across a US border.

Valuation Verification

CIF(CIP) 5   Cost of merchandise 1 Insurance 1 Prepaid Freight.
CF 5   Cost of merchandise 1 Prepaid Freight.
FoB(FCA) 5   Cost of merchandise Dutiable Value (7501 column 33).
FAS 5   Free alongside carrier 2 Cost of merchandise alongside the export carrier.
Ex works(Ex factory) 5   Cost of merchandise at shipper warehouse.

The objective is to arrive at the FoB(FCA) value in all cases.
Prepaid freight and insurance are nondutiable charges 5 NDC.
All NDCs can be deducted from the CIP(CIF), CF terms of sale to arrive at the correct FoB value.

- FAS, ex works are below the FoB value amount. There may exist values that must be added to these amounts to bring them up to an acceptable level as a true FoB value.
- Packing charges, if not already included in the invoice value, must be added to the value.
- Foreign loading and handling charges in the case of FAS terms of sale must be added.
- Assist values must be added to the terms of sale regardless of the terms.

For additional information, review CFR 152 in the CBP regulations.

Methods of Valuation

- *Transaction value.* The price actually paid or payable between a buyer and seller of imported merchandise.
- *Transaction value of identical or similar.* The price paid or payable between another buyer and another seller on merchandise that is entered at or around the same time, from the same region of the world, used on a separate importation for valuation purposes only (fair market value concept).
- *Deductive value.* The price after importation and US resale minus all nondutiable charges that are calculated back toward an acceptable value for customs purposes.
- *Computed value.* The sum of the cost of the merchandise including raw materials, labor, production, and assembly, generally added together as a computed valuation for customs purposes.
- *Value if no other value can be determined.* CBP will appraise a value based on general industry knowledge without the benefit of specifics; an educated guess of the value.

Commissions

- *Selling commission.* Commission that is paid as a condition of the sale or from the sale; dutiable commission.
- *Buying commission.* Commission that is paid, not as a condition of sale; a true buying agent will receive payment regardless of the existence of the sale; nondutiable commission.

Customs Powers of Attorney

Importer of record. A person or party who is responsible for duties, fees, taxes, and penalties as a result of imported goods entering the United States.

- *Customs broker.* A person or party who is licensed by the DoT to conduct customs business on behalf of an importer of record.
- *Bureau of Customs and Border Protection.* The enforcement agency that administers the laws governing the importation of merchandise, baggage, and collection of duties thereon.

All customs brokers must have a valid power of attorney to conduct customs business on behalf of an importer of record. The penalty for conducting customs business on behalf of an importer without a valid power of attorney (PoA) is an amount up to the value of the merchandise for each transaction and/or loss of the broker's license.

PoA

The PoA extends the authority to a broker to become an extension of the traffic department of the importer. Caution must be exercised when executing a PoA.

Revocation

All PoAs should be dated with a date of expiration as a supervision and control issue. A letter of revocation to the Port Director of Customs stating an importer's request to revoke a previously issued PoA will be in effect on the date that CBP receives the request.

IRS #_____

CUSTOMS POWER OF ATTORNEY
Check the appropriate box.

_____ Individual
_____ Partnership
_____ Corporation
_____ Sole Proprietorship

KNOW ALL MEN BY THESE PRESENTS: That _____
_____
(Full name of person, partnership, corporation, or sole proprietorship [Identify]) a corporation doing business under the laws of the State of ____
_____
____ or a _____ doing business as
_____
residing at _____
having an office and place of business at _____
_____
_____ hereby constitutes and appoints each of the following
persons: _____
_____

Customs Brokerage Service Provider

as a true and lawful agent and attorney of the grantor named above for and in the name, place, and stead of said grantor from this date and in all

Customs Districts, and in no other name, to make, endorse, sign, declare, or swear to any entry, withdrawal, declaration, certificate, bill of lading, carnet, or other document that is required by law or regulation in connection with the importation, transportation, or exportation of any merchandise that is shipped or consigned by or to said grantor; to perform any act or condition that may be required by law or regulation in connection with such merchandise; and to receive any merchandise that is deliverable to said grantor.

To make endorsements on bills of lading conferring the authority to transfer title, make entry or collect drawback, and to make, sign, declare, or swear to any statement, supplemental statement, schedule, supplemental schedule, certificate of delivery, certificate of manufacture, certificate of manufacture and delivery, abstract of manufacturing records, declaration of proprietor on drawback entry, declaration of exporter on drawback entry, or any other affidavit or document that may be required by law or regulation for drawback purposes, regardless of whether such bill of lading, sworn statement, schedule, certificate, abstract, declaration, or other affidavit or document is intended for filing in any customs district;

To sign, seal, and deliver for and as the act of said grantor any bond that is required by law or regulation in connection with the entry or withdrawal of imported merchandise or merchandise exported with or without benefit of drawback, or in connection with the entry, clearance, lading, unlading or navigation of any vessel or other means of conveyance that is owned or operated by said grantor, and any and all bonds that may be voluntarily given and accepted under applicable laws and regulations, consignee's and owner's declarations that are provided for in section 485, Tariff Act of 1930, as amended, or affidavits in connection with the entry of merchandise;

To sign and swear to any document and to perform any act that may be necessary or required by law or regulation in connection with the entering, clearing, lading, unlading, or operation of any vessel or other means of conveyance that is owned or operated by said grantor;

To authorize other Customs Brokers to act as grantor's agent; to receive, endorse, and collect checks that are issued for Customs duty refunds in grantor's name that is drawn on the Treasurer of the United States; if the grantor is a nonresident of the United States, to accept the service of process on behalf of the grantor;

And generally, to transact at the customhouses in any district any and all customs business, including the making, signing, and filing of protests under section 514 of the Tariff Act of 1930, in which said grantor is or may be concerned or interested and which may properly be transacted or performed by an agent and attorney, giving to said agent and attorney full power and authority to do anything whatever requisite and necessary to be done in the premises as fully as the said grantor could do if present and acting, hereby ratifying and confirming all that the said agent and attorney shall lawfully do by virtue of these presents; the foregoing power of attorney to remain in full force and effect until the ____ day of ____, 20 ___ , or until the notice of revocation in writing is duly given to and received by a District Director of Customs. If the donor of this power of attorney is a partnership, the said power shall in no case have any force or effect after the expiration of two years from the date of its execution.

IN WITNESS WHEREOF, the said _____

Has caused these presents to be sealed and signed:

(Signature) _____

(Capacity) _____ (Date) _____

WITNESS:

_____

(Corporate seal)

Customs Power of Attorney Completion Instructions

IRS # _____ Please input your company IRS # for the entity acting as importer of record.

Know all men by these presents that _____

_____ Please state the full name of the importer of record who is issuing the customs power of attorney.

A corporation doing business under the laws and the state of _____

_____ Please input the state in which your corporation filed for its corporate status.

Doing business as _____ Only to be completed if there is a dba name under which the importer conducts import business.

Residing at _____ Only to be completed if the importer is doing business from their home address.

Having an office and a place of business at _____

_____

Please state the full business address for the importer of record. Hereby constitutes and appoints the following persons: _____

_____

Please input the name of the Customs Broker that the importer of record is granting the customs power of attorney to. If this field is completed, please verify that this company is the same company under which you intend to represent you in your customs business affairs.

Has caused these presents to be sealed and signed _____

_____

Must be signed by a corporate officer of the importer of record.

Capacity _____ Title of the corporate officer who signed the PoA.

Date _____ This is the date that you want the power of attorney to go into effect.

Please sign and return the fax copy and note that the original will be sent in the mail to your attention. Also, please endorse it and return it to The Alston Group as soon as possible to keep within the regulations.

Certificate of Registration

The certificate of registration is a documentary tool that allows merchandise to be exported from the United States and return to the United States without the payment of duty, on the value previously exported. Certificates of registration are originally intended for foreign commodities, yet may also prove valuable for American-made products returning to the United States without proof of US manufacture status. Articles are subject to examination before exportation and reimportation. Any value added to merchandise while outside the United States is dutiable upon return to the United States.

It is to the exporter's advantage to utilize the privilege of a certificate of registration if there is a 1% chance that the merchandise will return to the United States. Certificate of registrations are completed on a CF 4455.

Foreign Shipper's Repair/Manufacturer's Affidavit

A foreign shipper's repair affidavit is a documentary tool that is used by importers to declare to the United States the actual repair, further manufacturing, and added value to an imported item that was previously exported and now being returned. This document is prepared on the foreign shipper's letterhead. It should contain the following information:

- Name and address of the shipper or manufacturer
- Detailed description of the commodity

- Valuation itemized listing of values added due to repair, alteration, or further processing
- Date received into the commerce of the shipper's or manufacturer's country
- Value declared upon receipt of merchandise before repair, alteration, or manufacturing
- Name of responsible person with knowledge of the pertinent facts of the shipment

This document may be used when an exporter has failed to register merchandise before export as an alternative privilege. Customs will accept this in lieu of the certificate of registration, though the first preference is a CF 4455 registration with an opportunity to examine merchandise prior to export.

Importation and Customs Clearance Process

1. Prefile privileges
   a. *Air Shipment—Wheels Up Policy.* The broker can present or transmit customs entry import declaration to CBP when the airlines has certified that the cargo has physically left the ground in the country of export.
   b. *Ocean Shipment—5-Day Policy.* The broker can present or transmit the customs entry import declaration to CBP five days before the arrival of the importing vessel or carrier.
   c. *Documentary requirements.* The broker can submit faxes or photocopies of the original import documentation for most import shipments. Original documents may be requested for certain special classes of merchandise (textiles, quota items, restricted merchandise requiring commodity specialist review, etc.).
2. The right to make entry
   a. Every importer has the right to make entry, the right to import the merchandise into the commerce of the United States for consumption for its own use or for sale. The consumption entry is the most common type of importation into the commerce of the United States.
      i. *Section 1321 sample shipment exemption.* Merchandise valued under $200, and meeting sample definitions, is exempt from entry requirements.

    ii. *Informal entries.* Merchandise not exceeding $2000 is eligible for informal entry procedures.

    iii. *Formal consumption entries.* Merchandise valued over $2000 must be entered under a formal consumption entry.

3. Privileged entries
    a. *Temporary importation entry.* Merchandise entered into the United States temporarily without the payment of duties for a period not to exceed one year.
    b. *Bonded warehouse entries.* Merchandise imported and stored in a customs bonded warehouse for a period of five years from the date of importation without the payment of duties, fees, or taxes. Duties are paid when the goods are withdrawn from the warehouse for consumption.
    c. *In-bond entries.* The transportation of merchandise not yet cleared through customs authority from one bonded location to another customs bonded location. There are three main types of in bond entries, as follows:
        i. Immediate transportation (IT)
        ii. Transportation and exportation (TE)
        iii. Immediate exportation (IE)

Import Declaration

Import declaration (entry) is a two-part process.

Part I: Release Phase (Customs Form 3461)

Filing of documentation or the electronic transmission of information to determine whether the merchandise may be released from CBP custody can be done by any of the following ways:

- Before arrival (prefile)
- Upon take off of aircraft (wheels up)
- Five days before the arrival of the ocean carrier
- After arrival of the importing conveyance

Release status notification is as follows:

- *Paperless release.* No entry documentation needs to be presented. Examination of cargo not required.

- *Entry documents required (EDR) declaration.* CF 3461, invoice, packing list, bond, etc., must be submitted to CBP for further review.
- *General examination/conditional release.* After EDR, no examination required, and shipment can be released.
- *Intensive examination.* CBP examination required. Release authorized after intensive examination if applicable.

Part II: Duty Payment

Duty payment takes place as follows:

- By electronic transfer (Automated Clearing House) from broker's or importer's bank account.
- By check directly from importer to CBP or broker to CBP.

Entry Summary Filing   Entry summary must be filed and duty paid by the tenth business day from the date of release under Part I. Failure to do so may result in liquidated damages (penalty) against the importer. The amount of the penalty is determined as follows:

Unrestricted merchandise 5 Value 1 Duties 1 Fees 1 Taxes
Restricted merchandise 5 Three times the import value

Liquidation   Liquidation is determined by the final computation or ascertainment by CBP of regular and special duties accruing on an entry. To protest, a formal disagreement with a CBP decision is to be filed within 90 days from the date of liquidation. If allowed, reliquidation is to follow. If denied, the importer can file a summon (legal action) against CBP in the Court of International Trade within 180 days from the date of denial.

Recordkeeping

All records that pertain to the merchandise and are maintained in the normal course of business must be maintained in the United States. Records containing information and financial data needed to substantiate the correctness of information contained in the entry import declaration must be kept for five years from the date of entry. Drawback claims must be retained for five years from the date of entry and three years from the date that the claim is paid.

All records, including the purchase inquiry, purchase order, commercial invoice, letter of instructions, CF 3461, CF 7501, brokerage communications, customs communications, notice of liquidation, and other documents as outlined in CFR 163 on a list known as the (a)(1)(a) listing must be retained.

The penalties for failure to keep records are as follows:

- $100,000 or 75% of dutiable value for each release for willful failure
- $10,000 or 40% of the dutiable value for each release for negligence

Recordkeeping Requirements

The important points for maintaining records are as follows:

- All the records that pertain to the merchandise and are maintained in the normal course of business must be kept.
- Records containing information and financial data needed to substantiate the correctness of information contained in the entry (import declaration) must be kept.
- Records identified specifically by customs under a list commonly known as the (a)(1)(a) Records list in CFR Pt 163 of the Customs Federal Regulations must be kept.
- Records must be kept for five years from the date of entry. For drawback claims, they must be kept for three years from the date that the claim is paid.
- Records must be available to CBP in the United States for examination upon reasonable demand.

Recommendations of Compliance

All records should be kept in a centralized location within the importer's establishment or by a designated recordkeeping service provider.

Importers The necessary import transactional communication records for importers include the following:

- Purchase inquiry
- Purchase verifications
- Purchase negotiations between the buyer and seller of importer merchandise
- Purchase order communications

- Commercial invoice
- Packing list information
- Special customs declarations/certifications
- Customs Import Declaration (CF 3461)
- Customs Entry Summary (CF 7501)
- All communication records between the customs broker and the import compliance/traffic department in reference to each import transaction
- Supervisory communication detailing the supervision and control of import decisions between the importer and broker, freight forwarder, consultants, and attorneys
- All records of communication received from CBP
- All records of communication relating to any statements or acts made to CBP
- Notice of liquidations communication records
- Communications records detailing receipt of merchandise into the importer's establishments or designated receiving stations
- Communication records detailing the disposition of the merchandise after receipt or distribution
- Records indicating actual proof of purchase of imported goods
- Records indicating contract of carriage agreements, airway bills, and bills of lading
- Records indicating the exact amount of prepaid international freight or insurance contained in the import sales transaction

Importers cannot delegate recordkeeping duties to the customs broker in lieu of maintaining records for themselves.

Customs Brokers   Records that must be maintained by customs brokers are as follows:

- CF 3461 original (as prepared and released)
- CF 7501 original
- Airway bill or bill of lading
- Invoices (rated)
- Packing lists
- Special customs invoices
- Importer letter of instructions
- Importer communications—inquiries and replies

- Customs communications—inquiries and replies
- Copies of all accounting transactions in which the broker is involved (monies received from the importer and laid out on behalf of the importer)
- Delivery orders and disposition of merchandise
- Food and Drug Administration and all other government agency declarations and dispositions

Methods of Storage of Records

CBP regulations state that if a record has been created in hard copy format, it must be maintained in hard copy format. Records that were never created in a hard copy format may be maintained in an alternative CBP-approved format, but this must be approved before the actual storage practice is implemented. Preapproval may be obtained from CBP at the following location:

Bureau of Customs and Border Protection
Director of Regulatory Audit Division
909 S.E. First Avenue
Miami, Florida 33131

Standards for alternative storage methods are those that are commonly used in standard business practices such as machine-readable data, CD-ROM, and microfiche. Methods that are in compliance with generally accepted business practices will normally satisfy CBP requirements.

The importer must be able to substantiate and ensure that the imaging and/or media storage process preserves the integrity, readability, and security of the information that is contained in the original records. A standardized retrieval process must be implemented and exercised.

Customs Bonds

A customs bond is a contract that obligates the importer to perform certain functions in the importing process. These include the following:

- Pay duties, taxes, and fees on a timely basis.
- Pay as demanded by CBP any additional duties, taxes, and fees subsequently found due.
- File complete entries.

- Produce documents in cases in which CBP releases the merchandise conditionally.
- Hold the merchandise at the place of examination until the merchandise is properly released.
- In a timely manner, redeliver merchandise to CBP custody, if, for example, the merchandise is admissible, or, more commonly, if it does not comply with the country of origin marking rules.

Parties to a Bond

The parties to a bond are as follows:

- Principal (importer)
- Surety (insurance company)
- Beneficiary (CBP)

Types of Bonds

A single transaction bond covers one particular entry at one port. A continuous bond covers all entries at all ports for one year.

A single transaction bond on unrestricted merchandise equals the value plus duties, fees, and taxes. A single bond on restricted merchandise equals three times the value.

A continuous bond equals 10% of all the duties, fees, and taxes that were paid in the preceding calendar year. If no duties, fees, and taxes were paid, then the bond is 10% of the estimated duties, fees, and taxes to be paid in the current calendar year.

For breach of bond, penalties (liquidated damages) were assessed in the following amounts:

- *Unrestricted merchandise.* Entered value plus all duties, taxes, and fees
- *Restricted merchandise.* Three times the value of the imported articles

Invoices

Invoices are the nucleus of the customs entry declaration. The types are as follows:

- *Commercial.* A document prepared by the overseas shipper or seller that contains pertinent information related to the transaction of sale between the buyer and seller of imported merchandise.

- *Pro forma.* A document prepared by the importer of record that contains pertinent information related to the transaction of sale between the buyer and seller of imported merchandise.

Invoice Requirements

Invoice requirements, as set forth in the CFR Pt 141.86, are a very crucial element of the customs clearance process. Many penalty case situations develop from incorrect invoices that are submitted on behalf of imported merchandise. It is the importer's responsibility to present to the broker a proper invoice as established in customs regulations. It is the broker's responsibility to ensure that a proper invoice is received from the importer for presentation to the CBP. If the invoice is incomplete or in violation of the rules and regulatory standards that are noted in Pt 141.86 of CBP regulations, the broker is to request from the importer a corrected invoice. Failure to correct the importer is a lack of reasonable care on behalf of the broker. The broker would then face possible fines and penalties as liquidated damages in connection with the specific customs clearance.

The invoice must contain the following information:

- Port of entry to which the merchandise is destined
- Name and address of the importer of record
- Name and address of the ultimate consignee (if different from the importer of record)
- Name and address of the manufacturer and shipper
- Detailed description of the merchandise, including the name by which each item is known in the country of sale
- Unit price of the merchandise in the currency of sale
- Total value of the merchandise indicating the terms of sale associated with the actual purchase (carriage and insurance paid to [CIP], carriage paid to [CPT], ex works, etc.)
- Country of origin of the merchandise
- Statement of use in the United States
- Any rebates offered on imported merchandise between buyer and seller
- Any discounts from price
- Any values of assist, such as dies, molds, tools, and engineering work provided to the manufacturer to assist in the production of the imported merchandise

- Packing list (itemizing each net packed item)
- Must be in the English language
- Must be endorsed by the person or party who prepared the invoice

In addition, the following must be observed:

- Care must be exercised by foreign manufacturers and shippers in the preparation of invoices and other documents for entry of goods into the United States.
- Each invoice must contain information required by law and regulation outlined in CFR 141.86 code of federal regulations.
- Every statement of fact contained in the invoice or document must be true and accurate.
- Any inaccurate or misleading statement of fact in an invoice or document presented to a CBP officer may result in delays in merchandise release, detention of the goods, or a penalty against the importer under provision U.S.C. 1592.
- The importer will be required to prove exercise of reasonable care to avoid sanctions on future import transactions.

Duty Drawback

Drawback entries are a request for a 99% refund of duties that are paid on merchandise that is exported or destroyed under CBP supervision within three years from the date of importation.

The categories of drawback entries are as follows:

- *Unused merchandise (same condition).* Merchandise that is imported and exported in the same condition and unused within three years from the date of importation
- *Rejected merchandise.* Merchandise that is imported, not conforming to the importer's standards of approval, and then exported within three years from the date of importation
- *Manufacturing drawback.* Merchandise that is imported and used in the production or manufacture of a US product and then exported from the United States within five years from the date of importation and so used in manufacture within three years from the date received at the manufacturing site

Drawback entries are filed on CBP forms 7551, 7552, and 7553. Drawback entries must be filed and approved before export unless a waiver of prior notice is approved, allowing the goods to be exported without examination. An exporter may qualify for a drawback refund even if it is not the original importer of record who paid the original duty.

Harmonized Tariff Classification

The Harmonized Tariff System of the United States (HTSUS) is a very detailed reference and guide to proper classification of merchandise upon entry into the United States. All articles subject to customs clearance must be properly classified for such clearance.

The references for HTSUS information appear in book format and online at the CBP website (http://www.cbp.gov).

Format

General Rules of Interpretation

The General Rules of Interpretation (GRI) are CBP's formal guide of interpretation for classification purposes. Classification is not an exact science. A customs classification agent is required to interpret in many cases the determining factors of what is being imported. There are differences in interpretations in most cases, so the CBP regulatory procedures are to follow the guidelines of interpretation that is established in the HTSUS GRI.

General Notes

The General Notes are located directly after the GRI to provide ease in usage of the reference itself. General Notes provides explanation and definition to Special Tariff Treaty Programs (i.e., GSP, North American Free Trade Agreement, etc.). The General Notes also contains a definition of symbols and abbreviations used throughout the reference material.

Chapter Notes

The HTSUS is formatted in numerical order by chapters. Each chapter deals with a specific class of merchandise. Each chapter is preceded by an instruction to the chapter that is titled Chapter Notes. Chapter Notes provides a detailed discussion of specific commodities. Definitions to terms and clarification principles are contained in this section.

Alphabetical Index

The alphabetical index is located at the rear of the reference. It provides a reference to respective headings (first four digits of the classification number).

Techniques of Classification

GRI Consideration

The most difficult task in applying classification principles is determining what it is that is to be classified. This requires consulting the GRI.

Alphabetical Index

Once the interpretation is clear, the topic can be referenced in the alphabetical index to determine the proper heading for the commodity classification.

Chapter Notes

Before the selection of the HTSUS number, the Chapter Notes must be reviewed for interpretative notes that might prevent the usage of the intended classification number. The Chapter Notes also provide definitions for terms that are mentioned in the chapter.

HTSUS Number Structure

The structure of the HTSUS number is as follows:

- *Heading and subheading.* First eight digits of the HTSUS number
- *Statistical suffix.* The last two digits of the HTSUS number
- *Article description.* A detailed description of articles for classification purposes
- *Rates of duty*
- *General.* Normal trade relations countries
- *Special.* Special tariff treaty program designations
- *Column 2.* Rates of duties that are related to non-normal trade relations countries
- *Sample administrative cases*

NEWSLETTER

Court Fines Ford Motor Company over $20,000,000 for Failure to Declare Assists and Supplemental Payments

August 1, 2005

In two recent decisions, the U.S. Court of International Trade ("C.I.T.") fined the Ford Motor Company over $20 million for civil violations of 19 U.S.C. §1592 in connection with a series of importations in the late 1980s and early 1990s.

In the first decision, Slip Op. 05-86, the Court fined Ford $3 million, concluding that the company was grossly negligent in not presenting proper value information to Customs at the time of entry. The Court stated that these omissions were the result of recklessness and utter lack of care of the company's statutory obligations.

In the second decision, Slip Op. 05-87, the Court fined Ford in the amount of $17,151,923 for negligence, concluding that the company did not establish it exercised reasonable care in failing to declare the value of more than $350 million of merchandise in a 5-year period, despite the fact that it had a customs compliance program.

U.S. v. Ford Motor Company, Slip Op. 05-86 (Ford I)

In the first decision, Customs sought collection of duties and penalties for the importation of 11 entries of dies for automotive parts made by Ford in 1989. Customs sought $184,495 for unpaid duties and civil penalties. Ford's defense was that the merchandise at issue was entered at the value known at the time of entry and, thus, the company did not violate any Customs law. Customs, on the other hand, alleged that Ford:

1. Failed to notify Customs that the prices declared at entry were provisional and subject to adjustment;
2. Certified on the entries that the prices declared were true and correct when, in fact, the invoices failed to include the cost of known engineering changes; and
3. Failed to notify Customs "at once" when post-importation information was received indicating that the declared prices needed to be increased due to the engineering changes.

After a ten-day trial, the Court held that Ford's conduct constituted gross negligence, and assessed the company a penalty in the amount of $3 million, plus interest. The company was also ordered to pay $184,495 in unpaid duties.

In reaching this decision, the Court noted that, although Ford had an informal procedure to advise Customs that invoice prices were provisional and not final, there was a lack of communication between Ford's internal units about the provisional value policy and when to use it. Further, the Court held that the company's failure to notify Customs of the engineering changes was a material omission and breach of its duty under 19 U.S.C. §1484 to present Customs "true and accurate" information at the time of entry. Finally, the Court held that Ford's failure to notify Customs "at once" of the engineering purchase orders was a material omission, in violation of 19 U.S.C. §1485.

In assessing the penalty, the Court determined that these violations did not constitute fraud, but did rise to the level of gross negligence under 19 U.S.C. §1592. The Court found that Ford's omission of information from entry documents was reckless and illustrated an utter lack of care about the company's statutory obligations at the time of entry. The Court also rejected Ford's prior disclosure claim because Customs was already investigating the dies, and the company "knew or should have known" it was being investigated by the time it disclosed the violations. Taking all of these factors into account, including the gravity of Ford's conduct, the Court determined that $3 million was a just penalty in this case.

U.S. v. Ford Motor Company, Slip Op. 05-87 (Ford II)

The second decision involved many of the same issues in Ford I. In this parallel case, Customs sought to collect duties and penalties arising out of entries of vehicles and components imported between 1987 and 1992. Customs sought unpaid duties in the amount of $68,178 and penalties in the amount of $34,576,559 for gross negligence, or in the alternative, $17,288,279 for simple negligence.

Again, Ford's problems were the result of omissions in the entry process. Specifically, the company provided assists but failed to declare them on its entry documents. Further, contrary to the requirements of 19 U.S.C. §1484, Ford failed to declare on its entry documents that the values stated therein were not final because the company was obliged to make lump sum payments to its vendors after entry. Finally, Ford failed to report these payments to Customs as soon as they were known, as required by 19 U.S.C. §1485.

The Court noted that while Ford had mechanisms in place to enable it to comply with its statutory obligations to properly enter merchandise, and that it made a good-faith effort to follow its internal compliance measures with respect to these entries, the company failed to follow through on its processes, and, thus, the company was negligent under 19 U.S.C. §1592.

The Court considered all of the mitigation factors in the case, including Ford's allegation that it made consistent efforts to comply with its statutory obligations. In the end, the Court concluded that there was overwhelming evidence that Ford failed to declare the correct transaction value at entry for more than $350 million of merchandise entered during the five-year period in question. Accordingly, the Court assessed the statutory maximum penalty for negligence under 19 U.S.C. §1592.

Conclusion

In both cases, Ford's problems were caused in large measure because of internal communication problems regarding assists and supplemental payments. In the second case, the Court noted that Ford had compliance measures in place to handle the issues discussed above, but its employees did not follow the company's own compliance manual to report those assists and supplemental payments to Customs.

Both decisions demonstrate the high standard of care expected by the Court and Customs when making entry. In particular, importers are required to declare the total correct value (inclusive of assists and supplemental payments) at the time of entry for known costs.

If the total correct value is not known at the time of entry, then the importer is expected to use the Customs Entry Reconciliation program to subsequently declare unknown costs.

If the company is not using the entry reconciliation program, they are expected to advise Customs that the entry values are provisional and to immediately report to Customs increases in those values when they occur. Finally, importers are expected to have adequate procedures in place within the company to report transactions that may affect the value in a timely manner to Customs.

Our office will provide companies with copies of these decisions on request, and answer any questions you may have regarding them, and their impact on the company's Custom compliance program, including accepted methods to identify and advise Customs of provisional values, and to report valued changes through Customs' entry reconciliation program.

If you have any questions with regard to this newsletter, please do not hesitate to contact George R. Tuttle at (415) 288-0425 or grt@tuttlelaw .com or George R. Tuttle, III at (415) 288-0428 or geo@tuttlelaw.com.

George R. Tuttle and George R. Tuttle, III are attorneys with the Law Offices of George R. Tuttle in San Francisco. The information in this article is general in nature, and is not intended to constitute legal advice or to create an attorney-client relationship with respect to any event or occurrence, and may not be considered as such.

PILLSBURY PAYS $6 MILLION PENALTY FOR COMMERCIAL FRAUD

Domino Sugar Pays $100,000 for the Same Allegation

NEW ORLEANS, La.—As a result of an investigation conducted by the New Orleans office of U.S. Immigration and Customs Enforcement (ICE), on September 4, Pillsbury Company paid a $6 million penalty for commercial fraud. DOMINO SUGAR Corporation (now known as Tate & Lyle Corporation) paid a $100,000 fine based on the same allegation.

The ICE investigation, which started in September 1999, revealed that in 1992 PILLSBURY and DOMINO SUGAR were directly involved in a scheme to trans-ship nearly 6900 metric tons of Guatemalan sugar through the island of Saint Kitts into the Port of New Orleans. Both companies claimed the country of origin to be Saint Kitts to avoid quota tariffs. ICE agents subsequently determined that the loss of revenue to the United States exceeded $2.5 million.

"We will continue to pursue those companies that circumvent duty requirements on imports," said New Orleans ICE Interim Special Agent-in-Charge Mike Holt. "Those companies that perpetrate commercial fraud pose a serious problem for our country and will continue to be the focus of our enforcement actions."

In addition to this commercial fraud investigation conducted by ICE, the Department of Justice filed a complaint against PILLSBURY and DOMINO SUGAR in the Court of International Trade. The Justice Department's complaint against both companies was settled with the September 4 payment of the fines.

The U.S. Immigration and Customs Enforcement (ICE) is the largest investigative arm of the Department of Homeland Security (DHS), responsible for the enforcement of border, economic, infrastructure, and transportation security laws. ICE seeks to prevent acts of terrorism by targeting the people, money and materials that support terror and criminal networks.

GUIDANCE ON REEXPORTS

The US Department of Commerce regulates the exports and reexports of *dual-use* items, that is, goods, software, and technologies with commercial and proliferation or military applications, through its Export Administration Regulations (EAR). If an entity outside of the United States wishes to export or reexport an item that is of US origin or that has a US connection (as described in more detail in Parts B through D below), the product may require a license from the US Department of Commerce's Bureau of Industry and Security (BIS). Certain additional restrictions are also outlined in Part E below.

EAR

An item is subject to the EAR if it meets any of the following conditions:

1. Was produced or originated in the United States (see Part A).
2. Is a foreign-made product that contains more than a specified percentage of US-controlled content (see Part B).
3. Is a foreign made-product based on certain US-origin technology or software and is intended for shipment to specified destinations (see Part C).
4. Was made by a plant or a major component of a plant that is located outside the United States, and if that plant or major component of a plant is the direct product of a certain US technology or software, and the product is intended for shipment to specified destinations (see Part D).

A. BIS License for Reexport

An importer may need to obtain a license to *reexport* an item that was produced or originated in the United States. A reexport is the shipment or transmission of an item that is subject to the EAR from one foreign country (i.e., a country other than the United States) to another foreign country. A reexport also occurs when there is *release* of technology or software (source code) that is subject to the EAR in one foreign country to a national of another foreign country.

Many items subject to the EAR do not need a license to be reexported from one foreign country to another. But certain items are controlled and will require a license or must qualify for a license exception. License requirements apply particularly to items that are controlled by multilateral export control regimes. In addition, some destinations and persons (individuals or groups) are subject to comprehensive export controls, including controls on widely traded consumer products.

To determine whether a US-origin product requires a license, an exporter needs the following three pieces of information:

1. *The Export Control Classification Number (ECCN)*. Certain items, notably those controlled by multilateral export control regimes, are on the Commerce Control List (CCL) (Part 774 of the EAR) and are included in a specific ECCN. If an item is not on the CCL, it may be classified as EAR99. EAR99 is a general category of goods and technology that encompasses many widely traded consumer and industrial items. The ECCN in the CCL will also explain the reason(s) for control.

2. *The ultimate destination of the item*. An exporter will need to match the reason(s) for control that are listed in ECCNs on the CCL (Part 774 of the EAR) with the country of ultimate destination in the Country Chart (Part 738 of the EAR). The reason(s) for control, when used in conjunction with the Country Chart, will help an exporter determine if a license is required to the ultimate destination. If the exporter determines that the reexport transaction requires a license, the exporter should review the EAR to determine if any license exceptions are available (Part 740 of the EAR). For general information on license exceptions, see Part E below.

3. *The end user and end use for the item*. Even if a license is not required based on the ultimate destination (or a license is required but a license exception would generally apply), an exporter may need to apply for a license because of the end use or end user. There are certain special restrictions that apply to persons (or entities) who are identified in the EAR, as well as to persons whom the exporter knows or has reason

to know are involved in weapons proliferation activities. In most instances, a license is required to persons who identified in Part 744 of the EAR for the reexport of all items that are subject to the EAR (i.e., all items on the CCL and all items that are classified as EAR99).

B. BIS License for US-Origin Content

As noted previously, certain foreign-produced items are also subject to the EAR because they contain more than a specified percentage value of US-origin controlled content. An exporter needs to first determine if the foreign-produced item is subject to the EAR. If an exporter determines that a foreign-produced item is subject to the EAR, the exporter will then follow the process that is outlined in Part A to determine if your foreign-produced item requires a license.

The following steps are provided as general guidance for determining whether a foreign-produced commodity that incorporates US-origin parts is subject to the EAR or qualifies for the *de minimis* exception to the EAR. This general guidance does not take into account specific items that are not eligible for *de minimis* treatment. Section 734.4 and Supplement 2 to Part 734 can be consulted for information on such items and the calculation of U.S.-controlled content.

1. *General guidance regarding incorporation of US parts or components into foreign-produced items.* A foreign company that incorporates US-origin parts or components in a foreign commodity needs to do the following:

   a. Classify the US-origin parts or components exported to the entity according to the classification system that is set forth in the EAR. The US exporter may be able to assist in determining the ECCN.

   b. Determine if the US parts or components are controlled content. (US-controlled content is content that would require a US license if it were to be reexported as separate parts or components to the country of ultimate destination.)

   c. Determine if the US-controlled content is greater than 25% of the value of the finished foreign product. (For designated terrorist-supporting countries, an exporter must determine if the US-controlled content is greater than 10% of the value of the finished product.) If the U.S.-controlled content is 25% or less of the value of the finished product (or 10% or less for applicable countries), the exporter qualifies for the *de minimis* exception that is set forth in 734.4 of the EAR, and the product is not subject to the EAR.

d. If the controlled content is greater than 25% (or 10% for applicable countries), the product is subject to the EAR. If your product is subject to the EAR, the exporter needs to determine if the item requires a license because of the ultimate destination or the end use or end user. The steps to do this are outlined in Section 734.4 and Part 734.

2. *Additional guidance regarding foreign software incorporating US-origin software and foreign technology commingled with or drawn from US-origin technology.* If an exporter incorporates US-origin software into foreign software or if foreign technology is commingled with or drawn from U.S.-origin technology, the exporter would follow a process that is similar to the one that is outlined above. That process and a related one-time reporting requirement are set forth in Section 734.4 and Supplement 2 to Part 734 of the EAR.

Note: The *de minimis* exception can be used only for items that are alike— hardware into hardware or software into software. The *de minimis* exception cannot be used for incorporating software into hardware.

C. BIS License for Direct Product of US Technology or Software

Direct products of US-origin technology are subject to the EAR only if they are intended for specified destinations, they would be subject to national security controls (if they were US-origin items), and the US-origin technology or software on which the foreign product is based required a written assurance from the recipient when it was exported from the United States. See EAR Sections 734.3(a)(4) and 736.2(b)(3).

D. BIS License for Product of a Plant or Major Component of a Plant Based on US Technology

The product of such a foreign plant or the major component of a plant is subject to the EAR only if it is intended for specified destinations, if it would be controlled for national security reasons (if it were a US-origin product), and if the technology on which the plant or major component of a plant is based required a written assurance from the recipient when it was exported from the United States. See Sections 734.3(a)(5) and 736.2(b)(3).

E. Product Eligibility for License Exception

In certain instances, if a reexport transaction requires a license, the exporter may be able to use one of the license exceptions that are set forth in Part 740 of the EAR. A license exception allows the reexport of an item without applying for a license, provided that the transaction meets all the terms and conditions of the license exception.

Special Restrictions

An exporter may not reexport an item that is subject to the EAR to a party whose export privileges have been denied by the BIS. Information on parties subject to denial orders is available at http://www.bis.doc.gov/dpl/default.shtm.

US persons may be subject to additional restrictions under the EAR. See Section 744.6 of the EAR. US persons may also be subject to restrictions under other U.S. government regulations, such as those that are issued by the Office of Foreign Assets Control (OFAC) of the US Department of the Treasury or other US government departments or agencies.

Export License Compliance Requirements

The Department of Commerce (DoC) has enforcement and protective measures that are available to ensure that the recipients of items subject to the EAR comply with the reexport license requirements of the EAR. If the DoC determines that an exporter has not complied with these requirements and restrictions, it may institute administrative enforcement proceedings, resulting in the possible imposition of civil penalties or denial of eligibility to receive U.S. exports (Part 764 of the EAR).

Reexport License

If a reexport requires a license and is not eligible for a license exception, application for a reexport license may be made electronically through the

Simplified Network Application Process (SNAP). Basic information on the SNAP program is available on the BIS website (http://www.bis.doc.gov/snap/index.htm). Before the first submission of an electronic application, a *PIN* request package must be completed.

Additional Information and Contacting the BIS

For assistance regarding a reexport license or product classification or to obtain other information on US export controls, consult the main BIS website (information is in English).

To speed the responses to requests for information and assistance, the BIS has a list of Web forms (in English) for different kinds of requests. Using the correct form will help provide a prompt response to an inquiry.

In addition, the Office of Exporter Services, BIS can be contacted directly at the following address:

U.S. Department of Commerce
P.O. Box 273 (for mail)
Room 1099 (for visitors)
14th Street and Pennsylvania Avenue, Northwest
Washington, DC 20044
Phone: 202-482-4811
Fax: 202-482-3617

All requests for information and assistance must be in English.

Disclaimer

This book and the BIS provide this Guidance on Reexports for information purposes only. The guidance does not provide an official interpretation or translation of the US export control law or regulations. This information does not relieve the readers of any duties or obligations regarding the knowledge of or compliance with all relevant US export control laws and regulations as they appear in the US Code of Federal Regulations and as modified by notices in the Federal Register.

FDA ENFORCEMENT

FDA and CBP Announce Revised Compliance Schedule for Enforcement of the Prior Notice Interim Final Rule and Contingency Plan for Prior Notice System Outages

The United States Food and Drug Administration (FDA) and U.S. Customs and Border Protection (CBP) today issued a revised compliance policy guide (CPG) that describes their strategy for enforcing the requirements of the prior notice interim final rule (IFR) while maintaining an uninterrupted flow of food imports.

The prior notice provision in the Public Health Security and Bioterrorism Preparedness and Response Act of 2002 (Bioterrorism Act) gives FDA advance information of imported food shipments. This allows the FDA to target inspections more effectively and helps to ensure the safety of imported food products before they enter domestic commerce. FDA and CBP began receiving prior notices on December 12, 2003, when the prior notice IFR took effect. Since February 2004, FDA and CBP have been receiving about 160,000 prior notice submissions a week. The prior notice IFR has proven to be an important tool in the nation's food defense efforts.

Under the revised CPG, FDA and CBP will enforce fully all provisions of the prior notice IFR on August 13, 2004, except for the following violations:

- The registration number submitted for the manufacturing facility is inaccurate or is invalid.
- The registration number for the shipper is not provided.
- The airway bill number or bill of lading number is not provided or is invalid.
- The name and address of the ultimate consignee is inaccurate because it contains the name and address of the express consignment operator or consolidator instead of the ultimate consignee.

For these violations, the two agencies generally will continue to exercise enforcement discretion until November 1, 2004, unless the violation reflects a history of the repeated conduct of a similar nature by a person who had been notified of such violations.

The revised CPG also states that the agencies will exercise enforcement discretion for prior notices that fail to include a required manufacturing facility registration number if the food imported or offered for import is for quality assurance, research, or analysis purposes only (i.e., not for human or animal consumption and not for resale).

FDA and CBP initially published the CPG in December 2003, and revised it in June 2004 to include additional guidance regarding food imported or offered for import for noncommercial purposes with a non-commercial shipper. Enforcement discretion for these shipments continues under the revised CPG.

FDA and CBP are also announcing a corresponding 3-month delay in their projected date for issuing the prior notice final rule from March 2005 to June 2005. This will allow FDA and CBP to retain the 3-month assessment period to determine whether the prior notice timeframes can be reduced further as they develop the prior notice final rule.

Lastly, the agencies are announcing the issuance of an updated prior notice compliance summary and a new "Guidance for Industry: Prior Notice of Imported Food Contingency Plan for System Outages." The compliance summary states that since increased enforcement began in June, entries submitted to FDA and CBP with no prior notice have been almost eliminated. Although some problems still exist, only a small percent fail to submit any prior notice information. Most prior notice data are being submitted; however, completion of registration number and bill of lading is lower than completion of most other data elements.

FDA and CBP also are looking more closely at the validity and consistency of the data that are being entered. For example, although a consignee is entered on 100 percent of the submissions through automated commercial system (ACS), almost 2 percent of consignee data (which as an example, equated to 2466 for the week ending July 3rd) indicates unknown/consolidated consignee, and not the ultimate consignee as required by the prior notice IFR.

FDA and CBP now are actively identifying specific submitters and transmitters (broker/filers) whose submissions tend to be error prone and are providing information to industry to encourage better compliance. The agencies also are using the results of our compliance information to review some of the most problematic compliance areas to determine how to best improve compliance rates. The agencies intend to continue their education and outreach efforts to industry through November 1, 2004.

The Contingency Plan provides guidance on submitting prior notice of imported food during system outages affecting the applicable FDA and CBP computer program systems. The contingency plan identifies seven potential system downtime scenarios that could have an impact on transmission, confirmation, and processing of prior notice submissions and explains recommended submission options for each of the identified scenarios. In any of the scenarios described in the contingency plan, where the alternative submission options include both e-mail and facsimile (fax) transmissions, e-mail transmission is strongly encouraged as the more efficient means.

All documents may be found on FDA's website (http://www.fda.gov/oc /bioterrorism/bioact.html).

TIPS FOR NEW IMPORTERS AND EXPORTERS

To avoid potential problems in the clearance of merchandise through the U.S. Customs and Border Protection (CBP), the Office of Trade Relations strongly recommends familiarization with CBP policies and procedures before actually importing or exporting goods. Companies should also be aware of any entry requirements, including those of other federal agencies, specific to the particular commodity being imported or exported. The following tips are for new importers and exporters:

CBP Website

CBP recommends that importers review the topics on the CBP import page (select the import tab on the CBP home page: http://CBP.gov), particularly the information that is contained in the section that is titled infrequent importer/traveler. There are many topic-specific links to explore, but it might be best to begin with U.S. Import Requirements, found in the box that is titled Publications in the SEE ALSO column. This will lead to information on CBP import requirements, the arrival of goods, formal entry versus informal entry, classification, protest, mail shipments, restricted merchandise, and more. For other agency requirements for frequent importers with higher-valued shipments, it is important to read *Importing into the United States*. This publication (available online and in hard copy) contains more in-depth information and is valuable reading for anyone who is seriously venturing into the importing business. From the CBP home page, select the import tab, then select communications to the trade (on the left side of the page), then under Publications, select Importing into the United States. It is also important to read the informed compliance material on the CBP website. CBP has prepared a number of

Informed Compliance publications (ICPs) in the "What Every Member of the Trade Community Should Know About..." series on a variety of issues. Select the Import tab on the CBP home page, and then, on the left, scroll down to the link that is titled informed compliance. If business requires international travel, review the traveler information in the Know Before You Go! Online Brochure. From the CBP home page, click on the tab Import, scroll down to select the link infrequent importer/traveler, and select the Know Before You Go! online brochure link in the SEE ALSO column on the right.

Contacting the CBP Office at the Port of Entry

A complete directory of the various ports of entry can be found on the CBP website. Select the ports tab on the CBP home page, and then the state and service (if the port is not known, choose a nearby port of entry). Ask to speak with a CBP import specialist who is assigned to the commodity you are importing. Import specialists are commodity-specific and can provide classification advice, commodity-specific requirements, and advisory duty rates and respond to questions on filing an entry (although in many ports, questions regarding entry filing are handled by entry specialists). Before calling the port, the importer should do as much research as possible. For the import specialist to provide the best assistance, it is important to exactly describe the merchandise to be imported. The importer should be able to provide a full and complete description of the article and provide specific information such as the country of origin of the merchandise, the composition of the merchandise, and the intended use of the item. For more information on the classification of merchandise select import, then select duty rates/hts link, then the Harmonized Tariff Schedule (HTS), which contains the actual HTS and Tariff Classification guidelines that explain how to properly classify merchandise. An electronic version of the HTS is available online.

CBP Written Ruling for Harmonized Tariff System of the United States Classification and Rate of Duty for Merchandise

For information on CBP ruling letters, select the legal tab on the CBP home page, then select the link rulings, and finally the link, What Are Ruling Letters. When requesting a binding ruling, importers should follow the procedures outlined in Part 177 of the Customs Regulations

(19 C.F.R. 177). The Customs Regulations may be accessed via the legal tab. Results of previous ruling requests can be researched by using Customs Rulings Online Search System (CROSS). CBP may have already issued rulings on similar products that can be used for guidance. To access CROSS, select the legal button on the CBP home page and then select the CROSS link.

Valuable Information Regarding Exporting

If future plans call for exporting merchandise from the United States, an exporter should review the information found in the export section of the CBP website. This section contains links to information on export issues such as the New Shipper's Export Declaration (SED) Form, Automated Export System (AES), Exporting a Motor Vehicle, and Industry Alerts. Although CBP enforces many export regulations for various other government agencies, specific questions pertaining to licensing requirements for a particular commodity should be directed to the related agency. Other agency contact information as well as information on commodities that may require export licenses can be obtained by visiting the DOC BIS websites (http://www.bis.doc.gov). Questions regarding export licenses may also be directed to CBP officers at the port where the merchandise will exit the country. A complete directory of the various ports of entry can be found on the CBP website. Select the ports tab on the CBP home page, and then the state and port.

Consulting a Licensed Customs Broker

Those importing merchandise either for their own use or for commercial transactions, particularly if they find importing procedures complicated, may hire a customs broker. Customs brokers are private businesses that can handle the clearance of merchandise on behalf of importers and exporters. To view a list of customs brokers licensed to conduct CBP business in a specific port, select the ports tab on the CBP home page, and then the state and port. Then scroll down and select the link, Brokers: View List. There is also an Informed Compliance Publication about customs brokers that appears under the Legal tab. Select the informed compliance publications link and then scroll down to the Entry section. Remember, even when using a broker, the importer of record is ultimately responsible for the correctness of the entry documentation presented to CBP and all applicable duties, taxes, and fees.

Researching Quota Requirements

Import quotas control the amount or volume of various commodities that can be imported into the United States during a specified period of time. United States import quotas may be divided into two types: absolute and tariff-rate. Absolute quotas limit the quantity of goods that may enter the commerce of the United States in a specific period. Tariff-rate quotas permit a specified quantity of imported merchandise to be entered at a reduced rate of duty during the quota period. Once a quota has been reached, goods may still be entered, but at a considerably higher rate of duty. Quota information is available on the CBP website. Select the Import tab and then the link textiles and quotas. This section contains links to information on subjects such as Textile Status Report for Absolute Quotas (Textiles and Quotas), Visa and Exempt Certification Requirements for Textiles, and Commodity Status Report for Tariff Rate and in the publications box of the RELATED LINKS column provides general information and the link Import Quotas.

Freedom of Information Act Procedures

When members of the trade community or individuals from the public request information from CBP, there are circumstances when the information being sought can be provided only if the request is in agreement with the provisions of the Freedom of Information Act (FOIA). The CBP website has a comprehensive explanation of the agency FOIA program, including background and general information about FOIA law and specific instructions for making a FOIA request. A hyperlink to the CBP FOIA information appears at the bottom center of the CBP main web page. The website also has a link to the Department of Justice FOIA web page.

CBP Billing for Shipment Examination

Under Title 19, section 1467, of the United States Code (19 U.S.C. 1467), CBP has the right to examine any shipment imported into the United States. It is important for the importer to know that the importer must bear the cost of such cargo examinations. Per the CBP regulations, it is the responsibility of the importer to make the goods available for examination: "The importer shall bear any expense involved in preparing the merchandise for CBP examination and in the closing of packages" (19 C.F.R. 151.6). Household effects are not exempt. No distinction is made between commercial and personal shipments. In the course of normal operations, CBP does not charge for cargo examinations. However, there may still be costs involved for the importer. For example, if a shipment is selected for examination, it will generally be moved to a centralized examination station (CES) for the CBP examination to take place. A CES is a privately operated facility, not in the charge of a CBP officer, at which merchandise is made available to CBP officers for physical examination. The CES facility will unload (devan) the shipment from its shipping container and will reload it after the examination. The CES will bill the importer for their services. There are also costs associated with moving the cargo to and from the examination site and with storage. Rates will vary across the country and a complete devanning may cost several hundred dollars. The CES concept fulfills the needs of both CBP and the importer by providing an efficient means to conduct examinations in a timely manner. CESs are discussed in part 118 of the Customs Regulations and are available for viewing on the CBP website (19 C.F.R. 118). Select the legal tab, then select Customs Regulations (CFR, multiple years) in the what's new column under quicklinks, and scroll down to Title 19–Customs Duties.

Import Licensing

CBP does not require an importer to have a license or permit, but other agencies may require a permit, license, or other certification, depending on the commodity being imported. CBP acts in a ministerial capacity for these other agencies. There is a listing of other government agencies in the appendix section of the publication Importing into the United States. A license may also be required from local or state authorities to do business. CBP entry forms require an importer number. This is either the IRS business registration number or, if a business is not registered with the IRS or the import is being done by an individual without a business, the Social Security number will be sufficient. As an alternative, a CBP-assigned number may be requested by completing Customs Form 5106 and presenting it to the Entry Branch at a CBP port of entry.

CBP Contact

For comments or concerns an importer thinks have not been resolved in an appropriate manner, contact the Office of Trade Relations at the following address:

Office of Trade Relations
Customs and Border Protection
Department of Homeland Security
1300 Pennsylvania Avenue, Northwest
Room 4.2A
Washington, D.C. 20229
Phone: 202-344-1440
Fax: 202-344-1969
traderelations@dhs.gov

MANAGING THE NORTH AMERICAN FREE TRADE AGREEMENT UNITED STATES/CANADA/MEXICO

Advance Rulings

An advance ruling is a written document that is received from the customs authority from a North American Free Trade Agreement (NAFTA) country. It provides binding information on specific NAFTA questions about the future imports of goods into Canada, Mexico, and the United States.

Annex 401

Annex 401 of NAFTA provides the specific rule of origin that is applied to determine whether a good qualifies as an originating good under the terms of NAFTA.

Appeals

Appeals procedures are used by importers, exporters, or producers of goods to request a second review of NAFTA decisions that are given by the customs administrations.

Certificate of Origin

The certificate of origin is a trilaterally agreed-upon form that is used by Canada, Mexico, and the United States to certify that goods qualify for the preferential tariff treatment that is accorded by NAFTA. The certificate of origin must be completed by the exporter. A producer or manufacturer may also complete a certificate of origin in a NAFTA territory to be used as a basis for an exporter's certificate of origin. To make a claim for NAFTA preference, the importer must possess a certificate of origin at the time that the claim is made.

Claiming Preferential Treatment

A claim for preferential treatment is usually made at the time of importation on the customs document that is used by the importing country. The agreement allows NAFTA claims up to one year from the date of importation. The procedures for presenting a NAFTA claim are different in Canada, Mexico, and the United States.

Commercial Samples

Under NAFTA, commercial samples can be imported duty free if the value, shipped individually or together, does not exceed US$1, or the equivalent amount in Canadian or Mexican currency, or if they are marked, torn, perforated, or otherwise unsuitable for sale or use except as commercial samples.

Commodity-Specific Information

This section contains NAFTA-specific information on certain traded commodities.

Confidentiality

Article 507(1) of NAFTA requires that each country protect the confidentiality of business information that is provided to them in the course of conducting government business. In addition, the governments of Canada, Mexico, and the United States must ensure that this business information is not disclosed to third parties and does not prejudice the competitive positions of the persons providing the information.

Country of Origin Marking

Country of origin marking is used to clearly indicate to the ultimate purchaser of a product where it is made. NAFTA marking rules are also used to determine the rate of duty, staging, and country of origin that are applicable for NAFTA goods.

Currency Conversion

Currency conversion is a means to determine the value of a good or material when currency is expressed in a currency other than that of the producer. The currency used in Canada is the Canadian dollar. In Mexico, it is the peso. The United States uses the American dollar.

Customs Procedures

Customs procedures topic includes various subjects such as the certificate of origin, advance rulings, NAFTA claims, verifications, determinations, and appeals to name a few. This information is gathered from a variety of CBP-published documents.

Denial of Benefits

Under NAFTA, the importing country has the right to deny NAFTA benefits if you do not follow NAFTA regulations. Benefits may also be denied if it is determined that an imported good does not qualify as originating in one of the NAFTA countries.

Determinations

Determinations are issued by the customs administrations as a result of a NAFTA verification. Determinations are binding on the exporter and producer and may be appealed.

Drawback

Drawback is a refund, reduction, or waiver in whole or in part of customs duties that is collected upon importation of an article or materials that are subsequently exported. Under NAFTA, this refunded amount is the lesser of the amount of duties that are paid upon importation into the NAFTA territory, and the total amount paid on the finished good is related to the NAFTA country to which it is exported. Drawback became effective for trade between Canada and the United States on January 1, 1996, and for trade between Mexico, the United States, and Canada, this program became effective on January 1, 2001.

Duty Deferral

Various duty deferral programs are available in Canada, Mexico, and the United States that allow deferring duty payment on materials that are used in the manufacture of a good that is later exported. The duty deferral program is designed to assist Canadian, Mexican, and US businesses to compete more favorably in the international market. The NAFTA Duty Deferral Program requires that duties must be paid on the foreign components one time within the NAFTA territory if entered into a duty deferral program and then exported into a NAFTA territory. The NAFTA Duty Deferral Program became effective for trade between Canada and the United States on January 1, 1996. For trade with Mexico, the effective date was January 1, 2001.

Duties (Tariff Elimination) and Fees

Goods brought into Canada, Mexico, and the United States are subject to customs duties and taxes. Each country has its own rate of duties. The amount of duties charged is based on the Harmonized Tariff System classification number of the good, value, and origin.

Customs User Fee

A customs user fee is an amount of money that is charged for processing goods through customs. NAFTA allows the parties to maintain existing merchandise processing fees; however, no party may adopt customs user fees for originating goods.

Intellectual Property Rights

NAFTA details specific conditions regarding the nature and scope of responsibility with respect to the intellectual property rights of the United

States, Mexico, and Canada. Intellectual property rights refer to copyright and related rights, trademark rights, patent rights, rights in the layout designs of semiconductor integrated circuits, trade secret rights, plant breeders' rights, rights in geographic indications, and industrial design rights.

Laboratory Standards

Laboratory standards are a list of harmonized laboratory methods that are accepted by the customs laboratories of Canada, Mexico, and the United States for determining the specified physical and chemical properties for customs processing including admissibility and classification within the Harmonized Tariff System.

NAFTA: A Guide to Customs Procedures

The NAFTA Customs Guide is a trilaterally agreed-upon guide that provides general information on various topics such as the rules of origin, certificate of origin, entry procedures, verifications, determinations, and appeals. The guide is written in layman's terms and is a great reference for newcomers to NAFTA.

NAFTA Public Law and Legislative History

NAFTA Rulings

NAFTA rulings are specific rulings that are issued by the customs authority on NAFTA issues.

NAFTA Verification/Audit Manual

The NAFTA Verification/Audit Manual is developed to support the verification of goods for which NAFTA preferential tariff treatment has been claimed and to help comply with the rules of origin. This trilateral guide details the recommended technical verification framework to be observed by each party when conducting NAFTA verifications. This trilaterally agreed-upon manual also provides significant automobile information.

North American Free Trade Agreement

The term *Agreement* refers to NAFTA. It is the actual text of the preferential trade agreement between Canada, Mexico, and the United States as implemented on January 1, 1994.

Objectives

NAFTA is a comprehensive agreement that came into effect on January 1, 1994, creating the world's largest free trade area. Article 102 of the agreement details the objectives of NAFTA. Among its main objectives are liberalizing trade between Canada, Mexico, and the United States; stimulating economic growth; and giving the NAFTA countries equal access to each others' markets.

Packaging

Under NAFTA, packaging and packing are used in different contexts. Packing refers to the materials and containers that are used to protect a good during transportation but does not include packaging materials and containers.

Penalties

Under NAFTA, Canada, Mexico, or the United States may impose criminal, civil, or administrative penalties for violation of their laws and customs procedures.

Postimportation NAFTA Claims

Generally, NAFTA claims are made at the time of importation. However, NAFTA allows for a NAFTA claim to be made by the importer within one year from the date of importation.

Recordkeeping

All the records that are related to a preferential duty claim under NAFTA must be kept for a minimum of five years.

Repairs and Alterations

Under NAFTA, Canada, Mexico, and the United States do not assess customs duties on goods that are imported or exported within the NAFTA territories for repairs or alterations regardless of origin.

Resources

The Resources is a list of resources that provide information on NAFTA.

Rules of Origin (Preference Criteria)

Rules of origin include both the general rules of origin, which are used to determine whether or not a good or material is eligible for NAFTA preferential treatment, and the specific rules of origin, which are used to determine if a foreign material is originating in the NAFTA territories.

Standards Document

The Standards document sets forth the uniform regulatory standards that are adopted by Canada, Mexico, and the United States for purposes of implementing the preferential tariff treatment and other customs-related provisions of NAFTA.

Temporary Importations

Article 305 of NAFTA provides for the duty-free temporary importation of certain classes of goods.

Transshipment

Under limited specific circumstances, NAFTA allows goods to leave the NAFTA territories and reenter the territories with a NAFTA claim.

Value (NAFTA)

This section covers specifics on calculating the NAFTA value, determining the regional value content of goods and materials, the regional value content for automobiles, etc.

Verifications

Verifications is the process that is used by the customs authorities to determine whether a good qualifies as NAFTA originating when a preferential duty rate has been claimed.

OUTLINE OF TERRORISM ACT OF 2002

The sections of the Outline of Terrorism Act of 2002 are presented here for review. Please refer to the actual document for purposes other than a brief review.

SECTION 1. SHORT TITLE; TABLE OF CONTENTS
SHORT TITLE.—This Act may be cited as the
"Terrorism Risk Insurance Act of 2002."

TABLE OF CONTENTS
The table of contents for this Act is as follows:
Sec. 1. Short title; table of contents.

TITLE I—TERRORISM INSURANCE PROGRAM
Sec. 101. Congressional findings and purpose.
Sec. 102. Definitions.
Sec. 103. Terrorism Insurance Program.
Sec. 104. General authority and administration of claims.
Sec. 105. Preemption and nullification of preexisting terrorism exclusions.
Sec. 106. Preservation provisions.
Sec. 107. Litigation management.
Sec. 108. Termination of Program.

TITLE II—TREATMENT OF TERRORIST ASSETS
Sec. 201. Satisfaction of judgments from blocked assets of terrorists, terrorist organizations, and State sponsors of terrorism.

TITLE III—FEDERAL RESERVE BOARD PROVISIONS
Sec. 301. Certain authority of the Board of Governors of the Federal Reserve System.

TITLE I—TERRORISM INSURANCE PROGRAM
SEC. 101. CONGRESSIONAL FINDINGS AND PURPOSE

FINDINGS.—The Congress finds that the ability of businesses and individuals to obtain property and casualty insurance at reasonable and predictable prices, in order to spread the risk of both routine and catastrophic loss, is critical to economic growth, urban development, and the construction and maintenance of public and private housing, as well as to the promotion of United States exports and foreign trade in an increasingly interconnected world.

Property and casualty insurance firms are important financial institutions, the products of which allow mutualization of risk and the efficient use of financial resources and enhance the ability of the economy to maintain stability, while responding to a variety of economic, political, environmental, and other risks with a minimum of disruption; the ability of the insurance industry to cover the unprecedented financial risks presented by potential acts of terrorism in the United States can be a major factor in the recovery from terrorist attacks, while maintaining the stability of the economy; widespread financial market uncertainties have arisen following the terrorist attacks of September 11, 2001, including the absence of information from which financial institutions can make statistically valid estimates of the probability and cost of future terrorist events, and therefore the size, funding, and allocation of the risk of loss caused by such acts of terrorism; a decision by property and casualty insurers to deal with such uncertainties, either by terminating property and casualty coverage for losses arising from terrorist events, or by radically escalating premium coverage to compensate for risks of loss that are not readily predictable, could seriously hamper ongoing and planned construction, property acquisition, and other business projects, generate a dramatic increase in rents, and otherwise suppress economic activity; and the United States Government should provide temporary financial compensation to insured parties, contributing to the stabilization of the United States economy in a time of national crisis, while the financial services industry develops the systems, mechanisms, products, and programs necessary to create a viable financial services market for private terrorism risk insurance.

PURPOSE.—The purpose of this title is to establish a temporary Federal program that provides for a transparent system of shared public and private compensation for insured losses resulting from acts of terrorism, in order to—protect consumers by addressing market disruptions and ensure the continued widespread availability and affordability of property and casualty insurance for terrorism risk; and allow for a transitional period for the private markets to stabilize, resume pricing of such insurance, and build capacity to absorb any future losses, while preserving State insurance regulation and consumer protections.

SEC. 102. DEFINITIONS.

In this title, the following definitions shall apply:

ACT OF TERRORISM.—

CERTIFICATION.—The term "act of terrorism" means any act that is certified by the Secretary, in concurrence with the Secretary of State, and the Attorney General of the 13 United States (i) to be an act of terrorism; (ii) to be a violent act or an act that is dangerous to—(I) human life; (II) property; or (III) infrastructure; (iii) to have resulted in damage within the United States, or outside of the United States in the case of—

(I) an air carrier or vessel described in paragraph (5)(B); or (II) the premises of a United States mission; and (iv) to have been committed by an individual or individuals acting on behalf of any foreign person or foreign interest, as part of an effort to coerce the civilian population of the United States or to influence the policy or affect the conduct of the United States Government by coercion.

LIMITATION.—No act shall be certified by the Secretary as an act of terrorism if—

(i) the act is committed as part of the course of a war declared by the Congress, except that this clause shall not apply with respect to any coverage for Workers' Compensation; or (ii) property and casualty insurance losses resulting from the act, in the aggregate, do not exceed $5,000,000.

DETERMINATIONS FINAL.—Any certification of, or determination not to certify, an act as an act of terrorism under this paragraph shall be final, and shall not be subject to judicial review.

NONDELEGATION.—The Secretary may not delegate or designate to any other officer, employee, or person, any determination under this paragraph of whether, during the effective period of the Program, an act of terrorism has occurred.

AFFILIATE.—The term "affiliate" means, with respect to an insurer, any entity that controls, is controlled by, or is under common control with the insurer.

CONTROL.—An entity has "control" over another entity, if—(A) the entity directly or indirectly or acting through 1 or more other persons owns, controls, or has power to vote 25 percent or more of any class of voting securities of the other entity; (B) the entity controls in any manner the election of a majority of the directors or trustees of the other entity; or (C) the Secretary determines, after notice and opportunity for hearing, that the entity directly or indirectly exercises a controlling influence over the management or policies of the other entity.

DIRECT EARNED PREMIUM.—The term "direct earned premium" means a direct earned premium for property and casualty insurance issued by any insurer for insurance against losses occurring at the locations described in subparagraphs (A) and 6 (B) of paragraph (5).

INSURED LOSS.—The term "insured loss" means any loss resulting from an act of terrorism (including an act of war, in the case of workers' compensation) that is covered by primary or excess property and casualty insurance issued by an insurer if such loss—

(A) occurs within the United States; or (B) occurs to an air carrier (as defined in section 40102 of title 49, United States Code), to a United States flag vessel (or a vessel based principally in the United States, on which United States income tax is paid and whose insurance coverage is subject to regulation in the United States), regardless of where the loss occurs, or at the premises of any United States mission.

INSURER.—The term "insurer" means any entity, including any affiliate thereof—

(A) that is—(i) licensed or admitted to engage in the business of providing primary or excess insurance in any State; (ii) not licensed or admitted as described in clause (i), if it is an eligible surplus line carrier listed on the Quarterly Listing of Alien Insurers of the NAIC, or any successor thereto; (iii) approved for the purpose of offering property and casualty insurance by a Federal agency in connection with maritime, energy, or aviation activity; (iv) a State residual market insurance entity or State workers' compensation fund; or (v) any other entity described in section 103(f), to the extent provided in the rules of the Secretary issued under section 103(f); (B) that receives direct earned premiums for any type of commercial property and casualty insurance coverage, other than in the case of entities described in sections 103(d) and 103(f); and (C) that meets any other criteria that the Secretary may reasonably prescribe.

INSURER DEDUCTIBLE.—The term "insurer deductible" means— (A) for the Transition Period, the value of an insurer's direct earned premiums over the calendar year immediately preceding the date of enactment of this Act, multiplied by 1 percent; (B) for Program Year 1, the value of an insurer's direct earned premiums over the calendar year immediately preceding Program Year 1, multiplied by 7 percent; (C) for Program Year 2, the value of an insurer's direct earned premiums over the calendar year immediately preceding Program Year 2, multiplied by 10 percent; (D) for

Program Year 3, the value of an insurer's direct earned premiums over the calendar year immediately preceding Program Year 3, multiplied by 15 percent; and (E) notwithstanding subparagraphs (A) through (D), for the Transition Period, Program Year 1, Program Year 2, or Program Year 3, if an insurer has not had a full year of operations during the calendar year immediately preceding such Period or Program Year, such portion of the direct earned premiums of the insurer as the Secretary determines appropriate, subject to appropriate methodologies established by the Secretary for measuring such direct earned premiums.

NAIC.—The term "NAIC" means the National Association of Insurance Commissioners.

PERSON.—The term "person" means any individual, business or non-profit entity (including those organized in the form of a partnership, limited liability company, corporation, or association), trust or estate, or a State or political subdivision of a State or other governmental unit.

PROGRAM.—The term "Program" means the Terrorism Insurance Program established by this title.

PROGRAM YEARS.—19 (A) TRANSITION PERIOD.—The term "Transition Period" means the period beginning on the date of enactment of this Act and ending on December 31, 2002.

PROGRAM YEAR 1.—The term "Program Year 1" means the period beginning on January 1, 2003 and ending on December 31, 2003.

PROGRAM YEAR 2.—The term "Program Year 2" means the period beginning on January 1, 2004 and ending on December 31, 2004.

PROGRAM YEAR 3.—The term "Program Year 3" means the period beginning on January 1, 2005 and ending on December 31, 2005.

PROPERTY AND CASUALTY INSURANCE.—The term "property and casualty insurance"—(A) means commercial lines of property and casualty insurance, including excess insurance, Workers' Compensation insurance, and surety insurance; and does not include—(i) Federal crop insurance issued or reinsured under the Federal Crop Insurance Act (7 U.S.C. 1501 et seq.), or any other type of crop or livestock insurance that is privately issued or reinsured; (ii) private mortgage insurance [as that term is defined in section 2 of the Homeowners Protection Act of 1998 (12 U.S.C. 4901)] or title insurance; (iii) financial guaranty insurance issued by monoline financial guaranty insurance corporations; (iv) insurance for medical malpractice; (v) health or life insurance, including group life insurance; (vi) flood insurance provided under the National Flood Insurance Act of 1968 (42 U.S.C. 4001 et seq.); or (vii) reinsurance or retrocessional reinsurance.

SECRETARY.—The term "Secretary" means the Secretary of the Treasury.

STATE.—The term "State" means any State of the United States, the District of Columbia, the Commonwealth of Puerto Rico, the Commonwealth of the Northern Mariana Islands, American Samoa, Guam, each of the United States Virgin Islands, and any territory or possession of the United States.

UNITED STATES.—The term "United States" means the several States, and includes the territorial sea and the continental shelf of the United States, as those terms are defined in the Violent Crime Control and Law Enforcement Act of 1994 (18 U.S.C. 2280, 2281).

RULE OF CONSTRUCTION FOR DATES.—With respect to any reference to a date in this title, such day shall be construed—(A) to begin at 12:01 a.m. on that date; 8 and (B) to end at midnight on that date.

SEC. 103. TERRORISM INSURANCE PROGRAM.

ESTABLISHMENT OF PROGRAM.—

IN GENERAL.—There is established in the Department of the Treasury the Terrorism Insurance Program.

AUTHORITY OF THE SECRETARY.—Notwithstanding any other provision of State or Federal law, the Secretary shall administer the Program, and shall pay the Federal share of compensation for insured losses in accordance with subsection (e).

MANDATORY PARTICIPATION.—Each entity that meets the definition of an insurer under this title shall participate in the Program.

CONDITIONS FOR FEDERAL PAYMENTS.—No payment may be made by the Secretary under this section with respect to an insured loss that is covered by an insurer, unless—(1) the person that suffers the insured loss, or a person acting on behalf of that person, files a claim with the insurer; (2) the insurer provides clear and conspicuous disclosure to the policyholder of the premium charged for insured losses covered by the Program and the Federal share of compensation for insured losses under the Program—

(A) in the case of any policy that is issued before the date of enactment of this Act, not later than 90 days after that date of enactment; (B) in the case of any policy that is issued within 90 days of the date of enactment of this Act, at the time of offer, purchase, and renewal of the policy; and (C) in the case of any policy that is issued more than 90 days after the date of enactment of this Act, on a separate line item in the policy, at the time of offer, purchase, and renewal of the policy; (3) the insurer processes the claim for the insured loss in accordance with appropriate business practices, and any reasonable procedures that the Secretary may prescribe; and (4) the insurer submits to the Secretary, in accordance with such reasonable procedures as the Secretary may establish—(A) a claim for payment of the Federal share of compensation for insured losses under the Program; (B) written certification—(i) of the underlying claim; and (ii) of all payments made for insured losses; and (C) certification of its compliance with the provisions of this subsection.

MANDATORY AVAILABILITY.—INITIAL PROGRAM PERIODS.—During the period beginning on the first day of the Transition Period and ending on the last day of Program Year 2, each entity that meets the definition of an insurer under section 102—shall make available, in all of its property and casualty insurance policies, coverage for insured losses; and (B) shall make available property and casualty insurance coverage for insured losses that does not differ materially from the terms, amounts, and other coverage limitations applicable to losses arising from events other than acts of terrorism.

PROGRAM YEAR 3.—Not later than September 1, 2004, the Secretary shall, based on the factors referred to in section 108(d)(1), determine whether the provisions of subparagraphs (A) and (B) of paragraph (1) should be extended through Program Year 3.

STATE RESIDUAL MARKET INSURANCE ENTITIES.—IN GENERAL.—The Secretary shall issue regulations, as soon as practicable after the date of enactment of this Act, that apply the provisions of this title to State residual market insurance entities and State workers' compensation funds.

TREATMENT OF CERTAIN ENTITIES.—For purposes of the regulations issued pursuant to paragraph (1) (A) a State residual market insurance entity that does not share its profits and losses with private sector insurers shall be treated as a separate insurer; and (B) a State residual market insurance entity that shares its profits and losses with private sector insurers shall not be treated as a separate insurer, and shall report to each private sector insurance participant its share of the insured losses of the entity, which shall be included in each private sector insurer's insured losses.

TREATMENT OF PARTICIPATION IN CERTAIN ENTITIES.—Any insurer that participates in sharing profits and losses of a State residual market insurance entity shall include in its calculations of premiums any premiums distributed to the insurer by the State residual market insurance entity.

INSURED LOSS SHARED COMPENSATION.

FEDERAL SHARE.

IN GENERAL.—The Federal share of compensation under the Program to be paid by the Secretary for insured losses of an insurer during the Transition Period and each Program Year shall be equal to 90 percent of that portion of the amount of such insured losses that exceeds the applicable insurer deductible required to be paid during such Transition Period or such Program Year.

PROHIBITION ON DUPLICATIVE COMPENSATION.—The Federal share of compensation for insured losses under the Program shall be reduced by the amount of compensation provided by the Federal Government to any person under any other Federal program for those insured losses.

CAP ON ANNUAL LIABILITY.—

9 (A) IN GENERAL.—Notwithstanding paragraph (1) or any other provision of Federal or State law, if the aggregate insured losses exceed $100,000,000,000, during the period beginning on the first day of the Transition Period and ending on the last day of Program Year 1, or during Program Year 2 or Program Year 3 (until such time as the Congress may act otherwise with respect to such losses)—(i) the Secretary shall not make any payment under this title for any portion of the amount of such losses that exceeds $100,000,000,000; and (ii) no insurer that has met its insurer deductible shall be liable for the payment of any portion of that amount that exceeds $100,000,000,000.

INSURER SHARE.—For purposes of subparagraph (A), the Secretary shall determine the pro rata share of insured losses to be paid by each insurer that incurs insured losses under the Program.

NOTICE TO CONGRESS.—The Secretary shall notify the Congress if estimated or actual aggregate insured losses exceed $100,000,000,000 during the period beginning on the first day of the Transition Period and ending on the last day of Program Year 1, or during Program Year 2 or Program Year 3, and the Congress shall determine the procedures for and the source of any payments for such excess insured losses.

FINAL NETTING.—The Secretary shall have sole discretion to determine the time at which claims relating to any insured loss or act of terrorism shall become final.

DETERMINATIONS FINAL.—Any determination of the Secretary under this subsection shall be final, unless expressly provided, and shall not be subject to judicial review.

INSURANCE MARKETPLACE AGGREGATE RETENTION AMOUNT.—For purposes of paragraph (7), the insurance marketplace aggregate retention amount shall be—(A) for the period beginning on the first day of the Transition Period and ending on the last day of Program Year 1, the lesser of—(i) $10,000,000,000; and (ii) the aggregate amount, for all insurers, of insured losses during such period; (B) for Program Year 2, the lesser of—(i) $12,500,000,000; and (ii) the aggregate amount, for all insurers, of insured losses during such Program Year; and (C) for Program Year 3, the lesser of—(i) $15,000,000,000; and (ii) the aggregate amount, for all insurers, of insured losses during such Program Year.

RECOUPMENT OF FEDERAL SHARE.

MANDATORY RECOUPMENT AMOUNT.—For purposes of this paragraph, the mandatory recoupment amount for each of the periods referred to in subparagraphs (A), (B), and (C) of paragraph (6) shall be the difference between—(i) the insurance marketplace aggregate retention amount under paragraph (6) for such period; and

(ii) the aggregate amount, for all insurers, of insured losses during such period that are not compensated by the Federal Government because such losses—(I) are within the insurer deductible for the insurer subject to the losses; or (II) are within the portion of losses of the insurer that exceed the insurer deductible, but are not compensated pursuant to paragraph (1).

NO MANDATORY RECOUPMENT IF UNCOMPENSATED LOSSES EXCEED INSURANCE.

MARKETPLACE RETENTION.—Notwithstanding subparagraph (A), if the aggregate amount of uncompensated insured losses referred to in clause (ii) of such subparagraph for any period referred to in subparagraph (A), (B), or (C) of paragraph (6) is greater than the insurance marketplace aggregate retention amount under paragraph (6) for such period, the mandatory recoupment amount shall be $0.

MANDATORY ESTABLISHMENT OF SURCHARGES TO RECOUP MANDATORY RECOUPMENT AMOUNT.—The Secretary shall collect, for repayment of the Federal financial assistance provided in connection with all acts of terrorism (or acts of war, in the case of workers compensation) occurring during any of the periods referred to in subparagraph (A), (B), or (C) of paragraph (6), terrorism loss risk-spreading premiums in an amount equal to any mandatory recoupment amount for such period.

DISCRETIONARY RECOUPMENT OF REMAINDER OF FINANCIAL ASSISTANCE.—To the extent that the amount of Federal financial assistance provided exceeds any mandatory recoupment amount, the Secretary may recoup, through terrorism loss risk-spreading premiums, such additional amounts that the Secretary believes can be recouped, based on— (i) the ultimate costs to taxpayers of no additional recoupment; (ii) the economic conditions in the commercial marketplace, including the capitalization, profitability, and investment returns of the insurance industry and the current cycle of the insurance markets; (iii) the affordability of commercial insurance for small- and medium-sized businesses; and (iv) such other factors as the Secretary considers appropriate.

POLICY SURCHARGE FOR TERRORISM LOSS RISK-SPREADING PREMIUMS.

POLICYHOLDER PREMIUM.—Any amount established by the Secretary as a terrorism loss risk-spreading premium shall—(i) be imposed as a policyholder premium surcharge on property and casualty insurance policies in force after the date of such establishment; (ii) begin with such period of coverage during the year as the Secretary determines appropriate; and (iii) be based on a percentage of the premium amount charged for property and casualty insurance coverage under the policy.

COLLECTION.—The Secretary shall provide for insurers to collect terrorism loss risk-spreading premiums and remit such amounts collected to the Secretary.

PERCENTAGE LIMITATION.—A terrorism loss risk-spreading premium (including any additional amount included in such premium on a discretionary basis pursuant to paragraph (7)(D)) may not exceed, on an annual basis, the amount equal to 3 percent of the premium charged for property and casualty insurance coverage under the policy.

ADJUSTMENT FOR URBAN AND SMALLER COMMERCIAL AND RURAL AREAS AND DIFFERENT LINES OF INSURANCE.

ADJUSTMENTS.—In determining the method and manner of imposing terrorism loss risk-spreading premiums, including the amount of such premiums, the Secretary shall take into consideration—(I) the economic impact on commercial centers of urban areas, including the effect on commercial rents and commercial insurance premiums, particularly rents and premiums charged to small businesses, and the availability of lease space and commercial insurance within urban areas; (II) the risk factors related to rural areas and smaller commercial centers, including the potential exposure to loss and the likely magnitude of such loss, as well as any resulting cross-subsidization that might result; and (III) the various exposures to terrorism risk for different lines of insurance.

RECOUPMENT OF ADJUSTMENTS.—Any mandatory recoupment amounts not collected by the Secretary because of adjustments under this subparagraph shall be recouped through additional terrorism loss risk-spreading premiums.

TIMING OF PREMIUMS.—The Secretary may adjust the timing of terrorism loss risk spreading premiums to provide for equivalent application of the provisions of this title to policies that are not based on a calendar year, or to apply such provisions on a daily, monthly, or quarterly basis, as appropriate.

CAPTIVE INSURERS AND OTHER SELF-INSURANCE ARRANGEMENTS.—The Secretary may, in consultation with the NAIC or the appropriate State regulatory authority, apply the provisions of this title, as appropriate, to other classes or types of captive insurers and other self-insurance arrangements by municipalities and other entities (such as workers' compensation self-insurance programs and State workers' compensation reinsurance pools), but only if such application is determined before the occurrence of an act of terrorism in which such an entity incurs an insured loss and all of the provisions of this title are applied comparably to such entities.

REINSURANCE TO COVER EXPOSURE.

OBTAINING COVERAGE.—This title may not be construed to limit or prevent insurers from obtaining reinsurance coverage for insurer deductibles or insured losses retained by insurers pursuant to this section, nor shall the obtaining of such coverage affect the calculation of such deductibles or retentions.

LIMITATION ON FINANCIAL ASSISTANCE.—The amount of financial assistance provided pursuant to this section shall not be reduced by reinsurance paid or payable to an insurer from other sources, except that recoveries from such other sources, taken together with financial assistance for the Transition Period or a Program Year provided pursuant to this section, may not exceed the aggregate amount of the insurer's insured losses for such period. If such recoveries and financial assistance for the Transition Period or a Program Year exceed such aggregate amount of insured losses for that period and there is no agreement between the insurer and any reinsurer to the contrary, an amount in excess of such aggregate insured losses shall be returned to the Secretary.

GROUP LIFE INSURANCE STUDY.

STUDY.—The Secretary shall study, on an expedited basis, whether adequate and affordable catastrophe reinsurance for acts of terrorism is available to life insurers in the United States that issue group life insurance, and the extent to which the threat of terrorism is reducing the availability of group life insurance coverage for consumers in the United States.

CONDITIONAL COVERAGE.—To the extent that the Secretary determines that such coverage is not or will not be reasonably available to both such insurers and consumers, the Secretary shall, in consultation with the NAIC—(A) apply the provisions of this title, as appropriate, to providers of group life insurance; and (B) provide such restrictions, limitations, or conditions with respect to any financial assistance provided that the Secretary deems appropriate, based on the study under paragraph 8 (1).

STUDY AND REPORT.

STUDY.—The Secretary, after consultation with the NAIC, representatives of the insurance industry, and other experts in the insurance field, shall conduct a study of the potential effects of acts of terrorism on the availability of life insurance and other lines of insurance coverage, including personal lines.

REPORT.—Not later than 9 months after the date of enactment of this Act, the Secretary shall submit a report to the Congress on the results of the study conducted under paragraph (1).

SEC. 104. GENERAL AUTHORITY AND ADMINISTRATION OF CLAIMS.

GENERAL AUTHORITY.—The Secretary shall have the powers and authorities necessary to carry out the Program, including authority—(1) to investigate and audit all claims under the Program; and (2) to prescribe regulations and procedures to effectively administer and implement the Program, and to ensure that all insurers and self-insured entities that participate in the Program are treated comparably under the Program.

INTERIM RULES AND PROCEDURES.—The Secretary may issue interim final rules or procedures specifying the manner in which—(1) insurers may file and certify claims under the Program; (2) the Federal share of compensation for insured losses will be paid under the Program, including payments based on estimates of or actual insured losses; (3) the Secretary may, at any time, seek repayment from or reimburse any insurer, based on estimates of insured losses under the Program, to effectuate the insured loss sharing provisions in section 103; and (4) the Secretary will determine any final netting of payments under the Program, including payments owed to the Federal Government from any insurer and any Federal share of compensation for insured losses owed to any insurer, to effectuate the insured loss sharing provisions in section 103.

CONSULTATION.—The Secretary shall consult with the NAIC, as the Secretary determines appropriate, concerning the Program.

CONTRACTS FOR SERVICES.—The Secretary may employ persons or contract for services as may be necessary to implement the Program.

CIVIL PENALTIES.

IN GENERAL.—The Secretary may assess a civil monetary penalty in an amount not exceeding the amount under paragraph (2) against any insurer that the Secretary determines, on the record after opportunity for a hearing—(A) has failed to charge, collect, or remit terrorism loss risk-spreading premiums under section 103(e) in accordance with the requirements of, or regulations issued under, this title; (B) has intentionally provided to the Secretary erroneous information regarding premium or loss amounts; (C) submits to the Secretary fraudulent claims under the Program for insured losses; (D) has failed to provide the disclosures required under subsection (f); or (E) has otherwise failed to comply with the provisions of, or the regulations issued under, this title.

AMOUNT.—The amount under this paragraph is the greater of $1,000,000 and, in the case of any failure to pay, charge, collect, or remit amounts in accordance with this title or the regulations issued under this title, such amount in dispute.

RECOVERY OF AMOUNT IN DISPUTE.—A penalty under this subsection for any failure to pay, charge, collect, or remit amounts in accordance with this title or the regulations under this title shall be in addition to any such amounts recovered by the Secretary.

SUBMISSION OF PREMIUM INFORMATION.

IN GENERAL.—The Secretary shall annually compile information on the terrorism risk insurance premium rates of insurers for the preceding year.

ACCESS TO INFORMATION.—To the extent that such information is not otherwise available to the Secretary, the Secretary may require each insurer to submit to the NAIC terrorism risk insurance premium rates, as necessary to carry out paragraph (1), and the NAIC shall make such information available to the Secretary.

AVAILABILITY TO CONGRESS.—The Secretary shall make information compiled under this subsection available to the Congress, upon request.

FUNDING.

FEDERAL PAYMENTS.—There are hereby appropriated, out of funds in the Treasury not otherwise appropriated, such sums as may be necessary to pay the Federal share of compensation for insured losses under the Program.

ADMINISTRATIVE EXPENSES.—There are hereby appropriated, out of funds in the Treasury not otherwise appropriated, such sums as may be necessary to pay reasonable costs of administering the Program.

SEC. 105. PREEMPTION AND NULLIFICATION OF PRE-EXISTING TERRORISM EXCLUSIONS.

GENERAL NULLIFICATION.—Any terrorism exclusion in a contract for property and casualty insurance that is in force on the date of enactment of this Act shall be void to the extent that it excludes losses that would otherwise be insured losses.

GENERAL PREEMPTION.—Any State approval of any terrorism exclusion from a contract for property and casualty insurance that is in force on the date of enactment of this Act, shall be void to the extent that it excludes losses that would otherwise be insured losses.

REINSTATEMENT OF TERRORISM EXCLUSIONS.—Notwithstanding subsections (a) and (b) or any provision of State law, an insurer may reinstate a preexisting provision in a contract for property and casualty insurance that is in force on the date of enactment of this Act and that excludes coverage for an act of terrorism only—(1) if the insurer has received a written statement from the insured that affirmatively authorizes such reinstatement; or (2) if—(A) the insured fails to pay any increased premium charged by the insurer for providing such terrorism coverage; and (B) the insurer provided notice, at least 30 days before any such reinstatement, of—(i) the increased premium for such 19 terrorism coverage; and (ii) the rights of the insured with respect to such coverage, including any date upon which the exclusion would be reinstated if no payment is received.

SEC. 106. PRESERVATION PROVISIONS.

STATE LAW.—Nothing in this title shall affect the jurisdiction or regulatory authority of the insurance commissioner (or any agency or office performing like functions) of any State over any insurer or other person—(1) except as specifically provided in this title; and (2) except that—(A) the definition of the term "act of terrorism" in section 102 shall be the exclusive definition of that term for purposes of compensation for insured losses under this title, and shall preempt any provision of State law that is inconsistent with that definition, to the extent that such provision of law would otherwise apply to any type of insurance covered by this title; (B) during the period beginning on the date of enactment of this Act and ending on December 31, 2003, rates and forms for terrorism risk insurance covered by this title and filed with any State shall not be subject to prior approval or a waiting period under any law of a State that would otherwise be applicable, except that nothing in this title affects the ability of any State to invalidate a rate as excessive, inadequate, or unfairly discriminatory, and, with respect to forms, where a State has prior approval authority, it shall apply to allow subsequent review of such forms; and (C) during the period beginning on the date of enactment of this Act and for so long as the Program is in effect, as provided in section 108, including authority in subsection 108(b), books and records of any insurer that are relevant to the Program shall be provided, or caused to be provided, to the Secretary, upon request by the Secretary, notwithstanding any provision of the laws of any State prohibiting or limiting such access.

EXISTING REINSURANCE AGREEMENTS.—Nothing in this title shall be construed to alter, amend, or expand the terms of coverage under any reinsurance agreement in effect on the date of enactment of this Act. The terms and conditions of such an agreement shall be determined by the language of that agreement.

SEC. 107. LITIGATION MANAGEMENT.
PROCEDURES AND DAMAGES.

IN GENERAL.—If the Secretary makes a determination pursuant to section 102 that an act of terrorism has occurred, there shall exist a Federal cause of action for property damage, personal injury, or death arising out of or resulting from such act of terrorism, which shall be the exclusive cause of action and remedy for claims for property damage, personal injury, or death arising out of or relating to such act of terrorism, except as provided in subsection (b).

PREEMPTION OF STATE ACTIONS.—All State causes of action of any kind for property damage, personal injury, or death arising out of or resulting from an act of terrorism that are otherwise available under State law are hereby preempted, except as provided in subsection (b).

SUBSTANTIVE LAW.—The substantive law for decision in any such action described in paragraph (1) shall be derived from the law, including choice of law principles, of the State in which such act of terrorism occurred, unless such law is otherwise inconsistent with or preempted by Federal law.

JURISDICTION.—For each determination described in paragraph (1), not later than 90 days after the occurrence of an act of terrorism, the Judicial Panel on Multidistrict Litigation shall designate 1 district court or, if necessary, multiple district courts of the United States that shall have original and exclusive jurisdiction over all actions for any claim (including any claim for loss of property, personal injury, or death) relating to or arising out of an act of terrorism subject to this section. The Judicial Panel on Multidistrict Litigation shall select and assign the district court or courts based on the convenience of the parties and the just and efficient conduct of the proceedings. For purposes of personal jurisdiction, the district court or courts designated by the Judicial Panel on Multidistrict Litigation shall be deemed to sit in all judicial districts in the United States.

PUNITIVE DAMAGES.—Any amounts awarded in an action under paragraph (1) that are attributable to punitive damages shall not count as insured losses for purposes of this title.

EXCLUSION.—Nothing in this section shall in any way limit the liability of any government, an organization, or person who knowingly participates in, conspires to commit, aids and abets, or commits any act of terrorism with respect to which a determination described in subsection (a)(1) was made.

RIGHT OF SUBROGATION.—The United States shall have the right of subrogation with respect to any payment or claim paid by the United States under this title.

RELATIONSHIP TO OTHER LAW.—Nothing in this section shall be construed to affect—(1) any party's contractual right to arbitrate a dispute; or (2) any provision of the Air Transportation Safety and System Stabilization Act (Public Law 107–42; 49 U.S.C. 40101 note).

EFFECTIVE PERIOD.—This section shall apply only to actions described in subsection (a)(1) that arise out of or result from acts of terrorism that occur or occurred during the effective period of the Program.

SEC. 108. TERMINATION OF PROGRAM.

TERMINATION OF PROGRAM.—The Program shall terminate on December 31, 2005.

CONTINUING AUTHORITY TO PAY OR ADJUST COMPENSATION.—Following the termination of the Program, the Secretary may take such actions as may be necessary to ensure payment, recoupment, reimbursement, or adjustment of compensation for insured losses arising out of any act of terrorism occurring during the period in which the Program was in effect under this title, in accordance with the provisions of section 103 and regulations promulgated thereunder.

REPEAL; SAVINGS CLAUSE.—This title is repealed on the final termination date of the Program under subsection (a), except that such repeal shall not be construed—

(1) to prevent the Secretary from taking, or causing to be taken, such actions under subsection (b) of this section, paragraph (4), (5), (6), (7), or (8) of section 103(e), or subsection (a)(1), (c), (d), or (e) of section 104, as in effect on the day before the date of such repeal, or applicable regulations promulgated thereunder, during any period in which the authority of the Secretary under subsection (b) of this section is in effect; or

(2) to prevent the availability of funding under section 104(g) during any period in which the authority of the Secretary under subsection (b) of this section is in effect.

STUDY AND REPORT ON THE PROGRAM.

STUDY.—The Secretary, in consultation with the NAIC, representatives of the insurance industry and of policy holders, other experts in the insurance field, and other experts as needed, shall assess the effectiveness of the Program and the likely capacity of the property and casualty insurance industry to offer insurance for terrorism risk after termination of the Program, and the availability and affordability of such insurance for various policyholders, including railroads, trucking, and public transit.

REPORT.—The Secretary shall submit a report to the Congress on the results of the study conducted under paragraph (1) not later than June 30, 2005.

TITLE II—TREATMENT OF TERRORIST ASSETS

SEC. 201. SATISFACTION OF JUDGMENTS FROM BLOCKED ASSETS OF TERRORISTS, TERRORIST ORGANIZATIONS, AND STATE SPONSORS OF TERRORISM.

IN GENERAL.—Notwithstanding any other provision of law, and except as provided in subsection (b), in every case in which a person has obtained a judgment against a terrorist party on a claim based upon an act of terrorism, or for which a terrorist party is not immune under section 1605(a)(7) of title 28, United States Code, the blocked assets of that terrorist party (including the blocked assets of any agency or instrumentality of that terrorist party) shall be subject to execution or attachment in aid of execution in order to satisfy such judgment to the extent of any compensatory damages for which such terrorist party has been adjudged liable.

PRESIDENTIAL WAIVER.

IN GENERAL.—Subject to paragraph (2), upon determining on an asset-by-asset basis that a waiver is necessary in the national security interest, the President may waive the requirements of subsection (a) in connection with (and prior to the enforcement of) any judicial order directing attachment in aid of execution or execution against any property subject to the Vienna Convention on Diplomatic Relations or the Vienna Convention on Consular Relations.

EXCEPTION.—A waiver under this subsection shall not apply to—

(A) property subject to the Vienna Convention on Diplomatic Relations or the Vienna Convention on Consular Relations that has been used by the United States for any nondiplomatic purpose (including use as rental property), or the proceeds of such use; or

(B) the proceeds of any sale or transfer for value to a third party of any asset subject to the Vienna Convention on Diplomatic Relations or the Vienna Convention on Consular Relations.

SPECIAL RULE FOR CASES AGAINST IRAN.—Section 2002 of the Victims of Trafficking and Violence Protection Act of 2000 (Public Law 106–386; 114 Stat. 1542), as amended by section 686 of Public Law 107–228, is further amended—

(1) in subsection (a)(2)(A)(ii), by striking "July 27, 2000, or January 16, 2002" and inserting "July 27, 2000, any other date before October 28, 2000, or January 16, 2002";

(2) in subsection (b)(2)(B), by inserting after "the date of enactment of this Act" the following: "(less amounts therein as to which the United States has an interest in subrogation pursuant to subsection (c) arising prior to the date of entry of the judgment or judgments to be satisfied in whole or in part hereunder)"; (3) by redesignating subsections (d), (e), and (f) as subsections (e), (f), and (g), respectively; and (4) by inserting after subsection (c) the following new subsection (d): "(d) DISTRIBUTION OF ACCOUNT BALANCES AND PROCEEDS INADEQUATE TO SATISFY FULL AMOUNT OF COMPENSATORY AWARDS AGAINST IRAN.—

"(1) PRIOR JUDGMENTS.

"(A) IN GENERAL.—In the event that the Secretary determines that 90 percent of the amounts available to be paid under subsection (b)(2) are inadequate to pay the total amount of compensatory damages awarded in judgments issued as of the date of the enactment of this subsection in cases identified in subsection (a)(2)(A) with respect to Iran, the Secretary shall, not later than 60 days after such date, make payment from such amounts available to be paid under subsection (b)(2) to each party to which such a judgment has been issued in an amount equal to a share, calculated under subparagraph (B), of 90 percent of the amounts available to be paid under subsection (b)(2) that have not been subrogated to the United States under this Act as of the date of enactment of this subsection.

"(B) CALCULATION OF PAYMENTS.—The share that is payable to a person under subparagraph (A), including any person issued a final judgment as of the date of enactment of this subsection in a suit filed on a date added by the amendment made by section 686 of Public Law 107–228, shall be equal to the proportion that the amount of unpaid compensatory damages awarded in a final judgment issued to that person bears to the total amount of all unpaid compensatory damages awarded to all persons to whom such judgments have been issued as of the date of enactment of this subsection in cases identified in subsection (a)(2)(A) with respect to Iran.

"(2) SUBSEQUENT JUDGMENT.

"(A) IN GENERAL.—The Secretary shall pay to any person awarded a final judgment after the date of enactment of this subsection, in the case filed on January 16, 2002, and identified in subsection (a)(2)(A) with respect to Iran, an amount equal to a share, calculated under subparagraph (B), of the balance of the amounts available to be paid under subsection (b)(2) that remain following the disbursement of all payments as provided by paragraph (1).

The Secretary shall make such payment not later than 30 days after such judgment is awarded.

"(B) CALCULATION OF PAYMENTS.—To the extent that funds are available, the amount paid under subparagraph (A) to such person shall be the amount the person would have been paid under paragraph (1) if the person had been awarded the judgment prior to the date of enactment of this subsection.

"(3) ADDITIONAL PAYMENTS.

"(A) IN GENERAL.—Not later than 30 days after the disbursement of all payments under paragraphs (1) and (2), the Secretary shall make an additional payment to each person who received a payment under paragraph (1) or (2) in an amount equal to a share, calculated under subparagraph (B), of the balance of the amounts available to be paid under subsection (b)(2) that remain following the disbursement of all payments as provided by paragraphs (1) and (2).

"(B) CALCULATION OF PAYMENTS.—The share payable under subparagraph (A) to each such person shall be equal to the proportion that the amount of compensatory damages awarded that person bears to the total amount of all compensatory damages awarded to all persons who received a payment under paragraph (1) or (2).

"(4) STATUTORY CONSTRUCTION.—Nothing in this subsection shall bar, or require delay in, enforcement of any judgment to which this subsection applies under any procedure or against assets otherwise available under this section or under any other provision of law.

"(5) CERTAIN RIGHTS AND CLAIMS NOT RELINQUISHED.—Any person receiving less than the full amount of compensatory damages awarded to that party in a judgment to which this subsection applies shall not be required to make the election set forth in subsection (a)(2)(B) or, with respect to subsection (a)(2)(D), the election relating to relinquishment of any right to execute or attach property that is subject to section 1610(f)(1)(A) of title 28, United States Code, except that such person shall be required to relinquish rights set forth—" (A) in subsection (a)(2)(C); and

"(B) in subsection (a)(2)(D) with respect to enforcement against property that is at issue in claims against the United States before an international tribunal or that is the subject of awards by such tribunal."

"(6) GUIDELINES FOR ESTABLISHING CLAIMS OF A RIGHT TO PAYMENT.—The Secretary may promulgate reasonable guidelines through which any person claiming a right to payment under this section may inform the Secretary of the basis for such claim, including by submitting a certified copy of the final judgment under which such right is claimed and by providing commercially reasonable payment instructions. The Secretary shall take all reasonable steps necessary to ensure, to the maximum extent practicable, that such guidelines shall not operate to delay or interfere with payment under this section."

DEFINITIONS.—In this section, the following definitions shall apply:

(1) ACT OF TERRORISM.—The term "act of terrorism" means—(A) any act or event certified under section 102(1); or (B) to the extent not covered by subparagraph (A), any terrorist activity (as defined in section 212(a)(3)(B)(iii) of the Immigration and Nationality Act (8 U.S.C. 1182(a)(3) (B)(iii))).

BLOCKED ASSET.—The term "blocked asset" means—(A) any asset seized or frozen by the United States under section 5(b) of the Trading With the Enemy Act (50 U.S.C. App. 5(b)) or under sections 202 and 203 of the International Emergency Economic Powers Act (50 U.S.C. 1701; 1702); and (B) does not include property that—(i) is subject to a license issued by the United States Government for final payment, transfer, or disposition by or to a person subject to the jurisdiction of the United States in connection with a transaction for which the issuance of such license has been specifically required by statute other than the International Emergency Economic Powers Act (50 U.S.C. 1701 et seq.) or the United Nations Participation Act of 1945 (22 U.S.C. 287 et 17 seq.); or (ii) in the case of property subject to the Vienna Convention on Diplomatic Relations or the Vienna Convention on Consular Relations, or that enjoys equivalent privileges and immunities under the law of the United States, is being used exclusively for diplomatic or consular purposes.

CERTAIN PROPERTY.—The term "property subject to the Vienna Convention on Diplomatic Relations or the Vienna Convention on Consular Relations" and the term "asset subject to the Vienna Convention on Diplomatic Relations or the Vienna Convention on Consular Relations" mean any property or asset, respectively, the attachment in aid of execution or execution of which would result in a violation of an obligation of the United States under the Vienna Convention on Diplomatic Relations or the Vienna Convention on Consular Relations, as the case may be.

TERRORIST PARTY.—The term "terrorist party" means a terrorist, a terrorist organization (as defined in section 212(a)(3)(B)(vi) of the Immigration and Nationality Act (8 U.S.C. 1182(a)(3)(B)(vi))), or a foreign state designated as a state sponsor of terrorism under section 6(j) of the Export Administration Act of 1979 (50 U.S.C. App. 2405(j)) or section 620A of the Foreign Assistance Act of 1961 (22 U.S.C. 2371).

TITLE III—FEDERAL RESERVE BOARD PROVISIONS
SEC. 301. CERTAIN AUTHORITY OF THE BOARD OF GOVERNORS OF THE FEDERAL RESERVE SYSTEM.

Section 11 of the Federal Reserve Act (12 U.S.C. 248) is amended by adding at the end the following new subsection: "(r)(1) Any action that this Act provides may be taken only upon the affirmative vote of 5 members of the Board may be taken upon the unanimous vote of all members then in office if there are fewer than 5 members in office at the time of the action.

"(2)(A) Any action that the Board is otherwise authorized to take under section 13(3) may be taken upon the unanimous vote of all available members then in office, if—

"(i) at least 2 members are available and all available members participate in the action;

"(ii) the available members unanimously determine that—" (I) unusual and exigent circumstances exist and the borrower is unable to secure adequate credit accommodations from other sources; "(II) action on the matter is necessary to prevent, correct, or mitigate serious harm to the economy or the stability of the financial system of the United States;

"(III) despite the use of all means available (including all available telephonic, telegraphic, and other electronic means), the other members of the Board have not been able to be contacted on the matter; and "(IV) action on the matter is required before the number of Board members otherwise required to vote on the matter can be contacted through any available means (including all available telephonic, telegraphic, and other electronic means); and "(iii) any credit extended by a Federal reserve bank pursuant to such action is payable upon demand of the Board. "(B) The available members of the Board shall document in writing the determinations required by subparagraph (A)(ii), and such written findings shall be included in the record of the action and in the official minutes of the Board, and copies of such record shall be provided as soon as practicable to the members of the Board who were not available to participate in the action and to the Chairman of the Committee on Banking, Housing, and Urban Affairs of the Senate and to the Chairman of the Committee on Financial Services of the House of Representatives."

KEY INTERNATIONAL WEBSITES

1travel.com: http://www.onetravel.com

A UK service for small businesses that provides preliminary information on trade: http://www.dti.uk/ots/explorer/trade.html

Addresses & Salutations: http://www.bspage.com

Admission temporary admission (ATA) Carnet (Merchandise Password): http://www.uscib.org

Africa Online: http://www.africaonline.com

AgExporter: http://www.fas.usda.gov

Air Cargo News: http://www.aircargonews.com

Air Cargo Week: http://www.aircargoweek.com

Air Cargo World: http://www.aircargoworld.com

Airforwarders Association: http://www.airforwarders.org

Airline toll-free numbers and websites: http://www.princeton.edu/Main/air800.html

American Association of Port Authorities: http://www.aapa-ports.org

American Computer Resources, Inc.: http://www.the-acr.com

American Countertrade Association: http://www.countertrade.org

American Institute for Shippers' Associations: http://www.shippers.org

American Journal of Transportation: http://www.ajot.com

American River International: http://www.worldest.com/

American Shipper: http://www.americanshipper.com

American Short Line and Regional Railroad Association: http://www.aslrra.org

American Stock Exchange: http://www.amex.com

American Trucking Association: http://www.trucking.org

Australian stock exchange (ASX) Traders: http://www.ASX.com

Automated Export System Direct: http://www.aesdirect.gov

Automated teller machines around the world: http://www.fita.org/marketplace/travel.html#atm

Aviation Consumer Action Project: http://www.acap1971.org

Aviation Week: http://www.aviationnow.com

Bureau of Customs and Border Protection: http://www.cbp.gov

Bureau of Industry and Security: http://www.bis.doc.gov

Bureau of National Affairs, International Trade Reporter Export Reference Manual: http://www.bna.com

Business Advisor: http://www.business.gov

Business Traveler Info Network: http://www.business-trip.com

Career China: http://www.dragonsurf.com

Cargo Systems: http://www.cargosystems.net

Cargovision: http://www.cargovision.org

Census Bureau, Foreign Trade Division: http://www.census.gov/foreign trade/www

Central Europe Online: http://www.centraleurope.com

Chicago Stock Exchange: http://www.chicagostockex.com

Chinese News (in English): http://www.einnews.com/china

Classification schedules: http://www.census.gov/ftp/pub/foreign-trade/www/schedules.html

Commerce Business Daily: http://www.cbdnet.gpo.gov

Commercial Carrier Journal: http://www.etrucking.com

Commercial Encryption Export Controls: http://www.bis.doc.gov/Encryption/Default.htm

Correct way to fill out the Shipper's Export Declaration: http://www.census.gov/ftp/pub/foreign-trade/www/correct.way.html

Country Risk Forecast: http://www.controlrisks.com/html/index.php

Create Your Own Newspaper: http:/www.crayon.net

Culture and Travel: http://www.ciber.bus.msu.edu/busres/static/culture-travel-language.htm

Currency: http://www.oanda.com

Daily intelligence summary: http://www.dtic.mil/doctrine/jel/doddoct/data/d

Database at the United Nations World Bank: http://www.worldbank.org/data/onlinedatabases/onlinedatabases

Department of Transportation: http://www.dot.gov

Department of Transportation's Office of Inspector General: http://www.oig.dot.gov

Diverse languages of the modern world: http://www.unicode.org

Dr. Leonard's Healthcare Catalog: http://www.drleonards.com

Dun & Bradstreet: http://www.dnb.com

Economic Times (India): http://www.economictimes.com

Economist: http://www.economist.com

Electronic embassy: http://www.embassy.org

Embassies and consulates: http://www.embassyworld.com

Embassy web: http://www.embassy.com

European Union: http://www.europa.eu.int

Excite Travel: http://www.excite.com/travel

Export Administration Regulations: http://www.ntis.gov/products/type/database/export
 -regulations.asp
Export Assistant: http://www.cob.ohio-state.edu
Export Hotline: http://www.exporthotline.com
Export Legal Assistance Network: http://www.fita.org/elan
Export–Import Bank of the United States: http://www.exim.gov
Far Eastern Economic Review: http://www.feer.com
Federal Register Notice on the Status of Automated Export System and AERP: http://www
 .access.gpo.gov
Federation of International Trade Associations: http://www.fita.org
Financial Times: http://www.ft.com
For female travelers: http://www.journeywoman.com
Global Business: http://www.gbn.org
Global Business Information Network: http://www.bus.indiana.edu
Global Information Network for Small and Medium Enterprises: http://www.gin.sme
 .ne.jp/intro.html
Global law and business: http://www.law.com
Glossary of internalization and localization terms: http://www.bowneglobal.com/bowne
 .asp?page59&language51
Glossary of ocean cargo insurance terms: http://www.tsbic.com/cargo/glossary.htm
Government resources: http://www.ciber.bus.msu.edu/busres/govrnmnt.htm
Hong Kong Trade Development Counsel: http://www.tdctrade.com
iAgora Work Abroad: http://www.iagora.com/pages/html/work/index.html
Import–Export Bulletin Board: http://www.iebb.com
Inbound Logistics: http://www.inboundlogistics.com
Incoterms 2000: http://www.iccwbo.org/home/menu_incoterms.asp
Independent Accountants International: http://www. accountants.org
Industrial materials exchange (IMEX) Exchange: http://www.imex.com
Information on diseases abroad: http://www.cdc.gov
Inside China Today: http://www.einnews.com
Intellicast Weather (four-day forecast): http://www.intellicast.com/LocalWeather/World
Intermodal Association of North America: http://www.intermodal.org
International Air Transport Association: http://www.iata.org
International Association for Medical Assistance to Travelers: http://www.iamat.org
International Business: Strategies for the Global Marketplace Magazine: http://www.inter
 nationalbusiness.com
International Chamber of Commerce: http://www. iccwbo.org
International Commercial Law Monitor: http://www.lexmercatoria.org
International Economics and Business: dylee.keel.econ.ship.edu/econ/index.html
International Executive Service Corps : http://www.iesc.org
International Freight Association: http://www.ifa-online.com
International Law Check: http://www.law.comindex.shtml
International Maritime Organization: http://www.imo.org
International Monetary Fund: http://www.imf.org
International Society of Logistics: http://www.sole.org
International Trade Administration: http://www.ita.doc.gov
International trade shows and business events: http://www.ciber.bus.msu.edu/busre
International trade/import–export jobs: http://www.internationaltrade.org/jobs.html
International Trade/Import–Export Portal: http://www.imakenews.com

International warehousing logistics association (IWLA): http://www.warehouselogistics
.org

InterShipper: http://www.intershipper.com

Journal of Commerce Online: http://www.joc.com

Latin Trade: http://www.latintrade.com

Libraries: http://www.libraryspot.com/librariesonline.htm

Library of Congress: http://www.loc.gov

Local times around the world: http://www.times.clari.net.au

Logistics management and distribution report: http://www.manufacturing.net/magazine
/logistic

London Stock Exchange: http://www.londonstockexchange.com

Mailing lists: http://www.ciber.bus.msu.edu/busres/maillist.htm

Marine Digest: http://www.marinedigest.com

Market Research: http://www.imakenews.com

Matchmaker site: http://www.ita.doc.gov/efm

Medical conditions around the world: http://www.cdc.gov/travel/blusheet.htm

More trade leads: http://www.ibrc.bschool.ukans.edu

National Association of Foreign Trade Zones: http://www.NAFTZ.org

National Association of Purchasing Management: http://www.napm.org

National Association of Rail Shippers: http://www.railshippers.com

National Business Travel Association: http://www.biztraveler.org

National Customs Brokers and Forwarders Association of America: http://www.ncbfaa.org

National Institute of Standards and Technology: http://www.nist.gov

National Law Center For Inter-American Free Trade: http://www.natlaw.com

National Motor Freight Traffic Association: http://www.nmfta.org

New Records Formats for Commodity Filing and Transportation Filing: http://www
.customs.ustreas.gov

New York Times: http://www.nytimes.com

North American Free Trade Association Customs: http://www.nafta-customs.org

North American Industry Classification System: http://www.census.gov/epcd/www/naics
.html

Office of Anti-Boycott Compliance: http://www.bis.doc.gov/AntiboycottCompliance

Online Chambers of Commerce: http://www.online-chamber.com

Online newspapers: http://www.onlinenewspapers.com

Original Notice/Bureau of Census re: a classification of the definition of the exporter of
record for SED rep. Purp.: http://www.access.gpo.gov

Overseas Private Investment Corporation: http://www.opic.gov

Pacific Dictionary of International Trade and Business: http://www.pacific.commerce.ubc
.ca/ditb/search.html

Passenger rights: http://www.passengerrights.com

Port Import/Export Reporting Service: http://www.PIERS.com

Ports and Maritime Service Directory: http://www.seaportsinfo.com

Resources for international job opportunities: http://www.dbm.com/jobguide/internat.html

Reuters: http://www.reuters.com

Russia Today: http://www.russiatoday.com

Schedule B Export Codes: http://www.census.gov/foreign-trade/schedules/b

Search engine: http://www.google.com

Service Corps of Retired Executives: http://www.score.org

Shipping International: http://www.aajs.com/shipint

Shipping Times (Singapore): http://www.business-times.asia1.com.sg/shippingtimes
Small Business Administration: http://www.sba.gov
Small Business Administration Office of International Trade: http://www.sba.gov/oit
Small Business Administration Offices and Services: http://www.sba.gov/services
Small Business Association: http://www.sbaonline.gov
Small Business Development Centers: http://www.sba.gov/sbdc
Standard Industrial Classification Codes: http://www.trading.wmw.com/codes/sic.html
Statistical data sources: http://www.ciber.bus.msu.edu/busres/statinfo.htm
Statistics USA (STAT-USA) and National Transportation Data Base (NTDB): http://www
.stat-usa.gov
Telephone directories on the Web: http://www.teldir.com
The Expeditor: http://www.theexpeditor.com
The Export Practitioner (export regulations): http://www.exportprac.com
The Exporter: http://www.exporter.com
The Global Business Forum: http://www.gbfvisa.com
The Import–Export Bulletin Board: http://www.iebb.com/sell.html
The International Air Cargo Association: http://www.tiaca.org
The Times: http://www.londontimes.com
The Trade Compass: http://www.thetradecompass.com
The Trading Floor: http://www.trading/wmw.com
The World Academy: http://www.TheWorldAcademy.com
Tokyo Stock Exchange: http://www.tse.or.jp
Trade and Development Agency: http://www.tda.gov
Trade Information Center: http://www.ita.doc.gov/td/tic
Trade law website: http://www.hg.org/trade.html
Trade Net: http://www.tradenet.gov
Trade Point USA: http://www.tradepoint.org
Trade Statistics: http://www.ita.doc.gov/media
Trading Floor Harmonized Code Search Engine: http://www.trading.wmw.com
Traffics World: http://www.trafficsworld.com
Transportation Intermediaries Association: http://www.tianet.org
Transportation jobs and personnel: http://www.quotations.com/trans.htm
TravLang: http://www.travlang.com
Unibex: http://www.unibex.com
United Nations: http://www.un.org
United Nations Conference on Trade and Development: http://www.uncad-trains.org
United Nations International Trade Center: http://www.intracen.org
Universal Travel Protection Insurance: http://www.utravelpro.com
US Business Advisor: http://www.business.gov
US Census Bureau: http://www.census.gov
US Census Bureau Economic Indicators: http://www.census.gov/econ/www
US Census Bureau Foreign Trade Division Harmonized Tariff Classification Schedule:
http://www.census.gov/foreign-trade/www/schedules.html
US Council for International Business: http://www.uscib.org
US Customs Services: http://www.cbp.gov
US Department of Agriculture Foreign Agricultural Service: http://www.fas.usda.gov
US Department of Agriculture Shipper and Export Assistance: http://www.ams.usda
.gov/tmd/tsd
US Department of Commerce: http://www.doc.gov

US Department of Commerce Commercial Service: http://www.export.gov/com_svc/
US Department of Commerce International Trade Administration: http://www.ita.doc.gov
US Department of Commerce Trade Information Center: http://www.trade.gov/td/tic
US Export Assistance Centers: http://www.export.gov/eac.html
US Export Portal: http://www.export.gov
US Federal Maritime Commission: http://www.fmc.gov
US foreign trade zones: http://www.ia.ita.doc.gov/ftzpage
US government glossary and acronyms of international trade terms: http://www.joc.com
    /handbook/glossaryofterms.shtml
US Patent and Trademark Office: http://www.uspto.gov
US State Department Travel Advisory: http://www.travel.state.gov
US Trade Representative: http://www.ustr.gov
USA/Internet: http://www.stat-usa.gov
US–Mexico Chamber of Commerce: http://www.usmcoc.org/nafta.html
Various utilities and useful information: http://www.ciber.bus.msu.edu/busres/statics
    /online-tools-utilities.htm
Wall Street Journal: http://www.wsj.com
Wells Fargo: http://www.wellsfargo.com
World Bank Group: http://www.worldbank.org
World Chambers of Commerce Network: http://www.worldchambers.com
World Customs Organization: http://www.wcoomd.org
World Factbook: http://www.odci.gov/cia/publications/factbook/index.html
World Intellectual Property Organization: http://www.wipo.int
World newspapers online: http://www.virtourist.com/newspaper
World Trade Analyzer: http://www.tradecompass.com
World Trade Centers Association: http://www. iserve.wtca.org
World Trade Magazine: http://www.worldtrademag.com
World Trade Organization: http://www.wto.org
World Wide Shipping: http://www.ship.com
WorldPages: http://www.worldpages.com

ADVANCE MANIFEST RULES FOR CARGO INFORMATION: "2-HOUR RULE," "24-HOUR RULE," ETC.

(Affecting United States importers and exporters and their trading partners.)

Introductory Note: The following is an overview of the basic provisions of the U.S. Customs and Border Protection (CBP) advance cargo information requirements (known as the "24-Hour Rule"). For actual text of the "Final Rule," a series of FAQs (Frequently Asked Questions) with answers, plus additional information go to the CBP Web site at: www.cbp.gov. Please note that the rules and their enforcement are evolving and therefore subject to change.

BACKGROUND

In response to the terrorist attacks in New York and Washington, DC, on September 11, 2001, the U.S. government made substantive changes to the structure of numerous governmental agencies and enacted laws designed to better secure the country against possible future terrorist attacks.

The 200-plus year old U.S. Customs Service was renamed the Bureau of Customs and Border Protection, (CBP) and was consolidated, along with a number of other existing government agencies into the new Department of Homeland Security (DMS).

Importantly, the Trade Act of 2002 (section 343(a)) required that the CBP establish rules for the mandatory collection of electronic cargo information prior to the arrival of cargo in the United States (inbound cargo or imports) or its departure from the United States (outbound cargo or exports) by any mode of commercial transportation (sea, air, rail, or truck).

On December 5, 2003, U.S. Customs and Border Protection (CBP) published a notice (Final Rule) in the Federal Register (68 FR 68140) announcing changes in the Customs Regulations to require the advance electronic presentation of information for cargo in all modes of transportation, both inbound and outbound.

THE NEW REGULATIONS ("FINAL RULE")

68 FR 68140 amends the Customs Regulations to provide that the Bureau of Customs and Border Protection (CBP) must receive, by way of a CBP-approved electronic data interchange system (EDI), information pertaining to cargo (manifest data) before the cargo is either brought into or sent from the United States by any mode of commercial transportation (sea, air, rail, or truck).

The cargo information required is that which is reasonably necessary to enable high-risk shipments to be identified for purposes of ensuring cargo safety and security and preventing smuggling pursuant to the laws enforced and administered by CBP. These regulations are specifically intended to effectuate the provisions of section 343(a) of the Trade Act of 2002, as amended by the Maritime Transportation Security Act of 2002.

WHO IS AFFECTED?

Carriers and NVOCCs (non-vessel operating common carriers) are directly affected by the new regulations. Both groups must comply by sending manifest data to CBP according to the regulations (details follow).

Foreign exporters to the U.S., domestic exporters and importers, and foreign importers of U.S. products are also affected by these new regulations, because the bulk of the data forwarded to CBP by the carriers and NVOCCs originates from these groups. If transmittal of information is either incomplete, misleading, or not timely, it can cause a number of potentially serious problems including:

1. CBP may issue a "No Load" order to the carrier, effectively keeping the shipment at port and subjecting the shipment to storage charges and the importer and exporter to possible lost commercial opportunities.
2. Having the shipment become the target of additional scrutiny by CBP and possibly subjecting it to intense cargo examinations.
3. Potential denial or delays in obtaining permission to unlade the cargo at a U.S. port.

Obviously, importers and exporters will need to work closely with their foreign counterparts, carriers, NVOCCs and logistics firms to ensure compliance.

It should be noted that these new regulations are for the purpose of national security and that CBP is taking a very firm stance regarding compliance.

INBOUND TRANSMISSION TIMES

The regulations require that carriers send the required data to the CBP using the Automated Manifest System (AMS) and that the data be received by CBP according to the following timetable:

	Inbound—Transmission Received by CBP in AMS
Vessel	24 hours (before lading at foreign port) for nonbulk shipments
	24 hours before arrival for bulk shipments
Air	4 hours before *wheels up* from North American Free Trade Agreement (Canada and Mexico) and Central and South America above the equator
Rail	2 hours before arrival in United States
Truck	1 hour before arrival for non-Free and Secure Trade (FAST) participants
	30 minutes before arrival for FAST participants

The time requirements for bulk and break-bulk carriers to submit their cargo declaration information to CBP in SEA AMS is as follows:

	Cargo Declaration Data (CBP Form 1302) Including FROB*	
Type of Cargo	Qualifier	Time of Receipt by CBP in AMS
Containerized	None	24 hours prior to loading
Break bulk (nonexempt)	None	24 hours prior to loading
Bulk cargo	Voyage more than 24 hours	24 hours prior to arrival
Bulk cargo	Voyage less than 24 hours	Time of sailing
Break bulk cargo (exempt)	Voyage more than 24 hours	24 hours prior to arrival
Break bulk cargo (exempt)	Voyage less than 24 hours	Time of sailing

* FROB = Foreign remaining on board cargo.

The 24-hour period prior to loading begins from CBP receipt of information. The information is transmitted to CBP and must pass system edits and validations with a receipt message back to the transmitter to be considered received.

EFFECTIVE DATES

The "Final Rule" became effective January 5, 2004. However, within the Final Rule there were various implementation dates for automated transmissions for each mode of transportation. Carriers and/or automated NVOCCs are required to submit an electronic cargo declaration to CBP for all vessels loading on or after March 4, 2004. Any vessel that began its voyage on or after March 4, 2004 must comply with the specified reporting timeframe. Those vessels that were between foreign ports of call on March 4, 2004 were not required to comply with the electronic requirement for that voyage. The implementation dates were as follows:

Inbound	Implementation Date
Air	Beginning August 13, 2004 (see below)
Rail	Beginning July 12, 2004 (see below)
Truck	Beginning November 15, 2004 (see below)
Vessel	Voyages commencing March 4, 2004 or later

US DEPARTMENT OF COMMERCE, BUREAU OF INDUSTRY AND SECURITY, OFFICE OF EXPORTER SERVICES EXPORT MANAGEMENT AND COMPLIANCE DIVISION

Freight Forwarder Guidance

February 2012

Members of the international forwarding community play a key role in ensuring the security of the global supply chain, stemming the flow of illegal exports and helping to prevent weapons of mass destruction and other sensitive goods and technologies from falling into the hands of proliferators and terrorists.

The Forwarding Community's Forwarding agents have compliance responsibilities under the EAR even when their actions are dependent upon the information or instructions that are given by those who use their services. However, hiring an agent, whether a freight forwarder or some other agent, to perform various tasks does not relieve a party of its compliance responsibilities.

Agents are responsible for the representations that they make in filing export data. Moreover, no person, including an agent, may proceed with any transaction knowing that a violation of the EAR has, is about to, or is intended to occur. It is the agent's responsibility to understand its obligations.

Agents, especially those acting as the *exporter* in routed export transactions (see below), should understand the *Know Your Customer* guidance and *Red Flags* that are found in supplement no. 1 to part 732 of the EAR. Agents and exporters should determine if Red Flags are present, exercise due diligence in inquiring about them, and ensure that suspicious circumstances are not ignored. Failure to do so could constitute a violation of the EAR.

Agents should be thoroughly familiar with the ten General Prohibitions that are set forth in part 736 of the EAR and with the violations that are outlined in part 764 of the EAR. Engaging in prohibited conduct or committing the violations set out in the EAR may subject violators to significant penalties—up to 20 years imprisonment and fines of up to $1 million upon criminal conviction, and penalties of up to $250,000 per violation and/or a denial of export privileges for administrative offenses.

Routed and NonRouted Export Transactions' Primary responsibility for compliance with the EAR falls on the *principal parties in interest (PPI)* in a transaction. Generally, the PPIs in an export transaction are the US seller and foreign buyer. See the following parts and sections of the EAR for additional information: section 748.5, regarding parties to a transaction, part 758 on export clearance, and relevant definitions in part 772.

In a *routed export transaction*, in which the foreign PPI authorizes a US agent to facilitate the export of items from the United States, the USPPI obtains from the foreign PPI a writing in which the foreign PPI expressly assumes responsibility for determining the licensing requirements and obtaining authorization for the export. In this case, the US agent acting for the foreign PPI is the *exporter* under the EAR and is responsible for determining the licensing authority and obtaining the appropriate license or other authorization for the export.

An agent representing the foreign PPI in this type of routed export transaction must obtain a power of attorney or other written authorization in order to act on behalf of the foreign PPI.

In this type of routed export transaction, if the USPPI does not obtain from the foreign PPI the writing that is described above, then the USPPI is the exporter and must determine the licensing authority and obtain the appropriate license or other authorization. This is true even if the transaction is considered a routed export transaction for purposes of filing electronic export information pursuant to the Foreign Trade Regulations (15 C.F.R. part 30).

In a routed export transaction in which the foreign PPI assumes responsibility for determining the appropriate authorization for the export, the USPPI obtains from the foreign PPI a writing wherein the foreign PPI expressly assumes responsibility for determining the licensing requirements and obtaining the licensing authority. The EAR requires the USPPI to furnish the foreign PPI and its agent, upon request, with the correct Export Control Classification Number (ECCN) or sufficient technical information to determine the ECCN. In addition, the USPPI must provide the foreign PPI and its agent with any information that it knows will affect the determination of licensing authority. The USPPI also has a responsibility under the Foreign Trade Regulations (15 C.F.R. part 30) to provide certain data to the agent for the purposes of filing electronic export information.

In a transaction that is not a routed export transaction, if the USPPI authorizes an agent to prepare and file the export declaration on its behalf, the USPPI is the exporter under the EAR and is required to (A) provide the agent with the information that is necessary to complete the AES submission, (B) authorize the agent to complete the AES submission by power of attorney or other written authorization, and (C) maintain documentation to support the information that is provided to the agent for completing the AES submission.

If authorized by either the US or foreign PPI, the agent is responsible for (A) preparing the AES submission based on the information that is received from the USPPI, (B) maintaining documentation to support the information that is reported on the AES submission, and (C) upon request, providing the USPPI with a copy of the AES that is filed by the agent. Both the agent and the PPI who has authorized the agent are responsible for the correctness of each entry that is made on an AES submission. Good faith reliance on information obtained from the PPI can help protect an agent, but the careless use of *No-License-Required*, or unsupported entries, can get an agent into trouble. Agents without the appropriate technical expertise should avoid making commodity classifications and should obtain support documentation for ECCNs.

Additionally, upon written request, Census will provide companies with twelve months of AES data free of charge every 365 days. The Census Bureau's Foreign Trade Division currently provides USPPIs, and other filers requesting their AES data, with all the ten data elements that are required in routed export transactions.

As noted above, forwarders may be subject to criminal prosecution and/or administrative penalties for violations of the EAR. The BIS has not hesitated to hold forwarders liable for participating in illegal transactions.

Bad publicity alone can cost companies incalculable sums, in terms of future business, not to mention costs that are associated with lengthy and costly litigation, or administrative or criminal penalties. For example, in August 2009, after a government investigation lasting for more than five years, DHL reached a $9,444,744 Settlement Agreement with the BIS and Treasury's OFAC in a case involving hundreds of shipments to Iran, Sudan, and Syria, and a failure to adhere to government recordkeeping requirements.

This case, and many others involving forwarders, demonstrate the need for forwarders to know their customers and be aware of suspicious circumstances and Red Flags that may be present in an export transaction. When presented with Red Flags, forwarders have an obligation to inquire about the facts of the transaction, evaluate all of the information after inquiry, and refrain from engaging in the transaction if the Red Flags cannot be resolved. These steps help protect not only the forwarder but also the forwarder's client, who may be unknowingly engaging in a prohibited transaction.

Forwarders can take steps to mitigate their own and their clients' risks of liability by establishing a compliance program that scrutinizes export transactions and checks the parties to transactions against BIS's and other US Government agencies' various Lists to Check (see http://www.bis.doc .gov/complianceandenforcement/liststocheck.htm). Forwarders should also familiarize themselves with the types of activities to avoid in suspicious transactions as described in the BIS publication, Don't Let This Happen to You, also on the BIS website (http://www.bis.doc.gov/compliance andenforcement/dontletthishappentoyou-2008.pdf).

Although in a nonrouted transaction, the primary burden of compliance rests with the USPPI, section 758.3 of the EAR states that "[a]ll parties that participate in transactions subject to the EAR must comply with the EAR." Therefore, some compliance responsibility also rests with the freight forwarder. Parts 744, 760, 736, 732 supplement no. 3, and 764, among others, discuss how export transactions may not be conducted with certain parties; that dealing with certain parties may have additional licensing requirements; that dealing with certain parties should raise Red Flags for exporters; and that certain countries, activities, and items have certain restrictions under the EAR.

While the EAR allows flexibility in the manner in which US companies meet these compliance requirements in a number of different methods, the BIS strongly recommends that all parties dealing with export transactions maintain a vigorous and effective Export Management and Compliance Program (EMCP), incorporating the nine key elements (check the EMCP weblink at http://www.bis.doc.gov/complianceandenforcement/emcp.htm), and especially the screening of all parties to transactions, as part of their overall due diligence.

The BIS, however, also recommends striking the right balance. Compliance activities would differ depending on the nature of the items being exported and the destinations to which they are exported, but err on the side of caution to ensure that our US-origin dual-use goods and technologies are exported in compliance with the EAR.

Freight forwarders and exporters are symbiotically situated to work together to develop compliance procedures for their mutual benefit and sustainability. Building compliance partnerships and sharing compliance strategies with each other and other parties to transactions as part of standard operating procedures will give all who are involved a competitive edge. Once the investment is undertaken and the procedures are in place and continually maintained, export transactions will proceed predictably, safely, and with consistent application of the appropriate research and analysis of parties and uses/applications. The more compliance processes are integrated into existing business processes, the more seamless your entire export process will be. As you share and learn compliance techniques with your business partners and build synergies while also building business relationships, you will ensure your mutual longevity and bottom lines.

Even if forms like the BIS-711, the Destination Control Statement, and the Letter of Acceptance of License Conditions are not required by the EAR from your overseas business partners, as part of your own compliance processes, you may wish to draft a document, including language that is similar to these, and require their use in certain situations to enhance compliance.

Concerning documentation requirements, refer to the EAR's part 762 (applicable to all transactions that are subject to the EAR) regarding records that have to be maintained, records that don't have to be maintained, requirements for producing records, retention period, etc. There are also recordkeeping requirements from, inter alia, Customs (19 CFR part 163), the Department of State (ITAR and 22 CFR part 122.5), the Census Bureau (15 CFR 30.66(c)), and Treasury's Office of Foreign Assets Control (31 CFR part 501).

The BIS's Export Management and Compliance Division (EMCD, at 202-482-0062 and through the BIS website) is available to assist with compliance questions; our Outreach and Educational Services Division (OESD, at (202) 482-4811, 949-660-0144, and through the BIS website) is available to assist with general questions involving exporting, and, for licensing issues, it may be helpful to speak with one of the BIS's expert Licensing Officers who deals with your particular line of products. Your local Export Enforcement Field Office would also be able to give you guidance; to find your local office, call (202) 482-1208, or check the BIS Program Offices website at http://www.bis.doc.gov/about/programoffices .htm#ee, and for a regulatory perspective, you may also contact the BIS's Regulatory Policy Division (RPD) at (202) 482-2440 and through the BIS website.

Notably for freight forwarders, in the EAR, see, inter alia, sections 758.1 through 758.6, 748.4, and 750.7(d). Section 758.3(b) notes the difference in definitions between Census and the BIS for the term exporter. Section 758.8 discusses the return or unloading by forwarders, or other entities, of shipments at the direction of US government officials, and part 730, supplement no. 3, notes that export control responsibilities for Ocean Freight Forwarders are with the Federal Maritime Commission's Office of Freight Forwarders.

You may additionally set up information briefings, whereby you invite the EMCD, Customs and Border Protection (CBP), the BIS's Export Enforcement, and/or representatives from other government entities to make presentations to your company and your business partners, in order to support you in educating all regarding compliance. Make use of the BIS website and the other government websites, and send staff to BIS seminars and seminars that are offered by other government agencies.

Parties who believe they may have committed a violation of the EAR are encouraged to submit a Voluntary Self-Disclosure (VSD) to BIS. VSDs are an important indicator of a party's desire to bring their export activities into compliance and may provide important information to the BIS, helping to identify foreign proliferation networks. Parties submitting VSDs may be eligible for significant reductions in administrative penalties, and those with well-implemented EMCPs may expect further significant reductions of administrative penalties. The procedures for submitting VSDs may be found in section 764.5 of the EAR.

The procedures detailed in section 764.5 do not apply to VSDs involving violations of the antiboycott provisions of the EAR. The procedures for submitting VSDs for boycott violations are found in section 764.8 of the EAR.

The Office of Export Enforcement (OEE) and the Office of Exporter Services (which includes the EMCD, OESD, and RPD) welcome the opportunity to work with the international forwarding community to help ensure compliance with US export requirements. While it is important to protect yourselves and your clients from engaging in transactions that might constitute violations, it is equally important that the BIS be able to fulfill its mission of keeping the most sensitive goods out of the most dangerous hands. Development of effective, well-integrated, and well-implemented EMCPs, prompt notification by forwarders to the OEE of suspicious transactions, and assistance to OEE Special Agents in gathering the evidence that is necessary to disrupt illicit proliferation networks and bringing export violators to justice are important steps in helping to achieve these private- and public-sector goals.

Don't just read about it—practice it!

Bring the skills and tools that you have learned in life at this hands-on seminar!

Export/Import Procedures and Documentation
Seminar #1267

Get your products to and from customers and suppliers on time and hassle-free—and protect your company's investment!

The opportunities for exporting and importing have never been greater. But the details involved in these operations have never been more complex!

Learn how to deal successfully with banks, freight forwarders, customs brokers, and foreign customers. And find out how to use the necessary documents to obtain the greatest cost benefit for your company and a timely execution of your orders!

Who Should Attend

Export/import managers, traffic managers, shipping department personnel, international marketing managers, customer service staff, credit managers, controllers, purchasing managers, and directors of procurement or logistics.

How You Will Benefit

- Discover the latest export/import guidelines
- Get freight forwarders and bankers to work together to solve your logistics problems

- Maximize the services of general and bonded warehouses
- Prevent excessive duties by using foreign trade zones
- Avoid the pitfalls of improper documentation

What You Will Cover

- Document your shipment
- Execute smooth import transactions
- Comply with NAFTA and other origin requirements, trademarks, and copyright regulations
- Observe industry standards
- Avoid customs penalties
- Get help from freight forwarders and customs brokers
- Establish mutually beneficial relationships
- Get paid and make payments using letters of credit and documentary collections

For complete seminar content and schedule information, call 1-800-262-9699 or visit http://www.amanet.org.

Great Resource for Foreign Trade Zone Information

Welcome to the Foreign-Trade Zone Resource Center. This site was designed to provide information to virtually anyone who is involved in the foreign trade zone (FTZ) program. Although FTZs have grown since their creation by the Foreign-Trade Zones Act of 1934, there are still very few sources of information about FTZs. Recognizing this, we have produced the Foreign-Trade Zone Resource Center.

Potential FTZ grantees and FTZ users, as well as existing FTZ grantees and users, will find valuable information on this site. We will be adding additional FTZ information to this site as time permits. Meanwhile, if you have a document or information that you think would be helpful to other people who are interested in the Foreign-Trade Zones program, please feel free to submit it to our FTZ editor for review at editor@foreign-trade -zone.com.

List of Abbreviations

ACE	Automated Commercial Environment
ACS	Automated Commercial System
AES	Automated Export System
AIDC	Automated Identification and Data Collection
AIS	Automatic Identification System
AIU	American International Underwriters
AMA	American Management Association
APIS	Advance Passenger Information System
BASC	Business Anti-Smuggling Coalition
BIS	Bureau of Industry and Security
BSI	Border Safety Initiative
BTA	Bioterrorism Act
C4ISR	Command, Control, Communications, Computers, Intelligence, Surveillance, and Reconnaissance
CBP	Customs and Border Protection
CCL	Commerce Control List
CEO	Chief Executive Officer
CFC	Chlorofluorocarbon
CFR	Code of Federal Regulations; cost and freight
CIF	Cost, Insurance, and Freight
CIP	Carriage and Insurance Paid to
CNE&D	Confiscation, Nationalization, Expropriation, and Deprivation
COAC	Customs Operating Advisory Committee
CPT	Carriage Paid to
CROSS	Customs Rulings Online Search System
CSA	Canada Customs Self-Assessment
CSA	Customs Self-Assessment
CSC	Container Service Charge
CSI	Container Security Initiative
C-TPAT	Customs–Trade Partnership Against Terrorism
DaF	Delivered at Frontier
DDP	Delivered Duty Paid
DDU	Delivered Duty Unpaid

DEQ	Delivered Ex Quay
DES	Delivered Ex Ship
DHS	Department of Homeland Security
DoC	Department of Commerce
DoD	Department of Defense
DoT	Department of Transportation
DPL	Denied Parties List
EAR	Export Administration Regulations
ECCN	Export Control Classification Number
EDI	Electronic Data Interchange
EMS	Export Management System
EPA/OC	Environmental Protection Agency/Office of Compliance
EXW	Ex Works
FAS	Free Alongside Ship
FAST	Free and Secure Trade
FCA	Free Carrier
FCIA	Foreign Credit Insurance Association
FCPA	Federal Corrupt Practices Act
FDA	Food and Drug Administration
FEMA	Federal Emergency Management Agency
FIFRA	Federal Insecticide, Fungicide, and Rodenticide Act
FMC	Federal Maritime Commission
FoB	Free on Board
FRoB	Freight Remaining on Board
FTSR	Foreign Trade Statistical Regulations
FTZ	Foreign Trade Zone
GAO	Government Accounting Office
GATT	General Agreement on Tariffs and Trade
GIS	Geographic Information System
GPS	Global Positioning System
GSP	Generalized System for Preferences
HMR	Hazardous Materials Regulations
HSA	Homeland Security Act
HTSUS	Harmonized Tariff System of the United States
IBET	Integrated Border Enforcement Team
IBIS	Interagency Border Inspection Systems
ICC	International Chamber of Commerce
ICE	Immigration and Customs Enforcement
ILO	International Labor Organization

IMO	International Maritime Organization
INCOTerms	International Commercial Terms
IOMA	Institute of Management and Accounting
IPRR	Intellectual Property Rights e-Recordation Online System
IRS	Internal Revenue Service
ISA	Importer Self-Assessment
ISI	Immigration Security Initiative
ISIS	Integrated Surveillance Intelligence System
ISO	International Organization of Standards; Insurance Services Office, Inc.
ISPS Code	International Ship and Port Facility Security Code
ISSC	International Ship Security Certificate
ITAR	International Traffic in Arms Regulations
LC	landed cost, letter of credit
MEI	Maritime Education Initiative
MoT	Materials of Trade
MSST	Maritime Safety and Security Teams
MTSA	Maritime Transportation Security Act
NII	Nonintrusive Inspection
NTC	National Targeting Center
OECD	Organisation for Economic Co-operation and Development
OFAC	Office of Foreign Asset Controls
OIT	Office of Information and Technology
OPIC	Overseas Private Investment Corporation
ORM	Other Regulated Materials
OSC	Operation Safe Commerce
OSHA	Occupational Safety and Health Administration
PACMAN	Professional Association of Import/Export Compliance Managers
PAPS	Pre-Arrival Processing System
PCB	Polychlorinated Biphenyl
PFSO	Port Facility Security Officer
PIC	Prior Informed Consent
PIP	Partners in Protection (Canada)
PoA	Power of Attorney
PRD	Personal Radiation Detector
PSC	Port State Control

PSN	Proper Shipping Name
PST	Port Security Team
RCRA	Resource Conservation Recovery Act
RFID	Radio Frequency Identification
RIIDS	Radiation Isotope Identification Detection System
RoI	Return on Investment
RSO	Recognized Security Organization
RVSS	Remote Video Surveillance System
SCAC	Standard Carrier Alpha Code
SEC	Securities and Exchange Commission
SED	Shipper's Export Declaration
SENTRI	Secure Electronic Network for Travelers' Rapid Inspection
SEVIS	Student Exchange Visitor System
SNAP	Simplified Network Application Process
SOP	Standard Operating Procedure
SOX	Sarbanes–Oxley
SR&CC	Strikes, Riots, and Civil Commotions
SSA	Ship Security Alert
SSO	Ship Security Officer
SSP	Ship Security Plan
SSTL	Smart and Secure Trade Lanes
TPL	Third-Party Logistics
TRIA	Terrorism Risk Insurance Act
TSA	Transportation Security Administration
TSC	Transportation Security Card
TSCA	Toxic Substance Control Act
TWIC	Transportation Worker Identification Credential
UAV	Unmanned Aerial Vehicle
UN	United Nations
USCG	US Coast Guard
USML	US Munitions List
USPPI	US Principal Party in Interest
VSD	Voluntary Self-Disclosure
WCO	World Customs Organization

Author

Thomas Cook (Tom) is the managing director of Blue Tiger International (http://www.bluetigerintl.com), a premier international business consulting company on supply chain management, trade compliance, purchasing, sales and business development, global trade, and logistics.

Tom was the former chief executive officer of American River International in New York and Apex Global Logistics Supply Chain Operation in Los Angeles.

He has over 30 years' experience in assisting companies all over the world in managing their global operations.

He is a member of the New York District Export Council, sits on the board of numerous corporations, and is considered a leader in the business verticals that he works in.

Tom has been engaged by the American Management Association since 1981. He has been a course developer and leader/instructor in a host of areas, such as, but not limited to, project management, import and export, global supply chain, purchasing, risk management, negotiation skills, sales, marketing, and business development.

He has now authored over 15 books on global trade and is in the middle of writing an eight-book series titled *The Global Warrior: Advancing on the Necessary Skill Sets to Compete Effectively in Global Trade*. He has also authored books on sales management, customer service, and growth in world markets.

Tom has been, or is, involved with a number of organizations in education and training in a number of industry verticals such as, but not limited to, Institute of Supply Chain Managers (ISM), Council of Supply Chain Managers (CCS), Transpiration Intermediaries Association (TIA), Air Forwarders Association (AFA), US Chamber of Commerce, Department of Commerce, Conference Board, the State University of New York (SUNY), Dale Carnegie, California State University, Long Beach, and New York Institute of Technology (NYIT).

Tom is also the director of the National Institute of World Trade (http://niwt.org), a 30-year-old educational and training organization based in New York.

Tom is a former US naval and merchant marine officer. He holds a BS and Masters Degree in Business Management from the SUNY Maritime College, Fort Schuyler, New York.

Tom can be reached at tomcook@bluetigerintl.com or 516-359-6232.

Index